TALES OF
THE SMITHS

A Graphic Biography

Con Chrisoulis

T0322615

TALES OF
THE SMITHS

A Graphic Biography

Con Chrisoulis

OMNIBUS PRESS

London / New York / Paris / Sydney / Copenhagen / Berlin / Madrid / Tokyo

Exclusive Distributors
Music Sales Limited
14–15 Berners Street
London, W1T 3LJ.

Music Sales Pty Ltd
Australia and New Zealand
Level 4, 30–32 Carrington Street
Sydney NSW 2000
Australia

Every effort has been made to trace the copyright holders of the photographs
in this book but one or two were unreachable. We would be grateful if the
photographers concerned would contact us.

Printed in Malta.

A catalogue record for this book is available from the British Library.

Visit Omnibus Press on the web at www.omnibuspress.com

To Marilyn

INTRODUCTION

When Omnibus editorial director Chris Charlesworth asked me to write an introduction for a graphic biography titled *Tales Of The Smiths* I was quietly surprised. Previously, Omnibus had commissioned comparable volumes on the Sex Pistols and the Ramones but their careers had a more cartoon-like quality in keeping with punk mythology. The nearest I'd seen Morrissey portrayed in such a fashion was a graphic publication back in the early nineties in which he was featured doing unspeakable things. Probably for legal reasons, this anarchic tome was never reviewed or sold in book shops and I have no idea of its collectible value. I also recall Granada TV presenting an animated depiction of Morrissey in the documentary *These Things Take Time* and *Select* magazine using sketches of several Smiths for a feature on the famous 1996 court case. Neither of these prepared me for the arrival of a graphic biography but, on reflection, it makes sense. For many fans, The Smiths' story has become an almost mythical saga, even bearing strained comparison with that of The Beatles.

I was therefore expecting something along the lines of the various television documentaries on The Smiths, mainly with emphasis on the 1982–87 period. Instead, what we have in Volume 1 is the pre-history of The Smiths, terrain that has always fascinated me as a biographer. When I completed *Morrissey & Marr: The Severed Alliance* in 1992, that entire period was virgin territory. True, Morrissey had alluded to the pain of his troubled adolescence, schooling and celibacy in various interviews, but he was the only one talking. The other Smiths, particularly Joyce and Rourke, were silence personified, while Marr had only done a couple of in-depth interviews, at best. Detailing Morrissey's adventures alone meant tracking down countless associates and even family members, none of whom had ever spoken about him. It was the same with Marr. What emerged was a history with flesh on the bones. Much of it is rendered here, abetted by the wealth of Smiths-related commentary that has followed in its wake. Over the past couple of decades it seems that no Smiths 'anniversary' is allowed to pass without a 'special' from one of the monthly rock magazines.

Drawing a graphic biography is a very different challenge from writing one. Choosing key moments for visual emphasis requires an ability to combine gritty realism with mythological whimsy. It's amusing to see some minor moments, exclusively from the pages of *The Severed Alliance*, that unexpectedly appear here: the CJs, two pals from Morrissey's school who formed a band, get a surprise small-starring role; his private revelation about applying for a job as an Au Pair Boy is featured; and Angie, the girl who died, whom Morrissey has never mentioned in print, gets a page to herself. Plus, some of the comments from Morrissey's father to me are dramatised herein in slightly different form. Stephen Pomfret and Robin Allman, who never conducted any interviews before or after *The Severed Alliance,* also receive fairly lavish coverage.

As a lover of context, it's pleasing to see so many side stories, not just the expected (the Sex Pistols, Buzzcocks, Bowie, Sparks, New York Dolls), but also Ian Curtis, Jobriath and The Clash, among others. As a graphic biography for a modern audience, some of the vernacular has a more contemporary ring. Inevitably, there's some necessary poetic license and reiteration of old myths amid the careful documentation. Morrissey's mother is transformed into a cake-baking assistant librarian. I don't know if she ever baked a cake, and she was not working at a library in any capacity for the duration of her son's adolescence as some suppose. Of course, in early interviews and retrospectives, writers couldn't resist the 'library' angle, as it was such good copy. There's a reference to Morrissey studying for 'university entrance exams' (if only) but he never even studied for A-levels, and his parents did not divorce or sign such papers until quite a time after their separation in 1976. But these are the kind of broad brushstrokes that a graphic artist has to apply at times. As no photos have been published of many of the minor characters, it's funny to see the imagined depictions of people like Pomfret, Phil Fletcher and various teachers and associates.

I couldn't help wondering what Morrissey and Marr – or Joyce and Rourke for that matter – might make of this book. How strange must it be to have your life not merely documented in magazines and books but effectively transformed into cartoon-like animation. It's akin to seeing yourself in another dimension – funny, poignant and possibly disturbing.

JOHNNY ROGAN
Author of *Morrissey & Marr: The Severed Alliance.*

FOREWORD

I played but a small part in the development and formation of one of Britain's finest bands. I turned down The Smiths. Within a year, the band began to take off, standing apart from the mainstream pop fodder, capturing a certain zeitgeist and giving voice to disaffected youths amidst the desolation of early 80s Britain. Their legacy endures to this day, but in those early days, I didn't see it coming. Given a fork in the road and no signpost, which do you take?

My association with the band began one night in 1982, when I got a phone call out of the blue from Johnny Maher.

"Si, I want you to play drums in my new band. We're called The Smiths…"

Johnny hadn't been on my radar for months. I'd met him in late 1980 in a pub called The Vine in Sale, where I'd hang out with my schoolmates, Ian Brown and John Squire. We had a band called The Patrol, inspired by the DIY ethos of punk, which, in truth, had lost momentum. Johnny had cut a striking figure as he strode into the pub, cool as you like, gift of the gab, cocksure and funny. He seemed to be on a mission: I'm looking for a drummer, I've been told you might be interested? I was.

The next day, I went to pick up the guitarist from Wythenshawe and found him in his box room, casually playing Classical Gas, the theme tune from Granada TV's *This is Your Right*, on his acoustic. I was well impressed. We went over to see his classmate, Andy Rourke, the bass player for our new band, Freak Party, whose playing I was also blown away by. Andy's house, with his dad often away on business, became a base for us but also a way station for various dealers and druggies. We would listen to sounds from the likes of A Certain Ratio, Grandmaster Flash and Funkadelic, sitting around smoking hash, watching TV news: football hooligans, picketing miners, Moss Side riots. The sum total of the band was this: we jammed, we rehearsed, we recorded a demo and searched in vain for a singer for our experimental funk.

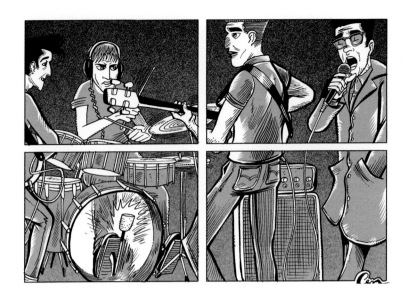

I hadn't seen or heard anything from Johnny since the last Freak Party rehearsal in Ancoats. That particular night, we had a visit from the Serious Crime Squad, who'd come to arrest Johnny after his name had come up in connection with a stolen Lowry. Andy and I were released later the same night, but Johnny got fined for handling stolen goods. It seemed he was keeping his head down. Now, all of sudden, he was back. I paced the floor of my parents' bedroom as Johnny explained that he'd tracked down a singer called Stephen Morrissey and needed to record a demo urgently. I had my reservations, but I agreed.

At the studio, Johnny ran through the songs: 'Suffer Little Children', which had obvious references to the Moors Murders, and 'The Hand That Rocks the Cradle', which was less depressing, in the circumstances. Studio engineer and key holder, Dale Hibbert, was on bass. Morrissey came in with his long dog-eared tweed coat, winkle pickers and a carrier-bag full of lyrics, giving the briefest of a shy smile in my direction. He seemed nice enough, but as soon as he started crooning I just knew it wasn't for me. His voice was tentative, quiet and too deep. There was no suggestion of the humour and swagger he would later attain and I missed Freak Party's funk bass lines and Chic-style guitar moves. I just didn't get it, whatsoever.

Who'd have thought, more than thirty years after my own decision, the band would continue to inspire and attract such a devoted legion of fans, and, much to the annoyance of Johnny Marr, be name-checked by a British Prime Minister eager to prove he had once been hip.

SI WOLSTENCROFT

2017

IRISH BLOOD, ENGLISH HEART

Following the sudden Irish influx during the 19th century Potato Famine, the north-west coast of England received ship after ship of starving families in search of a better future.

Consisting mostly of labourers, this new workforce flooded Manchester's factories and essentially became the backbone of the North's economy.

Irish immigrants themselves, Peter Morrissey and Elizabeth Dwyer, a hospital porter and assistant librarian respectively, moved to Manchester in the '50s, their second child being born there on the May 22nd, 1959.

Named after his father's stillborn brother, Steven Patrick Morrissey grew to become a champion of his adopted country, his songs encompassing an Englishness that never forgot its working class roots.

Recommended listening:
Morrissey's 'Irish Blood, English Heart' from the album *You Are the Quarry* (2004)

Suffer little children, and forbid them not, to come unto me: for of such is the kingdom of heaven. MATTHEW 19:14

Morrissey on the Moors Murders that took place from 1963 to 1965:
I did have a fixation on the Moors Murderers as a potential victim, if you like.

It was a very strong subject in Manchester throughout the late 1960s, very strong, almost an unspoken thing. It was too horrific for people to think about and to discuss.

In 1965, the same year that the committal proceedings opened against the Moors Murderers, both of Morrissey's grandfathers died, adding a sense of morbidity to the young boy's outlook on life.

To make matters worse, by December of the same year his mother's brother, Ernie, died of chronic alcohol abuse. The mourning family were in for another final shock, when the coffin proved too long to be placed in the grave.

Ernie Dwyer was the last male of the Dwyer line to bear the surname. He was 24 years old.

Quotes from a Morrissey interview to ITV's *South Bank Show* (Oct 18th, 1987)

Recommended listening:
The Smiths' 'Suffer Little Children' from their debut album *The Smiths* (1984)
Morrissey's '(I'm) The End of the Family Line' from the album *Kill Uncle* (1991)

I Know it's Over

Were you brought up in a religious household?
It was very religious, yes.
Then we had a couple of horrendous
family deaths and everyone turned
away from the Church. For a while.

Did it comfort you?
Nothing comforts me.

I think the world is a mesmerising mess.
I think human beings are mesmerising messes.

And there we are.

Quotes from a Morrissey interview with the BBC's Kirsty Young on *Desert Island Discs* (Nov 29th, 2009)

Recommended listening:
The Smiths' 'I Know it's Over' from their album *The Queen is Dead* (1986)

I HAVE FORGIVEN JESUS

Easter 1966.
St Wilfred's Church, Hulme.

Are you ready for your first communion, son?

Y-yes.

The blood of our Lord Jesus Christ, which was shed for thee, preserve thy body and soul unto everlasting life.

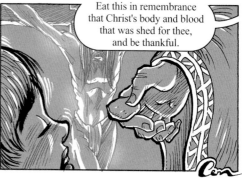

Eat this in remembrance that Christ's body and blood that was shed for thee, and be thankful.

Recommended listening:
Morrissey's 'I Have Forgiven Jesus' from the album *You Are the Quarry* (2004)
The Smiths' 'The Queen is Dead' from the album *The Queen is Dead* (1986)

Back to the Old House

1963

1964

1971

Recommended listening:
The Smiths' 'Back to the Old House', b-side to the single 'What Difference Does it Make?' (1984)
Dusty Springfield's 'I Only Want to Be with You' from the album *Stay Awhile/I Only Want to Be with...* (1964)
Sandie Shaw's single 'There's Always Something There to Remind Me' (1964)
T. Rex's 'Cosmic Dancer' from the album *Electric Warrior* (1971)

THE HEADMASTER RITUAL

Sept 24th, 1970.
St Mary's RC Secondary Modern School, Stretford.

Recommended listening:
The Smiths' 'The Headmaster Ritual' from the album *Meat is Murder* (1985)
The Smiths' 'Barbarism Begins at Home' from the album *Meat is Murder* (1985)

Angel, Angel,
Down We Go Together

1962. John Joseph Maher marries Frances Patricia Doyle; together they embark on a journey of no return, emigrating from Kildare, Eire, to Manchester.

Heading towards an unknown future, the young couple were separated from family at their country's docks.

Oh John, I feel so sad.

Don't feel sad, love. What other choice do we have? We're doing this for our unborn child.

I know, I know It's just that I fear that Manchester might change us ...change our child.

Fear not, my love. It won't be Manchester that will change our child, but our child that will change Manchester. Forever.

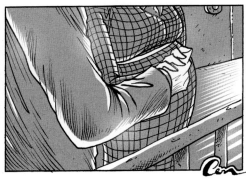

Frances gave birth to John Martin Maher on October 31st, 1963.

Recommended listening:
Morrissey's 'Angel, Angel, Down We Go Together' from the album *Viva Hate* (1988)

Hold On
to Your Friends

1975.
St Augustine's Grammar School, Manchester.

Recommended listening:
Morrissey's 'Hold On to Your Friends' from the album *Vauxhall and I* (1994)
Neil Young's 'Tonight's the Night' from the album *Tonight's the Night* (1975)

The Draize Train

Autumn 1975. Wythenshawe.
A young Andrew Rourke starts experimenting with pills and barbiturates.

Afterwards at St Augustine's Grammar School, Manchester.

In class that same day.

...and thus.

Recommended listening:
The Smiths' 'The Draize Train' from the live album *Rank* (1988)
Neil Young's 'Heart of Gold' from the album *Harvest* (1972)

My first lightning bolt came from Marc Bolan. I bought Jeepster by T. Rex purely because it was in the bargain singles box and it had a picture of Marc and Mickey Finn on the label, so I figured I was getting more for my 25p. When I played that record I heard magic. That magic is what I'm endlessly trying for. That's what keeps me breathing.

People as Places as People in which Johnny explains some of his early guitar heroes.

There's a sad song by Del Shannon called 'The Answer to Everything' that my parents used to play, and it struck a chord in me because it sounded so familiar.

That song was the inspiration for The Smiths' 'Please, Please, Please Let Me Get What I Want'.

Rory Gallagher came along at a time when I was at an age desperate for something to call my own. He had a very straightforward street image – jeans, plimsoles, a really battered guitar – and it just connected with me. I went to see him in concert and he scared the life out of me, honest! He was so intense I couldn't believe it – I wanted to get closer, but I was scared in case he made eye contact with me and the earth swallowed me.

Andrew Oldham inspired me because he wore hyper-activity like a badge of honour, and because he considers it impolite to be boring.

I like Keith Richards more for his ethic than his playing. He's the captain of the ship when it comes to being in a rock'n'roll band; he'll steer the band through anything, and go down with them if he has to. And he always looked good.

I've been listening to Melanie, Donovan, Davy Graham, Joni Mitchell's first album...

I don't want to hear music that uses a large vocabulary to say nothing. My attitude is: why use a lot of words when fuck off will do?

Quotes from Johnny Marr interviews for *The Guardian* (Jun 4th, 2004) and *The Guitar Magazine* (Jan 1997)

Recommended listening:
Modest Mouse's 'People as Places as People' from the album *We Were Dead Before the Ship Even Sank* (2007)
Del Shannon's 'The Answer to Everything' from the album *Hats Off to Del Shannon* (1962)
The Smiths' 'Please, Please, Please, Let Me Get What I Want' from the compilation *Hatful of Hollow* (1984)
Rory Gallagher's 'I'm Not Awake Yet' from the album *Deuce* (1971)
The Rolling Stones' 'Get Off My Cloud' from the album *December's Children (and Everybody's)* (1965)

Sorrow Will Come in the End in which
a young Michael Joyce hones his percussion skills.

I was born in Chorlton-on-Medlock, just by the Holy Name Church. A lot of back-to-backs there, the old style terrace houses. When I was about seven, I moved up to Fallowfield to a council estate. I know it sounds mad but it was like: "Ooh, there's an indoor toilet!"

It started at school. I was playing drums with a pair of files, practising on the desk – getting right into it.

I then started playing on the couch with a pair of knitting needles. I had to put a cover over it as I'd started to wear the couch down and my Mum saw it one day and gave me a clip round the ear! I said "Well, if I get a drum kit, that won't happen."

And I said "Look, to replace the couch, it's gonna cost as much as getting me a drum kit."

I got a second-hand one and played it in my little tiny bedroom upstairs.

Quotes from Mike Joyce interviews for Martin Hall's blog (Oct 6th, 2008) and the documentary *Inside The Smiths* (2007)

Recommended listening:
Drum intro to The Smiths' 'The Queen is Dead' from the album *The Queen is Dead* (1986)
Morrissey's 'Sorrow Will Come in the End' from the album *Maladjusted* (1997)

Saturday Night
and
Sunday Morning

Recommended listening:
The Smiths' 'This Night Has Opened My Eyes' from the compilation *Hatful of Hollow* (1984)

Recommended viewing:
John Schlesinger's *A Kind of Loving*, based on Stan Barstow's novel (1962)
Tony Richardson's *A Taste of Honey*, based on Shelagh Delaney's play (1961)
Karel Reisz's *Saturday Night and Sunday Morning*, based on Alan Sillitoe's novel (1960)
John Schlesinger's *Billy Liar*, based on Keith Waterhouse's novel (1963)
The Smiths' music video for their single 'Girlfriend in a Coma' (1987),
which features scenes from Sidney J. Furie's *The Leather Boys* (1964)

CHANGES

David Bowie admits to being bisexual in the 22nd Jan,1972 issue of *Melody Maker*, becoming the hero of a frustrated youth desperate for an alternative life and fashion style, thus paving the way for the punk movement.

Morrissey's dream to sing with Bowie was realised in 1995 when they toured together in Europe, until he fell out with him, quit the tour and disappeared altogether.

Recommended listening:
Morrissey's cover of David Bowie's 'Drive-In Saturday' from the album *Aladdin Sane* (1973), recorded live and featured as a b-side to Morrissey's single 'All You Need is Me' (2008)
David Bowie's 'The Bewlay Brothers' from the album *Hunky Dory* (1971)
The Smiths' 'Handsome Devil' from the compilation *Hatful of Hollow* (1984)

June 16th, 1972

at the Manchester Belle Vue

Recommended listening:
Morrissey's cover of T. Rex's 'Cosmic Dancer' from the album *Electric Warrior* (1971),
recorded live and featured as a b-side to Morrissey's 12" vinyl single 'Pregnant for the Last Time' (1991)
T. Rex's 'Teenage Dream' from the album *Zinc Alloy and the Hidden Riders of Tomorrow* (1974)

Recommended viewing:
Ringo Starr's T. Rex concert film *Born to Boogie* (1972)

ROCK 'N' ROLL
SUICIDE

Manchester Free Trade Hall
June 7th, 1973

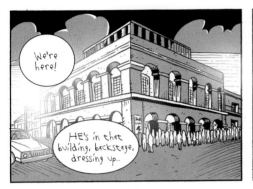

Later.

Recommended listening:
David Bowie's 'Rock 'n' Roll Suicide' from his concept album
The Rise and Fall of Ziggy Stardust and the Spiders from Mars (1972)
...heck, just listen to the whole album, it's impeccable.

Recommended viewing:
D.A. Pennebaker's *Ziggy Stardust and the Spiders from Mars: The Motion Picture* (1973)

THE RITUAL

I was a terrible bore when it came to athletics. I was just the type of person everyone despises, so I've carried on in that tradition.

I never wanted to get off P.E — it was the only intellectual subject in school. But I did used to get off all the other subjects.

I just used to be constantly ill — general manic depression mainly. I didn't need notes or anything. They just had to take one look at me and that was enough.

It was the only thing I was good at and I used to love it completely. The 100 metres was my raison d'être. Yes, I won everything.

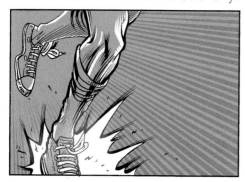

Quotes from a Morrissey interview for *Star Hits* (1985)

Recommended listening:
The Smiths' 'The Headmaster Ritual' from the album *Meat is Murder* (1985)

TALENT
IS AN
ASSET

Today I bought the album of the year.

The album is Kimono My House by Sparks.

STEVE MORRISSEY

384 Kings Road, Stretford, Manchester

SPACE CLOWN

1974. *The Midnight Special* TV show, NBC. Jobriath, the first openly gay rock artist, appears on television for the first time to launch his self-titled debut album.

A young Steve Morrissey is inspired by the man that many considered a Bowie imposter; this outsider status that Jobriath gained made the Mancunian a life-long fan.

After his record company dropped him due to poor sales, Jobriath descended into a drug-fuelled spiral, eventually changing his stage name to Cole Berlin and becoming a lounge singer. He died in 1983, one of the first victims of AIDS.

Years later, and striking obvious parallels with his own life, Morrissey reminisced:
At the time, the press either ridiculed him or didn't bother to write about him at all. He died in obscurity in the '80s.

In 2004 Morrissey personally oversaw the release of the first Jobriath compilation, *Lonely Planet Boy.*

Quotes from a Morrissey interview for *Index Magazine* (Feb 2004)

Recommended listening:
Jobriath's 'I'm a Man' from his self-titled debut album *Jobriath* (1973)

Recommended viewing:
Jobriath performing 'Rock of Ages' on NBC's *The Midnight Special* (1974)
Jobriath performing 'Sunday Brunch' as Cole Berlin on BBC's *Arena* documentary *Chelsea Hotel* (1981)
Kieran Turner's documentary *Jobriath A.D.* (2012)
Todd Haynes' motion picture love letter to glam rock, *Velvet Goldmine* (1998)

LONELY PLANET BOY

November 1973. *The Old Grey Whistle Test.*

The New York Dolls' historic UK TV appearance caught Steve Morrissey by such a surprise that he considered it:

My first real emotional experience.

Being devoted to the Dolls ruined my education. I was thrown off the track and football teams at school for turning up to games in desperately self-designed Dolls T-shirts.

In 1975, shortly after their demise, Morrissey set up and ran the New York Dolls' UK fan club from his bedroom in Stretford, Manchester.

Quotes from a Morrissey interview printed in Simon Goddard's *Mozipedia* (2010)

Recommended reading:
New York Dolls by Steven Morrissey, published by Babylon Books (1981)

Recommended viewing:
New York Dolls performing 'Jet Boy' on BBC2's *The Old Grey Whistle Test* (1973)

TIME

demanding Billy Dolls

November 9th, 1972.

Whilst living his own personal hell, the only hope that Steven Morrissey has left is the upcoming New York Dolls concert at the Hardrock theatre in his own neighbourhood of Stretford.

The Dolls would be opening for Roxy Music. This meant that the greatest bands of the glam rock era would be performing right before their greatest fan in their prime and in his home town.

David Bowie went on to write about Billy Murcia's untimely death in his song 'Time'.
Morrissey played a pivotal role in reuniting the surviving members of the New York Dolls, when he curated the 2004 Meltdown festival; he thus got to finally see them perform.

Quotes from a Morrissey interview with *Sonic* magazine (2004)

Recommended listening:
Morrissey's live cover of the New York Dolls' 'Trash' from their debut album *New York Dolls* (1973), offered as a b-side on the 7" reissue of Morrissey's classic single 'Suedehead' (2010)
David Bowie's 'Time' from the album *Aladdin Sane* (1973)

Recommended viewing:
Greg Whiteley's documentary about the last days of the Dolls' bassist, Arthur 'Killer' Kane, *New York Doll* (2005)

CPL 593H

how soon is
NOW?

384 Kings Road, Stretford, Manchester.

Trafford Library the following day.

Morrissey became a pro-feminist at a very young age. Years later he would use Marjorie Rosen's phrase "How Soon Is 'Now'?" from her book *Popcorn Venus* as the title of one of The Smiths' most celebrated singles.

Recommended listening:
The Smiths' 'How Soon is Now?' from their compilation *Hatful of Hollow* (1984)

Recommended reading:
Marjorie Rosen's *Popcorn Venus: Women, Movies and the American Dream* (1973)
Germaine Greer's *The Female Eunuch* (1970)
Molly Haskell's *From Reverence to Rape: The Treatment of Women in the Movies* (1974)

WILDLY

Recommended listening:
The Smiths' 'Cemetry Gates' from the album *The Queen is Dead* (1986)
The Smiths' 'Oscillate Wildly' from the compilation *The World Won't Listen* (1987)

Recommended viewing:
Brian Gilbert's biopic *Wilde* (1997)

DA DOO
RON RON

Even back then, I didn't so much listen to music as study it. I'd put on records, whether by a favourite group like T. Rex or just some naff pop record.

If the middle eight didn't appear where I thought it should or if the fade-out was too short, I'd get really frustrated!

Having my head buried in the speakers, listening out for those things sort of grew in tandem with my obsession for guitars.

When I heard Phil Spector's records, a whole new world opened up to me.

Quotes from a Johnny Marr interview for *The Guitar Magazine* (Jan 1997)

Recommended listening:
The Ronettes' 'Be My Baby' from the album *Presenting the Fabulous Ronettes Featuring Veronica* (1964)
The Crystals' 'Da Doo Ron Ron' from the compilation *The Crystals Sing the Greatest Hits, Volume 1* (1963)
The Shangri-Las' 'Leader of the Pack' from the album *Leader of the Pack* (1965)

LETNOMANSTEALYOURTHYME

One of my friends said they had found this amazing folk player. My idea of folk at the time was 'All Around My Hat', and he just put on this Pentangle record and it sounded very aggressive and free form; just cool, you know?

I had no idea where Bert Jansch was coming from, and I couldn't work out how he was doing what he was doing.

He was the only person that I ever really tried to work out stuff as a guitar player, fairly unsuccessfully.

And it's true that, if you actually sit in front of him and watch what he's doing, it's harder. It's better to just try to work it out by ear, because you'd need like a mirror, and you'd have to stand on your head to work out how he's doing it

Johnny befriended Bert Jansch in his later years and in 2003 they performed together at Jansch's 60th birthday celebration concert in London.

Quotes from Johnny Marr interviews for Roland.co.uk's blog (2009) and *The Guardian* (Oct 5, 2009)

Recommended listening:
Bert Jansch's album *Crimson Moon*, in which Johnny Marr participated (2000)
Pentangle's rendition of 'Let No Man Steal Your Thyme' from the album *The Pentangle* (1968)

Recommended viewing:
Pentangle performing 'Hunting Song' from their 1969 album *Basket of Light* on the BBC (1969)
Marr, Jansch and Bernard Butler performing 'The River Bank' at Jansch's 60th birthday celebration (2003)

SWEET&TENDER
HOOLIGAN

At 16 I had trials with Manchester City and Brian Clough's Nottingham Forest were sniffing around. But I didn't take football seriously enough to push it to the next level.

I'd go for a trial and take to the pitch wearing eyeliner. Half the opposition team were looking at the mascara and thinking "We'd better stay away from him"

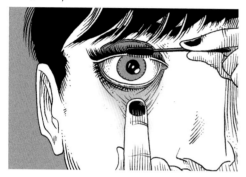

The other half just wanted to kick lumps out of me. My own team were probably thinking the same thing.

I was winging it, basically — having a laugh. My football career was always destined to be short-lived.

Quotes from a Johnny Marr interview for *The Daily Mail* (Aug 31, 2009)

Recommended listening:
The Smiths' 'Sweet and Tender Hooligan', b-side of their 12" single *Sheila Take a Bow* (1987)

STILL ILL

Recommended reading:
Viv Nicholson's autobiography *Spend, Spend, Spend*, co-written by Stephen Smith (1977)

Recommended listening:
The Smiths' 'Still Ill' from their self-titled debut album *The Smiths* (1983)
The Smiths' single 'Heaven Knows I'm Miserable Now' (especially its cover sleeve) (1984)

Late Night, Maudlin Street

I am depressed most of the time.
And when you're depressed it is so enveloping that it actually does control your life.

You cannot overcome it, and you can't take advice. People trying to cheer you up become infuriating and almost insulting.

Depression is very, very powerful. You can't simply go to a nightclub and have a quick Miller draft light, or whatever you call it, and come out of it.

I've tried Prozac and lithium. A lot of extreme things happen to you on them, which sometimes cannot seem to be worth it because I don't want something that's going to affect me in any way other than to perhaps cure me. I don't want anything that's going to make me different.

But having said all this, I function very well. I'm a reasonably well balanced person. I'm as strong as 90 percent of the people I know who would never, ever admit to depression. I think admitting it and talking about it is a strength.

Quotes from a Morrissey interview with *Details* magazine (Dec 1992)

Recommended listening:
Morrissey's 'Late Night, Maudlin Street' from the album *Viva Hate* (1988)

Recommended viewing:
Gerald Thomas' third *Carry On* comedy, *Carry On Teacher* (1959)

JOURNALISTS
WHO LIE

384 Kings Road, Stretford, Manchester.

Morrissey put together a weekly homemade pop magazine ever since he was a child.

CHATTERBOX

Dear James,

The Dolls lived in New York, I lived in Manchester. They hardly ever came to England so we never met and they never sent me any communications.

Finally, I have found a fellow New York Dolls obsessive...

I communicated with the secretary which wasn't quite the same thing, but I didn't mind. It was just a great honour to do what I did in those days. It was the first real adventure that I ever had.

Morrissey would continue running the New York Dolls UK fan club long after their break-up, using any pocket money he had to communicate with fellow fans.

Quotes from an article on Morrissey by the *Irish Independent* (Oct 21, 2013)

Recommended listening:
New York Dolls' 'Chatterbox' from the album *Too Much Too Soon* (1974)

MEAT IS MURDER

I became shy as a teenager because I became immersed in vegetarianism and I became very depressed by the existence of the abattoir.

I had a dawning when I was 11 or 12. Just the knowledge that such places existed. I saw a television documentary by accident when I was 11 and I was absolutely horrified.

I saw pigs and cows still thrashing about after they'd been supposedly stunned. I've never eaten meat since then.

It had such a profound effect on me as a teenager because I was very introverted. I felt I was on an alien planet.

Morrissey was honoured with the Linda McCartney Memorial Award from PETA in 2005 in recognition "of all of his hard work for animals" and for fighting for their rights for well over 20 years.

Quotes from a Morrissey interview with *Greenscene* magazine (issue 6, 1989)

Recommended listening:
The Smiths' 'Meat is Murder' from the album *Meat is Murder* (1985)

Recommended online reading:
www.peta.org

Come and Stay with Me

I was a small fat child in a welfare house; there was only one thing I dreamt about.
Yes.

Is that about you?
And fate has just handed it to me.
Yes, it is about the moment of singing.
Singing to an audience.

But I would stand on the table and sing.
You did?
Yes, I did, as a six year-old and I was off even at that stage.

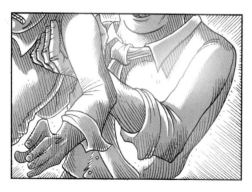

What was the first moment of singing to an audience? When did you first allow people to hear your voice?
That's a very good question.
Perhaps I was ten. And fat. In a council house.
It's embarrassing and I would never really say this apart from the fact that we're on national radio and I don't have much choice.

Now that we've gone this far, we may as well go further! What did you sing?
I sang the disc that you are about to play now, which was quite perverted of me, if you listen to the lyrics.
But I WAS SIX. Which is no excuse.

I'll send away all my false pride.

Quotes from a Morrissey interview with BBC's Kirsty Young on *Desert Island Discs* (Nov 29th, 2009)

Recommended listening:
Morrissey's 'All You Need is Me' from the album *Years of Refusal* (2009)
Marianne Faithfull's 'Come and Stay With Me' from the album *Marianne Faithfull* (1965)

bricks
and
mortar

The place where I grew up no longer exists apart from here, in the local history library's photographic evidence of Queen's Square and Old Trafford.

This is where I grew up and it was demolished in the late 1960s. And in a way it was like having one's childhood wiped away.

In Queen's Square my grandmother occupied the fourth house, we occupied the fifth house and the sixth house was occupied by my mother's sister and her family.

There's nothing at Queen's Square now, as you can see everything has just vanished.

I feel great anger and massive sadness. It's like a complete loss of childhood, because although I've always lived in Manchester, now when I pass through here it's just so foreign to me.

Quotes from a Morrissey interview on BBC2's *The Oxford Road Show* (March 22, 1985)

Recommended listening:
Morrissey's 'Late Night, Maudlin Street' from his first solo album *Viva Hate* (1988)
The Smiths' 'Paint a Vulgar Picture' from their final album *Strangeways, Here We Come* (1987)

bona drag

Nativity play, Christmas 1969.

Recommended listening:
Morrissey's 'November Spawned a Monster' from his early solo singles compilation *Bona Drag* (1990)

Recommended viewing:
Classic *Coronation Street* episodes (1960s-1970s)

SOLDIER BLUE

Recommended listening:
Buffy Sainte-Marie's 'Soldier Blue' from the album *She Used to Wanna Be a Ballerina* (1971)

hold on

It was the kind of school that gave no stroke whatsoever for individuality.

Did you have any friends amongst the other pupils?

I did. I must say that I did.

I did seem to attract the more obscure elements of school. The kind of person that never had any friends. The very lanky, bespectacled, spotted failure somehow was attracted to me and I thought that was quite interesting.

Because I was very good at athletics and I was the type who could have things very easy, if I really wanted to. Because, in working class schools, if you're good at athletics, you're the treasured student, everything you do is wonderful and you can get away with anything.

And I was that kind of student, but I kind of backed away from the very easy attainable things and I blended with the obscure pupils. Which was much more interesting than taking the easy route.

Quotes from a Morrissey interview on Channel 4's *Ear Say* television programme (June 1984)

Recommended listening:
Morrissey's 'Hold On to Your Friends' from the album *Vauxhall and I* (1994)

ghouls

It was quite an absurd school. The only thing you could possibly do was woodwork. And obviously when you left school you would go into a factory.

There was no question of being artistic, or of reading books, or thinking about anything specific. I remember at one point, in one instance, all the pupils were asked to write about their favourite book, and I wrote about the...

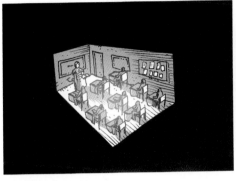

...THE DICTIONARY?

Uhh, yes! Luv it!

ARE YOU PUTTING ME ON, MISTER MORRISSEY?

And I remember I was virtually expelled for being so obstreperous and perverse.

YOU THINK THAT THIS IS FUNNY?

Expelled?! Oh Steven, what are we going to do with you?

Quotes from a Morrissey interview on Channel 4's *Ear Say* television programme (June 1984)

Recommended listening:
The Smiths' 'The Headmaster Ritual' from the album *Meat is Murder* (1985)

BOXERS

And what about your father, what sort of father was he when you were little?

He was quite happy and very good looking and out there enjoying life and very athletic.

So, therefore, when I hit my teens and I was very interested in things like the New York Dolls, he thought I was a bit of a lunatic. So that was the great separating point.

Quotes from a Morrissey interview with BBC's Kirsty Young on *Desert Island Discs* (Nov 29, 2009)

Recommended listening:
Morrissey's 'Boxers' from the singles compilation *World of Morrissey* (1995)

At the age of 12, Morrissey decided to become a scriptwriter for *Coronation Street*, the longest running British television soap opera, set in Manchester.

Recommended listening:
The Smiths' single 'Shakespeare's Sister' (1985),
the cover of which features actress Pat Phoenix as *Coronation Street*'s Elsie Tanner
The Smiths' 'That Joke Isn't Funny Anymore' from the album *Meat is Murder* (1985)

Recommended viewing:
Classic *Coronation Street* episodes, produced by Granada TV (1960s–1970s)

greased tea

Morrissey found the atmosphere of Coronation Street calming. The idea that people were happy with their lot, not fighting the past or the future, appealed to him.

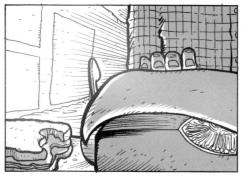

The community spirit no longer exists in England, but it's powerfully reflected in the soap. The dream for many people is to live a very uncomplicated life, where they cease to constantly question why they're here, where they're going, what value they have.

People within Coronation Street are happy to live in their houses, on their incomes, and they're very happy with the political situation. It's a dream.

Morrissey would continue submitting scripts to the producers of *Coronation Street* throughout his teenage years.

Quotes from a Morrissey interview with Len Brown, as published in the latter's book *Meetings with Morrissey* (2009)

Recommended listening:
Morrissey's 'Everyday is Like Sunday' from his debut solo album *Viva Hate* (1988)

life is a pigsty

Despite all the rejection letters from the producers of *Coronation Street*, young Steven Morrissey would continue submitting scripts to the soap opera.

Recommended listening:
Morrissey's 'Life is a Pigsty' from the album *Ringleader of the Tormentors* (2006)

viva hate

At one time though, I thought it was full of poetic instinct and it meant a great deal to many people.

But those days are certainly gone. I find the thing unbearable now.

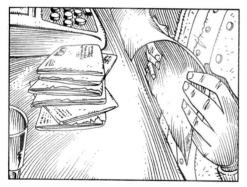

Even though Steven Morrissey's *Coronation Street* scripts were continuously rejected, he managed to begin a brief correspondence with *Corrie*'s chief scriptwriter, Leslie Duxbury, who was interested in the young lad's radical ideas for the series.

Quotes from a Morrissey interview in *Record Mirror* (Sept 1985)

Recommended listening:
Morrissey's 'Little Man, What Now?' from his debut solo album album *Viva Hate* (1988)

INTERLUDE

Morrissey's storylines were too wild for the Street.

I think the crux of the best script was them planting a juke box in the Rovers —much to the obvious horror of the regulars who, for some unknown reason, oppose any kind of change in their lives.

I think there were a couple of divorces in there somewhere... A few deaths — the odd strangulation thrown in.

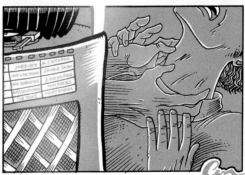

Quotes from a Morrissey interview in *Record Mirror* (Sept 1985)

Recommended listening:
Morrissey and Siouxsie's 12" single cover of Timi Yuro's 'Interlude' (1994)

beautiful creature

The basic fascination I have with cats is nothing unusual. I find them very intelligent and very superior. And I feel entranced by them.

I have a friend, Chrissie Hynde, she's exactly the same. You can be walking with her along the street, she sees a cat, she walks away.

You continue to walk on, talking to no one. You look around and she's crouched down with a cat in a hedge.

I have a cat in Manchester. She doesn't have a name. She was a stray — she responds to anything my mother says. She's very morbid, black and sullen. I had a cat called Tibby who died in September 1985, 23 human years of age. It was a big loss to me because he was practically like a brother.

Do you prefer the company of cats to the company of people?
Well, I don't have much choice. People don't like me.

Dedicated to Marilyn.

Quotes from Morrissey interviews with the *Smash Hits Yearbook* (1988) and *The Daily Telegraph* (June 17, 2011)

Recommended listening:
The Smiths' 'Meat is Murder' from the album *Meat is Murder* (1985)

Recommended online viewing:
www.morrisseywithcats.tumblr.com

you have killed me

When did you lose your virginity?

Actually it was in my early teens, 12 or 13. But it was an isolated incident, an accident. After that it was downhill. I've got no pleasant memories from it whatsoever.

Was your celibacy then prompted by a bad experience?

I've had very few experiences but they have been bad and they were a very long time ago. And it's not something that I would like repeated.

But this gets incredibly delicate and icy and it becomes almost too difficult to talk about.

I did lose the very idea that any communion between two people could possibly be enjoyable, I did lose that particular thread.

And I did become enormously depressed to the point where I believed that any kind of relationship was almost impossible.

Quotes from Morrissey interviews on Channel 4's *Ear Say* (June 1984) and with *i-D* magazine (Oct 1987)

Recommended listening:
Morrissey's 'You Have Killed Me' from the album *Ringleader of the Tormentors* (2006)

I NEVER HAD NO ONE EVER

Recommended listening:
The Smiths' 'Never Had No One Ever' from the album *The Queen is Dead* (1986)

no one ever

I think I was just considered to be unbalanced, which helped me greatly, because it simply confirmed everything I knew.

Steven, are you back?

I think it was fear, above anything else, of normality. I just didn't want the norm, in any way. And I didn't get it. And I'm very glad. I'm very, very glad indeed.

I didn't want to grow up to be anything that I knew. I wanted a completely different life and whatever that entailed.

Are you going to join the rest of us for din...

No.

I think my parents were very worried for a very long time. But then when you become successful it seems to authenticate any kind of insanity or madness, however people view it.

Not eating with the whole family now..? What's wrong with the lad now?

As long as he lives under this roof he can do as he pleases!

Quotes from a Morrissey interview with BBC's Kirsty Young on *Desert Island Discs* (Nov 29, 2009)

Recommended listening:
The Smiths' 'Never Had No One Ever' from the album *The Queen is Dead* (1986)

MEAT

Recommended listening:
The Smiths' 'Meat is Murder' from the album *Meat is Murder* (1985)

NOVEMBER SPAWNED A MONSTER

I went to stern, working-class Catholic schools which were very depressing and very repressive.

And it always seemed to me entirely wrong to inflict all these kind of foul, ugly images onto children- these images of serpents trampled underfoot with fire coming out of their nostrils and things like that.

And this constant belief at school that if you don't go to church it's a cardinal sin and you shall burn in hell, and God will strike you down.

This constant fear of whatever you do you're wrong, and whatever you do you're guilty, and just simply by reason of your existence you were absolutely guilty in every way.

I despised that. I often felt that Christianity and the Catholic Church were quite severely divided.

And I also looked upon Ireland, being the most Catholic country in the world, as being also the most repressed country in the world.

It seemed to me wrong; it seemed to me black. Because it didn't allow any degree of self-expression.

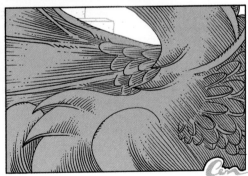

Quotes from a Morrissey interview on Channel 4's *Ear Say* (June 1984)

Recommended listening:
Morrissey's 'November Spawned a Monster' from his early singles compilation *Bona Drag* (1990)

CHELSEA GIRLS

Morrissey was educated, in the main, by his time spent at Paul Marsh's record shop in Moss Side, during the '60s.

I was fascinated by this little record shop with wooden floorboards exposed, with sawdust on the floor.

And I would go there as often as I could as a five-year-old, six-year-old.

And I would simply stand and examine everything, and read everything.

I was completely entranced by the song, recorded song, and the emotion that came from people singing...

And I still believe that

Quotes from a Morrissey interview with BBC's Kirsty Young on *Desert Island Discs* (Nov 29, 2009)

Recommended listening:
Nico's 'Chelsea Girls' from her debut solo album *Chelsea Girl* (1967)

Recommended listening:
avid Bowie's 'Ziggy Stardust' from his album *The Rise and Fall of Ziggy Stardust and the Spiders from Mars* (1972)
David Bowie's cover of The Easybeats' 'Friday on My Mind' from his covers album *Pin Ups* (1973)
Roxy Music's 'Re-Make/Re-Model' from their eponymous debut album *Roxy Music* (1972)

Blue Moon

My life was collecting seven-inch singles. That's what made me understand the beauty of pop music.

To have a song that was two minutes, nine seconds yet had volcanic emotion instead of elongated intros, dance outros...

I mean, all the great Elvis Presley records were under two minutes long and, to me, that's extreme talent to be able to shove everything in and condense it.

So many groups hit upon something and just repeat and repeat and repeat. The great moments in pop, I think, are very fleeting.

Quotes from a Morrissey interview with *Select* magazine (July 1991)

Recommended listening:
Elvis Presley's 'Blue Moon of Kentucky', featured as a b-side on his debut single 'That's All Right' (1954)
Elvis Presley's 'Blue Moon' and 'Blue Suede Shoes' from his debut album *Elvis Presley* (1956)
Elvis Presley's rendition of Mickey Newbury's 'An American Trilogy' from the album *Aloha From Hawaii* (1973)

SIZZLING BLOOD

I believe that everything went downhill from the moment the McDonald's chain was given licence to invade England. To me it was like the outbreak of war and I couldn't understand why English troops weren't retaliating.

The Americanisation of England is such a terminal illness I think England should be English and Americans should go home and spoil their own country.

Shopping centres are the worst — they're a boil on the face of the Earth. I regard modern architecture as more dangerous than nuclear war. It'll absolutely slaughter the human race.

And as for council houses — they can only be designed for the purpose of eliminating the working classes from the face of the Earth.

Quotes from a Morrissey interview with *Melody Maker* (Sept 26, 1987)

Recommended listening:
The Smiths' 'Meat is Murder' from the album *Meat is Murder* (1985)
The Smiths' 'Still Ill' from the album *The Smiths* (1984)
Morrissey's 'National Front Disco' from the album *Your Arsenal* (1992)

buck-toothed girls

I wrote to everyone.
I'd receive about 30 letters a day from no-one in particular.

I'd enter competitions.
I spent every solitary penny on postage stamps.

I had this wonderful arrangement with the entire universe without actually meeting anybody, just through the wonderful postal service.

The crisis of my teenage life was when postage stamps went up from 12p to 13p.

Quotes from a Morrissey interview with *The Face* (July 1984)

Recommended listening:
The Smiths' 'Ask' from the compilation *The World Won't Listen* (1987)

Lifeguard Sleeping

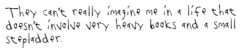

I swim a lot.
When I say that to people their heads spin around.

They can't really imagine me in a life that doesn't involve very heavy books and a small stepladder.

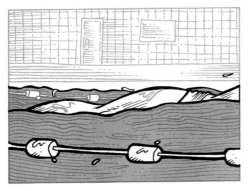

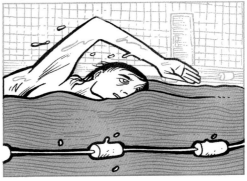

It's very nice to be underwater.
It gives you a very clear perspective on life.

I like diving between people's legs.
And obviously coming out the other side.
I don't loiter.

huff

pffh

Oh dear, oh dear! Another ten minutes and I was going to miss the street!

Quotes from a Morrissey interview with *Melody Maker* (Oct 14, 1997)

Recommended listening:
Morrissey's 'Lifeguard Sleeping, Girl Drowning' from the album *Vauxhall and I* (1994)

Please help the cause against loneliness

Wikipedia names Dusty Springfield as my first influence. I don't actually think I've ever even mentioned her name — and I was never remotely a fan.

'The Heart is a Lonely Hunter' by Carson McCullers was a big turning point for me when I was about 12.

Whenever I listened to music, I was ready to cry, usually with relief that someone understood...

...and that I was no longer alone in knowing whatever it was I thought I knew.

Quotes from a Morrissey interview with *The Columbus Dispatch* (Oct 2012)

Recommended listening:
Morrissey's 'Please Help the Cause Against Loneliness' from his early singles compilation *Bona Drag* (1990), written originally by him and Stephen Street for Sandie Shaw's comeback album *Hello Angel* (1988)

Recommended reading:
Carson McCullers' debut novel *The Heart is a Lonely Hunter* (1940)

Recommended viewing:
The motion picture adaptation of *The Heart is a Lonely Hunter*, directed by Robert Ellis Miller (1968)

In which we find young Steven Morrissey and his classmates being used as human targets by their gym teacher.

Recommended listening:
The Smiths' 'The Headmaster Ritual' from the album *Meat is Murder* (1985)

All the young dudes

Tell me about your final track and tell me why you've chosen Mott the Hoople.

This is Mott the Hoople from 1972, a track which made me feel quite charged and quite emotional and quite sad. And still does in its own way. And it's called 'Sea Diver'.

Following the break-ups of both The Spiders From Mars and Mott the Hoople, Steven Morrissey's last dose of glam rock was received when he attended the Hunter/Ronson concert at the Free Trade Hall, Manchester in March 1975.

As he did with most artists that collaborated with David Bowie, he obsessed over Mott the Hoople and the subsequent solo work that Ian Hunter produced. When Bowie's former right-hand man, Mick Ronson, joined Hunter to form new supergroup duo Hunter/Ronson, it seemed like a match made in heaven.

Just two years before this unlikely union, Steven would send letter after letter to the official Mott the Hoople fan club, pestering them for more information on his current favourite band.

In 1992 Morrissey would go full circle by befriending and employing Mick Ronson to produce one of his greatest solo albums and his love letter to glam, *Your Arsenal*. Ronson died a few months later from liver cancer.

Years later, when *Q* magazine asked him when and why he had last cried, he replied: "The death of Michael R."

Quotes from a Morrissey interview with BBC's Kirsty Young on *Desert Island Discs* (Nov 29, 2009)

Recommended listening:
Morrissey's Ronson-produced album, chock-full of glam moments, *Your Arsenal* (1992)
Mott the Hoople's 'Sea Diver' from their album *All the Young Dudes* (1973)
Mick Ronson's debut solo album *Slaughter on 10th Avenue* (1974)

Recommended viewing:
Promo video of Hunter/Ronson performing *Once Bitten Twice Shy* (1975)

RAW POWER

I fell in love with it before I even heard it, staring at this amazing Mick Rock picture of Iggy.
I've never really found an entire LP that I like better, really, and that's regardless of nostalgia.

Just looking at the sleeve, you get a whole story of not only that record, but what rock'n'roll should be in a 15-year-old's life: sexy, illicit, uncommercial, exciting, druggy. I wanted to sign up for all of that.

I put 'Gimme Danger' on first and couldn't believe it was exactly like the way I was playing... the way James Williamson played that riff, and then subsequently every riff on that record, made me think, "I should really find out more about what this guy's doing."

I spent almost a whole year learning that record. I would turn all the lights off in my bedroom and leave a little crack in the curtains so the orange street light would come through the window and create a super atmosphere.

Quotes from a Johnny Marr interview with Pitchfork.com (April 24, 2012)

Recommended listening:
The entire Stooges' album *Raw Power* (1973)

we hate it when our friends become successful

1975. After school rehearsal.

Recommended listening:
Morrissey's 'We Hate It When Our Friends Become Successful' from the album *Your Arsenal* (1992)
Steve Harley & Cockney Rebel's single 'Make Me Smile (Come Up and See Me)' (1975)

ROY'S KEEN

I am no longer strapped to the Women's Studies section of Waterstones on Kensington High Street night and day, as many people still seem to believe.
The world that I live in is quite broad. For instance, I go to the football whenever I can and whenever seems decent. And whenever I can get in for free.

Old Trafford Stadium, just around the corner from Steven Morrissey's bedroom.

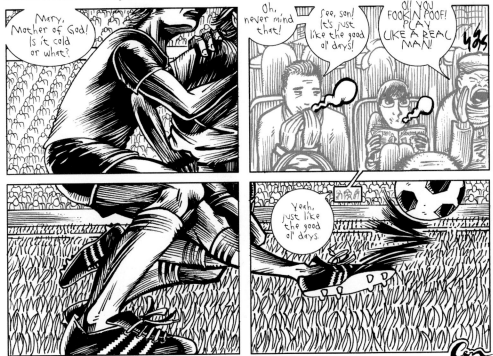

Excerpt from a Morrissey interview with *Select* (May 1994)

Recommended listening:
Morrissey's 'Roy's Keen' (an obvious pun on Manchester Utd's Roy Keane) from the album *Maladjusted* (1997)
Morrissey's 'Munich Air Disaster 1958' which refers to the plane crash that wiped out the 1958 Man Utd team,
b-side to his single 'Irish Blood, English Heart' (2004)

Recommended experiencing:
Morrissey fans chanting his name in football stadium fashion before he takes the stage

Munich Air Disaster 1958

I'm aware of how football has also been gagged, the television coverage and the newspaper coverage. I think snooker was introduced to strangulate football crowds. It's very, very sad...

I once bought a Manchester United hat, which I think was 12 shillings...

...and somebody ran up behind me and pulled it off and just ran ahead.

So I thought...

...and I decided to get my revenge on society.

Quotes from a Morrissey interview with the *NME* (Feb 20, 1988)

Recommended listening:
Morrissey's paean to football hooliganism 'We'll Let You Know' from the album *Your Arsenal* (1992)
Morrissey's 'Munich Air Disaster 1958' which refers to the plane crash that wiped out the 1958
Man Utd team, released as a b-side to his single 'Irish Blood, English Heart' (2004)

Listening to Lou Reed as a part of The Velvet Underground, we are really listening to the WH Auden of the modern world. Once again, not existing in print poetry but in recorded noise. And this is

the black angel's death song

At the age of 12 I went to see Lou Reed by myself.

At the time Lou Reed was singing exclusively about transsexuality and heroin and death and the beauty of death and the impossibility of life.

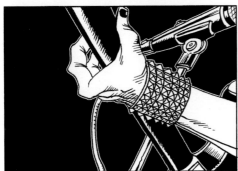

Quotes from Morrissey interviews with BBC's Kirsty Young on *Desert Island Discs* (Nov 29, 2009) and with *The Daily Telegraph* (June 17, 2011)

Recommended listening:
The Velvet Underground's flawless Andy Warhol-produced debut album *The Velvet Underground & Nico* (1967)
Lou Reed's flawless David Bowie/Mick Ronson-produced album *Transformer* (1972)

Recommended viewing:
Morrissey's cover of Lou Reed's 'Satellite of Love' live at Glastonbury Festival (2011)

What were you wearing back in '71?

I didn't religiously belong to any cult apart from when T. Rex happened and I bought a satin jacket. It was the first independent statement I made and it was extremely important to me.

Flares?

I did stray into a pair of loons on some occasions. Quite naturally green at the bottom and quite naturally yellow at the top.

Then later, when the New York Dolls happened, I tried to buy a pair of knee-length platform boots but I was very wisely stopped!

A Crombie?

I slept in a Crombie, with a Lancashire rose on it. You could quite easily be duffed up by those wearing a Yorkshire rose.

There were constant territorial, vicious, antagonising reasons for small-time anarchy. Everybody got their head kicked in... it's made me what I am today.

Quotes from a Morrissey interview with the *NME* (Feb 13, 1988)

Recommended listening:
T. Rex's first hit single 'Ride a White Swan' (1970)
Morrissey's 'Glamorous Glue' from his chock-full of glam moments, Mick Ronson-produced album *Your Arsenal* (1992)

SUEDEHEAD part one

Correct me if I'm wrong, but I thought the skinhead was an entirely British invention. I'm incapable of racism, even though I'm delighted that an increasing number of my audience are skinheads in nail varnish.

Most youth cultures come from the U.S.A. That the rest of the world around us looks upon skinheads as people who tattoo swastikas on their foreheads and throw fruit at innocent football supporters is a shame.

The original idea of skinheads was just about clothes and music. And in England it still is to a pretty great extent.

Style and everything it involves for me have their roots in the British working class. That's where all culture I appreciate passes on and in some degree is updated.

The British working class and its youth cultures are never vulgar or excessive. Whereas the middle class never has created a bit.

Quotes from Morrissey interviews with *Slitz* magazine (Sept 1992) and the *NME* (May 18, 1991)

Recommended listening:
Morrissey's 'Suedehead' from his debut solo album *Viva Hate* (1988)

Recommended reading:
Richard Allen's novel *Suedehead*, sequel to his cult paperback *Skinhead* (1971)

Recommended viewing:
Morrissey's music video for his single 'Our Frank' (1991)

SUEDEHEAD part two

For starters, surely 'Suedehead' has something to do with Richard Allen's pre-punk seminal trash novel of the same name? Yet there's no mention of suedeheads in the lyrics?
No, I'd noticed that. Does the song have anything to do with the title? But really I just like the word 'suedehead'!

So it's not even based on an episode from *Suedehead*?
No, not really.

And it's not about anyone in particular?
Yes, it is, but I'd rather not give any addresses and phone numbers at this stage.

Did you read all the Richard Allen books?
Skinhead, Suedehead, Smoothies...?
Yes, they were quite risqué little books at the time, certainly for 13-year-olds, who were the only people who read them

Did your mother know?
No, but she wasn't a suedehead. She was heavily into reggae. I don't think she even read Suedehead!

Weren't the books full of fighting and fornicating?
Yes, but I skipped those bits.

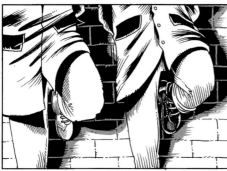

Quotes from a Morrissey interview with the *NME* (Feb 13, 1988)

Recommended viewing:
Morrissey's music video for his single 'Alma Matters', in which he sports a quasi-suedehead look (1997)

SUEDEHEAD part three

I think 'Starman' was the beginning, but the whole notion of Bowie being this despised person I found very encouraging. The daily tabloids wrote hateful things and there were only one or two people at school who'd actually confess to liking David Bowie.
I don't think that level of outrage exists anymore, people have forgotten how dramatic and serious it really was.

The Slade and Faces contingents were particularly aggressive people, while those who liked Bowie, Mott the Hoople and Lou Reed tended to be slightly more passive and easily picked on.

I remember standing outside concert halls in the early '70s, people would just walk past you and start kicking the queue. Everybody would just cower under a mass of Afghan coats.

Quotes from a Morrissey interview with the *NME* (Feb 13, 1988)

Recommended listening:
David Bowie's 'Starman' from the album *The Rise and Fall of Ziggy Stardust and the Spiders from Mars* (1972)

SUEDEHEAD part four

I began to hang around with a gang of people in Manchester who were very artistic and very expressive. They dyed their hair.

This led to a period of experimenting with bleach, documented in Morrissey's song 'I Know Very Well How I Got My Name'.

Yes, that's me. That's true. When I was 13 I did experiment with bottles of bleach and so forth.

I tried to dye it yellow and it came out gold. Then I tried to get rid of it and it came out purple. I was sent home from school.

How did your mother react?
Very tolerant, she'd had a lot of practice.

You weren't spanked?
No, that came much later in life, with the release of 'The Queen Is Dead'.

Quotes from a Morrissey interview with the *NME* (Feb 13, 1988)

Recommended listening:
Morrissey's 'I Know Very Well How I Got My Name', released as a b-side to his single 'Suedehead' (1988)
David Bowie's 'Moonage Daydream' from his concept album
The Rise and Fall of Ziggy Stardust and the Spiders from Mars (1972)

Recommended reading:
Richard Allen's novel *Suedehead*, sequel to his cult paperback *Skinhead* (1971)

SUEDEHEAD part five

And what exactly was a suedehead?

I think it was an outgrown skinhead. I don't mean a very, very large skinhead with a growth on his back. No, an outgrown skinhead who was slightly softer, not meant to be a football hooligan for instance... so obviously much less interesting.

Were you attracted to *Suedehead* and *Skinhead* because the heroes led very different lifestyles to your own?

They didn't really because youth cults in Manchester were very strong and suedeheads and skinheads and smoothies were very much part of daily life.

Morrissey would go to afternoon youth discos attended by violent club members, and enjoy the grime and the music, records including 'Young, Gifted and Black'.

There was a tremendous air of intensity and potential unpleasantness... On your way home you'd always get duffed up.

Were suedeheads the good guys?

Not really.
I don't think there were any good guys.
Everybody had several chips on several shoulders.
There was a great velocity of hate.

Quotes from a Morrissey interview with the *NME* (Feb 13, 1988)

Recommended listening:
Dave and Ansell Collins' 'Double Barrel' from the album *Double Barrel* (1971)
Aretha Franklin's cover of Nina Simone's 'Young, Gifted and Black' (1972)

FIVE YEARS

Do you pine for a mythical Britain?
Perhaps. It's certainly gone now. England doesn't only not rule the waves, it's actually sunk below them. And all that remains is debris... but in amongst the debris shine slits of positivity.

Midway through his *Diamond Dogs* Tour, David Bowie severed all ties with his glam rock past by renaming it The Soul Tour and embarked on another musical adventure/chapter, this time focusing on soul music. *Glam was officially over.*

Glam Rock 1971–1975
R.I.P.

Quotes from a Morrissey interview with *Spin* (April 1991)

Recommended listening:
The Smiths' 'The Queen is Dead' from the album *The Queen is Dead* (1986)
David Bowie's 'Five Years' from the album *The Rise and Fall of Ziggy Stardust and the Spiders from Mars* (1972)
David Bowie's 'Young Americans' from his soul phase album *Young Americans* (1975)

Recommended viewing:
David Bowie in full soul form performing 'Young Americans' live on *The Dick Cavett Show* (1974)

The End of the Family Line

Realising that your parents aren't compatible, I think, gives you a premature sense of wisdom that life isn't easy and it isn't simple to be happy.

Happiness is something you're very lucky to find.

Quotes from a Morrissey interview with *The Face* (July 1984)

Recommended listening:
Morrissey's '(I'm) the End of the Family Line' from the album *Kill Uncle* (1991)
Morrissey's 'Break Up the Family' from his debut solo album *Viva Hate* (1988)

Will Never Marry

My parents got divorced when I was 17...

...though they were working towards it for many years.

Quote from a Morrissey interview with *The Face* (July 1984)

Recommended listening:
Morrissey's 'Will Never Marry' from his early singles compilation *Bona Drag* (1990)

SOMETHING IS SQUEEZING MY SKULL part one

The Ramones burst on to the New York scene in 1974. Their minimalistic approach was the antithesis to the overproduced sounds of glam, hard and prog rock bands and they ushered in the punk rock era.

SOMETHING IS SQUEEZING MY SKULL part two

Morrissey became a regular contributor to the readers' letters columns of the UK music press.

He was unimpressed by The Ramones.

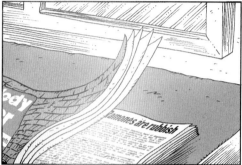

'… bumptious and degenerate no talents,' he called them in MM's Mailbag.

'… should be rightly filed and forgotten,' his letter concluded.

RAMONES are the latest bumptious band of degenerate
nts whose most notable achievement to date is their
o advance beyond the boundaries of New York City,
on the strength of a spate of convincing literature
the Ramones as God's gift to rock music.
been greeted with instant adulation by an army
s. Musically, they do not deal in subtlety or
y kind, their rule is to be as incompetent as

ieved to project the youth of America, New
e, anti-conformism, sex and struggle, or
miserably. And in the sober light of day
ave a field day.
the Stooges sound like concertmasters,
r place for their notoriously discordant
ntown Manhattan dives to which they

nd Patti Smith have proved that
away in the swamps and gutters
the only acts which originated
hy of any praise. The Ramones
that is of relevance or import-
d and forgotten. — STEVE
rd, Manchester.

Thirty-three years after writing the letter, and clearly remorseful, Morrissey was photographed hugging Johnny Ramone's memorial statue at his grave in the Hollywood Forever Cemetery for the cover of his single 'Something is Squeezing My Skull'.

Quotes from a letter Morrissey had published in *Melody Maker* (July 24, 1976).

Recommended listening:
Morrissey's 'Something is Squeezing My Skull' from the album *Years of Refusal* (2009)

SOMETHING IS SQUEEZING MY SKULL
part three

Thirty years after first hearing and hating it, the Ramones' album remains by Morrissey's side.

When I bought the Ramones' first album on import, I was enraged with jealousy because I felt they had booted the Dolls off the map.

I was 100% wrong. Three days after writing that Ramones piece, I realised that my love for The Ramones would outlive time itself.

And it shall. Well, it virtually has already.

If the Ramones were alive today, they'd be the biggest band in the world.

It takes the world 30 years to catch on, doesn't it?

I mean, look at poor Nico. Every modern teenager now seems to love Nico, yet while she was alive she couldn't afford a decent mattress.

Quotes from a Morrissey interview with *Billboard* (Oct 4, 2012)

Recommended listening:
Morrissey's 'Something is Squeezing My Skull' from his album *Years of Refusal* (2009)
The Ramones' self-titled debut album *The Ramones*. All of its 29 glorious minutes (1976)

REBEL
without
a cause
part one

I saw Rebel Without a Cause quite by accident when I was about six.

I was entirely enveloped.

I did research about him and it was like unearthing Tutankhamun's tomb.

His entire life seemed so magnificently perfect

When I mention James Dean to people they seem disappointed because it seems such a standard thing for a young person to be interested in — but I really can't help it

Quotes from Morrissey interviews with *Smash Hits* (June 21, 1984) and *Melody Maker* (Nov 3, 1984)

Recommended listening:
The Smiths' single 'Bigmouth Strikes Again', the cover featuring James Dean on his Czech Whizzer motorcycle (1986)

Recommended viewing:
Nicholas Ray's *Rebel Without a Cause*, released less than one month after Dean's fatal car crash (1955)

REBEL
without
a cause
part two

What he did on film didn't stir me that much, but as a person he was immensely valuable. Everything from his birth in a farming town to coming to New York, breaking into film and finding he didn't really want it when he had enormous success.

Even though he was making enormous strides with his craft, he was still incredibly miserable and obviously doomed.
Which is exactly the quality Oscar Wilde had. That kind of mystical knowledge that there is something incredibly black around the corner.

People who feel this are quite special

and always end up

in quite a mangled mess.

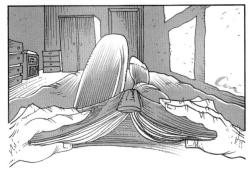

Quotes from a Morrissey interview with *Smash Hits* (June 21, 1984)

Recommended listening:
The three Smiths albums *Strangeways, Here We Come, Best I* (US) and *Best II* (US), the covers of which featured Dean's co-star, Richard Davalos, from Elia Kazan's *East of Eden* (1955)

REBEL without a cause
part three

He could wear an old rag and he was still quite stunning, and equally he could clamber into a tuxedo and it would also be incredibly fetching.

So for me he is the only person who looked perfect persistently.

Did you ever long for the kind of wild hedonism your hero James Dean was notorious for?

Yes I did. And it was a tremendous anti-climax waiting for it, and then suddenly I was 22 – the last thing I could remember was being 16!

What about a crush, an infatuation maybe?

Yes, I think I did... nothing I was about to put into practice in any way, it was always these very dark desires I had, mostly with people on television, which is utterly pointless anyway.
But in the real world... well I just wasn't really there. I never snogged on the corner, if that's what you mean!

I'm not really sure that he had any (acting skills). He was just a fascinating symbol of self-destruction. I had this incredible poetic union with James Dean. This blending of souls.

It's quite mystical and embarrassing. I felt this enormous affinity with almost every aspect of his life.

Quotes from Morrissey interviews with *Undress* (*NME* supplement) (July 1984), *Melody Maker* (Nov 3, 1984), *i-D* magazine (May 2004) and Channel 4's *Ear Say* (June 1984)

Recommended viewing:
George Stevens' *Giant* (1956)

My sister never experienced the kind of
isolation that I went through.

She always had quite a spirited social life.
She was never without the odd clump of friends.

Quotes from a Morrissey interview with *Melody Maker* (Nov 3, 1984)

Recommended listening:
The Smiths' 'Never Had No One Ever' from the album *The Queen is Dead* (1986)

Recommended reading:
Oscar Wilde's only published novel, *The Picture of Dorian Gray* (1890)

I have been steeped in personal depression for so long that I feel there is nothing any doctor or psychoanalyst can say to me.

I know all about depression and the weakening of the human spirit and struggle, and there is no one who can tell me anything about it, and there is nobody who can help me.

Quotes from a Morrissey interview with *Select* (May 1994)

Recommended listening:
The Smiths' 'Never Had No One Ever' from the album *The Queen Is Dead* (1986)

Margaret on the Guillotine

St Mary's RC Secondary Modern School, Stretford.
From day one the students were allocated to one of the school's four Houses. Each House would be encouraged to compete with the other and subsequently be rewarded in recompense for worthy behaviour or severely punished if they failed to prevail.

In Steven Morrissey's case he was allocated to House Clitherow. Named after the 16th century Catholic martyr, Margaret Clitherow, is it possible that her horrific death served as inspiration for the Joan of Arc reference in 'Bigmouth Strikes Again' or even the execution reference in 'Margaret on the Guillotine'?

In 1586, Margaret Clitherow was arrested and called before the York assizes for the crime of harbouring Roman Catholic priests.
She refused to plead to the case so there would be no trial, as that would entail her children being made to testify and therefore they would undoubtedly be tortured. Margaret was executed by being crushed to death on Good Friday.

She was stripped and had a handkerchief tied across her face, then laid out upon a sharp rock the size of a man's fist. A door was put on top of her and slowly loaded with an immense weight of rocks and stones (the small sharp rock would break her back when the heavy rocks were laid on top). Today Margaret is the patroness of the Catholic Women's League, a Roman Catholic lay organisation aimed at women in England and Wales.

Recommended listening:
The Smiths' 'Bigmouth Strikes Again' from the album *The Queen is Dead* (1986)
Morrissey's 'Margaret on the Guillotine' from his debut solo album *Viva Hate* (1988)

Recommended reading:
Peter Lake and Michael Questier's *The Trials of Margaret Clitherow: Persecution, Martyrdom and the Politics of Sanctity in Elizabethan England* (2011)

southpaw grammar

Did you get beaten by masters at school?

Yes. I wasn't really on the hit list. I wasn't one of those people who were dragged out every single day, but I found that I was certainly in the running for that.

I always found that I was hit and beaten for totally pointless reasons, which is what I'm sure every pupil would say.

But I think in my case I demand special consideration.

Stage 1: Hands in the air aka The Bluff

Stage 2: Hands on the desk aka The Inevitable

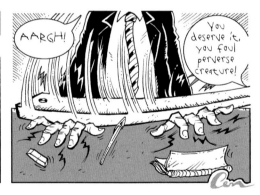

Quotes from a Morrissey interview with *Melody Maker* (Mar 16, 1985)

Recommended listening:
Morrissey's 'The Teachers Are Afraid of the Pupils' from the album *Southpaw Grammar* (1995)

...and so.

Recommended listening:
Morrissey's 'The Teachers Are Afraid of the Pupils' from the album *Southpaw Grammar* (1995)

hatful of hollow

Morrissey on attending sporting events for his school.

I had a terrible time and would have to go to places very far away.

I never wanted to do it, but if you were athletically capable you had to, otherwise you'd get beaten to death.

What do you mean you're not coming?

You're the fastest sprinter in the team, Morrissey!

My mother said I don't have to, if I don't want to.

YOUR... YOUR MOTHER?!

I always adored games but, because it was blindly compulsory, I went off the whole idea of athletics and movement.

I don't like anything that's enforced.

You're dead, when I return, Morrissey.

YOU HEAR ME? DEAD!

Go St Mary's

Quotes from a Morrissey interview printed in Johnny Rogan's *Morrissey & Marr: The Severed Alliance*, published by Omnibus Press (1992)

Recommended listening:
The Smiths' 'Back to the Old House' from the compilation *Hatful of Hollow* (1984)

Recommended viewing:
Lindsay Anderson's *if...* (1968)

Oh Mother

Recommended listening:
The Smiths' 'I Know It's Over' from the album *The Queen Is Dead* (1986)

Oscillate Wildly
part one

He had a life that was really tragic and it's curious that he was so witty.
Here we have a creature persistently creased in pain whose life was a total travesty.
He married, rashly had two children and almost immediately embarked on a love affair with a man. He was sent to prison for this.

It's a total disadvantage to care about Oscar Wilde, certainly when you come from a working class background. It's total self-destruction almost. My personal saving grace at school was that I was something of a model athlete.
I'm sure if I hadn't been, I'd have been sacrificed in the first year.
I got streams and streams of medals for running.

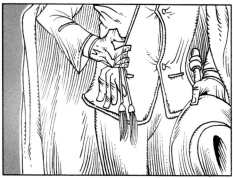

Quotes from a Morrissey interview with *Smash Hits* (June 21, 1984)

Recommended listening:
The Smiths' instrumental 'Oscillate Wildly' from the compilation *The World Won't Listen* (1987)

Recommended reading and listening:
Oscar Wilde's play *The Importance of Being Earnest* (1895), especially the recorded performance featuring John Gielgud, which Morrissey listened to on cassette obsessively (1953)

My mother, who's an assistant librarian, introduced me to his writing when I was eight. She insisted I read him and I immediately became obsessed.
Every single line affected me in some way. I liked the simplicity of the way he wrote. There was a piece called The Nightingale and the Rose that appealed to me immensely then.

A nightingale overhears a student lamenting the love of a professor's daughter, who will only dance with him if he brings her a red rose. After asking all the roses in the garden how she might find a red bud, the nightingale performs a ritual, singing the most beautiful song with her heart pressed against the thorn of a rose until it turns red, and the nightingale dies in the act. But the girl has in the meantime been given jewels by another man and rejects the student's gift. He, in turn, throws the rose into the gutter and returns to his studies swearing off love forevermore.

His hair is dark as the hyacinth-blossom, and his lips are red as the rose of his desire; but passion has made his face like pale ivory, and sorrow has set her seal upon his brow.

What a silly thing love is.

She said that she would dance with me if I brought her red roses.

Ah, on what little things does happiness depend!

Quotes from a Morrissey interview with *Smash Hits* (June 21, 1984) and
'The Nightingale and the Rose' by Oscar Wilde (1888)

Recommended reading and listening:
Read and listen to an audio reading of Oscar Wilde's short story 'The Nightingale and the Rose' (1888)
from his collection of stories for children *The Happy Prince and Other Tales* at
http://en.wikisource.org/wiki/The_Nightingale_and_the_Rose

Oscillate Wildly
part three

As I blundered through my late teens, I was quite isolated and Oscar Wilde meant much more to me. In a way he became a companion.

If that sounds pitiful, that was the way it was. I rarely left the house. I had no social life.

Then, as I became a Smith, I used flowers because Oscar Wilde always used flowers.

He once went to the Colorado salt mines and addressed a mass of miners there.

He started the speech with, 'Let me tell you why we worship the daffodil'.

Of course, he was stoned to death. But I really admired his bravery and the idea of being constantly attached to some form of plant. As I get older, the adoration increases. I'm never without him. It's almost Biblical. It's like carrying your rosary around with you.

Quotes from a Morrissey interview with *Smash Hits* (June 21, 1984)

Recommended listening:
The Smiths' 'Cemetery Gates' from the album *The Queen is Dead* (1986)

Recommended reading:
The Oscar Wilde Society of America's account of Wilde's trip to the United States of America in 1882
www.owsoa.org/wia.htm

Halfway to Paradise
part one

Billy Fury is virtually the same as James Dean. He was persistently unhappy and yet had a string of hit records.
He was discovered working on the docks in Liverpool, was dragged to London, styled and forced to make records.

He always wanted to make very emotionally over-blown ballads but he found himself in the midst of the popular arena.
He despised almost every aspect of the music industry and was very, very ill from an early age.

Did you cry when Billy Fury died?
Persistently. Loudly.

Quotes from Morrissey interviews with *Smash Hits* (June 21,1984) and *The Face* (July 1984)

Recommended listening:
The Smiths' single 'Last Night I Dreamt That Somebody Loved Me',
the front cover of which featured a young Billy Fury (1987)

Recommended viewing:
Michael Winner's musical *Play it Cool*, Britain's answer to the successful Elvis movies, starring Billy Fury (1962)

This album is the rarest I have. It was his first. Albums made in those days were thrust out to appeal to a mature audience.
Singles were for teenagers and I'm afraid I always preferred the singles.

As a child, Morrissey would wake with excitement on a Saturday morning, tearing down to the local record shop and spending hours immersed in its world.

Halfway to Paradise
part two

I'd leave about mid-day and go to bed and consider that a completely successful day.

I was really quite poor, so whatever record I could buy was like a piece of my heart something I couldn't possibly exist without Billy's singles are totally treasurable. I get quite passionate about the vocal melodies and the orchestration always sweeps me away.

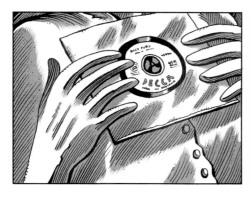

Quotes from a Morrissey interview with *Smash Hits* (June 21,1984)

Recommended listening:
Billy Fury's singles 'Halfway to Paradise' (1961) and 'Last Night Was Made for Love' (1962)
The Smiths' single 'Last Night I Dreamt That Somebody Loved Me' (1987), the front cover of which featured a young Billy Fury

Recommended viewing:
Kenneth Hume's *I've Gotta Horse*, Billy Fury's second musical comedy (1965)

TALES OF THE SMITHS & NICO
part one

Born Christa Päffgen in Nazi-controlled Cologne in 1938, Nico became one of Morrissey's greatest influences. Her life is a tragic tale of fate and circumstance.

Christa's father was a Yugoslavian adventurer who had already been drafted into Hitler's army by the time of her birth. He managed to instruct her mother to take her to her grandparents' house in Lowenau in order to evacuate them from Berlin.

He soon sustained head injuries at the front that caused severe brain damage, going insane within months. The Nazis sent him to a concentration camp where he died as an experimental medical subject.

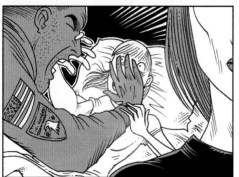 

After the country was liberated from Nazi control by the Allies, Christa moved to Berlin where she worked as a seamstress until, at age 15, she was raped by an American sergeant, who was consequently court-martialled.

Her song 'Secret Side', from her 1974 album *The End*, made oblique references to this event, while Lou Reed also referred to it in his song 'The Kids' from his 1973 album *Berlin*. Both albums are considered to have had a strong influence on Morrissey.

Recommended listening:
Nico's 'Secret Side' from the album *The End* (1974)
Lou Reed's 'The Kids' from the album *Berlin* (1973)

TALES OF THE SMITHS & NICO
part two

Discovered at 16 by photographer Herbert Tobias while both were working at a KaDeWe fashion show in Berlin, Tobias gave 'Nico' her adopted name, which she used for most of her life. Tobias named her after his ex-boyfriend, Greek filmmaker Nikos Papatakis.
Nico soon moved to Paris and began working for *Vogue*, *Tempo*, *Camera*, *Elle*, and other fashion magazines.

After appearing in several television advertisements, Nico got a small role in Alberto Lattuada's film *La Tempesta*. She also appeared in Rudolph Maté's *For the First Time*, with Mario Lanza, later that year. In 1959 she was invited to the set of Federico Fellini's *La Dolce Vita*, where she attracted the attention of the acclaimed director, who gave her a minor role in the film as herself.

In 1962 Nico gave birth to her son, Christian Aaron "Ari" Päffgen, commonly held to have been fathered by French actor Alain Delon, with whom she had a brief but passionate affair.
Delon always denied Ari's paternity.

Due to her developing drug dependency, the child was mostly raised by Delon's mother and her husband. Ari was eventually adopted by them, taking their surname, Boulogne.
Delon never spoke to his parents or Nico again.

Recommended listening:
Morrissey's 'You Have Killed Me' from the album *Ringleader of the Tormentors* (2006)

Recommended viewing:
Susanne Ofteringer's documentary *Nico Icon* (1995)
Federico Fellini's *La Dolce Vita* (1960)

Recommended reading:
Ari Päffgen's book about him and his mother, *L'Amour N'Oublie Jamais* (2001)

TALES OF THE SMITHS & NICO
part three

After splitting her time between New York and Paris, in 1963 Nico got the lead role in Jacques Poitrenaud's *Strip-Tease*.
She also recorded the title track, written by Serge Gainsbourg, initiating her career in music.
In 1965 Nico met Rolling Stones guitarist Brian Jones, with whom she had a brief affair.

She recorded her first single, 'I'm Not Sayin'' with the b-side 'The Last Mile', for The Rolling Stones' manager Andrew Loog Oldham's Immediate label.
The single was produced by The Yardbirds' (and future Led Zeppelin) guitarist Jimmy Page.
Later that summer in Paris, she was introduced to Bob Dylan. He played the song 'I'll Keep It with Mine' for her shortly after, which she'd later record.

After being introduced to Andy Warhol, Nico began working with Warhol and Paul Morrissey in New York on their experimental films, including *Chelsea Girls*, *The Closet*, *Sunset* and *Imitation of Christ*.
In 1967, while in L.A. she had a fling with The Doors' singer Jim Morrison, whose death inspired her later album, *The End*. When Warhol began managing Lou Reed and John Cale's experimental rock 'n' roll band, The Velvet Underground, he proposed that the group take on Nico as a chanteuse. They consented reluctantly, for both personal and musical reasons.

The group became the centrepiece of Andy Warhol's Exploding Plastic Inevitable, a multimedia performance featuring music, light, film and dance.
Nico sang lead vocals on three songs – 'Femme Fatale', 'All Tomorrow's Parties', 'I'll Be Your Mirror' – and backing vocal on 'Sunday Morning', on the band's debut album, *The Velvet Underground & Nico*.
Though it was poorly received at the time, it went on to become a timeless classic and is considered one of the most infuential albums of all time.

Recommended listening:
The Velvet Underground's entire groundbreaking debut album, *The Velvet Underground & Nico* (1967)
Nico's rendition of Serge Gainsbourg's 'Strip-Tease' (1963)

Recommended viewing:
Jacques Poitrenaud's *Strip-Tease* (1963)
Andy Warhol and Paul Morrissey's *Chelsea Girls* (1966)

TALES OF THE SMITHS & NICO
part four

Johnny Marr on The Velvet Underground influence:

I didn't realise that 'There Is A Light' was going to be an anthem, but when we first played it I thought it was the best song I'd ever heard.

There's a little in-joke in there just to illustrate how intellectual I was getting. At the time everyone was into The Velvet Underground and they stole the intro to 'There She Goes' — da da da-da, da da-da-da, Dah Dah! — from The Rolling Stones' version of 'Hitch Hike', the Marvin Gaye song. I just wanted to put that in to see whether the press would say, Oh it's The Velvet Underground! Cos I knew that I was smarter than that. I was listening to what The Velvet Underground was listening to.

During her tenure with The Velvet Underground, Nico and Lou Reed briefly became lovers. She had earlier been John Cale's lover, also a key member of The Velvets. Never truly accepted in the group, her presence caused constant tension in the studio.

Nico and Reed's relationship would often turn violent and soon after the release of the band's debut album she left the group to pursue a solo career.
Reconciling in the following year, Reed and Cale wrote songs for Nico's debut album *Chelsea Girl*.

Morrissey thought Nico's voice was an exquisite illustration of empty despair.

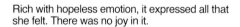

Rich with hopeless emotion, it expressed all that she felt. There was no joy in it.

Quotes from a Johnny Marr interview with *Select* (Dec 1993)

Recommended listening:
The Smiths' 'There is a Light That Never Goes Out' from the album *The Queen is Dead* (1986)
The Velvet Underground's 'There She Goes Again' from the album *The Velvet Underground & Nico* (1967)
The Rolling Stones' cover of Marvin Gaye's 'Hitch Hike' from their album *Out of Our Heads* (1965)
Marvin Gaye's 'Hitch Hike' from the album *That Stubborn Kinda Fellow* (1962)

TALES OF THE SMITHS & NICO
part five

Immediately following the end of her association with The Velvet Underground, Nico began work as a solo artist. On her debut album, 1967's *Chelsea Girl*, she recorded songs by Bob Dylan, Tim Hardin and Jackson Browne.

For *The Marble Index*, released in 1969, Nico wrote the lyrics and music. Accompaniment mainly centred around Nico's harmonium, while John Cale added an array of folk and classical instruments, and arranged the album.

The harmonium became Nico's signature instrument for the rest of her career. At this point she dyed her hair black and started donning darker clothes in order to physically represent her creative mood.

Nico released two more solo albums in the 1970s, on which she wrote the music, sang and played the harmonium. Cale produced and played most of the other instruments. *The End...* featured Brian Eno on synthesizer and she also collaborated with Roxy Music's Phil Manzanera.

During the Seventies, Nico made five films with French director Philippe Garrel. They met in 1969 and Nico contributed the song 'The Falconer' to Garrel's film *Le Lit de la Vierge*. Soon after, she moved in with Garrel and became a central figure in his professional and personal life.

After years of successfully avoiding class A drugs while recording with members of The Velvets, she became hooked on heroin whilst living with Garrel, a habit that she never truly managed to kick.

By now Nico's erratic behaviour was causing a lot of friction between her and Island Records and in 1975 the label dropped Nico from their roster.

Burnt out both physically and creatively, by the late '70s she had moved to the Salford area of Manchester.

Recommended listening:
Nico's masterpiece, 'Innocent and Vain', which was constantly on Morrissey's interval tapes prior to entering the stage from the '90s until 2002 and features Brian Eno's sonic bombardment. From her album *The End...* (1974)
Nico's 'Roses in the Snow' from the album *The Marble Index* (1969)
The Smiths' 'Miserable Lie' from their debut album *The Smiths* (1984)

Recommended viewing:
Philippe Garrel's *Le Lit de la Vierge* (1969)

LITTLE MAN,
WHAT NOW?
part one

Recommended listening:
Morrissey's 'Little Man, What Now?' from his debut solo album *Viva Hate* (1988)

Recommended reading:
Hans Fallada's novel *Kleiner Mann, was nun?* (*Little Man, What Now?*) (1932)

Recommended listening:
Morrissey's 'Little Man, What Now?' from his debut solo album *Viva Hate* (1988)

Recommended reading:
Oscar Wilde's essay *The Critic as Artist* (1891)

LITTLE MAN, WHAT NOW?
part three

D'you see that, Morrissey? Your fuckin' Irish mates just bombed hundreds of innocents in Birmingham.

They're NOT my mates... AND they DESERVE to have their own country ...or whatever!

Mick scum.

The following week:
Alright, Morrissey, ready for your final turn in Music Time?

Moreso than ever, sir.

Give Ireland back to the Irish.

Scumbag traitor.

I knew it

You suck, Morrissey!

Recommended listening:
Wings' debut single 'Give Ireland Back to the Irish' (1972)
Morrissey's 'Irish Blood, English Heart' from the album *You Are the Quarry* (2004)

Recommended viewing:
Paul Greengrass' *Bloody Sunday* (2002)
Steve McQueen's *Hunger* (2008)

Recommended listening:
The Smiths' 'The Headmaster Ritual' from the album *Meat is Murder* (1985)

Recommended viewing:
Stanley Kubrick's *A Clockwork Orange* (1971)

LITTLE MAN,
WHAT NOW?
part five

Recommended listening:
The New York Dolls' debut album *New York Dolls* (1973)

Jet Boy *part one*

I can't believe mum bought me a ticket for New York!

One year from today I'll be visiting my Aunt Mary for the summer!

Steve! How's it goin', man?

Wha!? David Johansen?!

GOD PLEASE DON'T MAKE THIS A DREAM

Hey man, me and the rest of the Dolls wanna thank you for all the hard work you did with the UK fan club, man!

Oh, don't mention it David!

And we wanna officially invite you to become a member of the band!

POP

...it's a dream.

Recommended listening:
The New York Dolls' 'Jet Boy' from their self-titled debut album (1973)

Recommended listening:
The New York Dolls' 'Trash' from their self-titled debut album (1973)

Recommended reading:
Oscar Wilde's essay *The Critic as Artist* (1891)

Jet Boy
part three

Summer 1975. Stretford, Manchester.

You again!

I told you to stop staring at me!

We're not leaving for another year!

Oh God.

I've got to get out of this place.

**September 1975.
Stretford Technical School, Manchester.**

Recommended listening:
The New York Dolls' 'Private World' from their self-titled debut album (1973)

Recommended listening:
The New York Dolls' 'Lonely Planet Boy' from their self-titled debut album (1973)

you've lost that lovin' feelin'

All the memories I have of life are not of people but of songs or films.
When I was a child I was obsessed with 'You've Lost That Lovin' Feelin'', the way the two voices were jumping around, and, when I saw it on Top of the Pops, the way Bill Medley and Bobby Hatfield would not look at each other and sing those two parts was extraordinary.
All the things that influenced me, in film and music, were quite haphazard and strange, and I felt that they could be gathered, blended and the final result would be something unique.

Quote from a Morrissey interview with *Mojo* (April 2006)

Recommended listening:
The Righteous Brothers' 'You've Lost That Lovin' Feelin'' (1964)

all you need is me
part one

Autumn 1975.
384 Kings Road, Stretford, Manchester.

Recommended listening:
Morrissey's 'My Dearest Love' released as a b-side to his 7" single 'All You Need is Me' (2008)

all you need is me
part two

Autumn 1975.
384 Kings Road, Stretford, Manchester.

Recommended listening:
Morrissey's 7" single 'All You Need is Me' (2008)

Recommended viewing:
Classic Granada TV *Coronation Street* episodes from the mid '70s (c. 1975)

all you need is me
part three

Autumn 1975.
Stretford Technical School, Manchester.

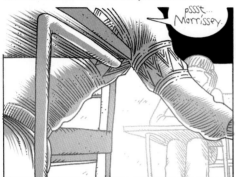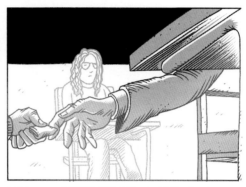

Recommended listening:
Morrissey's 'My Dearest Love' released as a b-side to his 7" single 'All You Need is Me' (2008)

all you need is me
part four

When I was young, I instantly excluded the human race in favour of pop music, and you can't live a fulfilled existence like that. People are invariably there. You have to go to school; you have to try to communicate with those around you.

Autumn 1975.
Stretford Technical School, Manchester.

But when you've sealed up your bedroom doors and you've blackened your windows, and all you want in the world are those tiny crackles that are about to introduce that record and you love the crackles that you hear from the needle on the vinyl...

...as much as you love what will follow then I don't think you will turn out to be a very level-headed human being. Music is like a drug, but there are no rehabilitation centres.

Quotes from a Morrissey interview with *Select* (July 1991)

Recommended listening:
Morrissey's 7" single 'All You Need is Me' (2008)

YEARS OF REFUSAL
PART ONE

In 1975, Britain's governing Labour Party declared the recession had ended, but the economy remained shaky. Inflation was high, strikes continued to cripple manufacturing and public services and unemployment rose above the 1,000,000 mark. Following the resignation of Harold Wilson as Prime Minister in March 1976, his successor James Callaghan was forced to call on the International Monetary Fund for a multi-billion pound bail-out in an attempt to bolster Britain's flagging economy.

Under these circumstances, a young Steven Patrick Morrissey chose to enroll at Stretford's Technical School in order to sit his O-Levels in the summer of 1976.

The subjects he chose to take were English literature, sociology, history and the general paper.

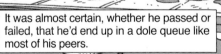

It was almost certain, whether he passed or failed, that he'd end up in a dole queue like most of his peers.

The year was 1975.

YEARS OF REFUSAL
PART TWO

With regard to 'Mama Lay Softly on the Riverbed'; I've read that your mother was a librarian. Did she influence your reading as a boy?

No, not really. My mother has masses and masses of books on Irish politics and Irish history, which I was never responsible enough to examine too deeply. When you're a teenager you want to read about people in your own situation because you need to compare whatever is happening to you with how other people manage when faced with your, uh, limitations. I went to a working-class school in Manchester so naturally there were never any books and no one ever suggested to us that we might want to read anything.

Quotes from a Morrissey interview with *Hot Press* (Apr 3, 2009)

Recommended listening:
Morrissey's 'Mama Lay Softly on the Riverbed' from the album *Years of Refusal* (2009)
Morrissey's 'Margaret on the Guillotine' from his debut solo album *Viva Hate* (1988)

YEARS OF REFUSAL
PART THREE

The British Conservative Party has chosen Margaret Thatcher as its new leader.
She will be the first woman to head a British political party after a landslide victory over the other four male candidates.

Mrs Thatcher, who served as Secretary of State for Science and Education in Ted Heath's government, exclaimed: *"It's like a dream."*

The MP for Finchley, north London, since 1959 rejected suggestions of great celebrations. She said:

Good heavens, no.

There's far too much work to be done.

At one point, talking about his childhood, Morrissey described the poverty he recalled in his school.

Children fainting through lack of food, absolute subsistence level, the dog ear of welfare. I never saw anybody speaking to me about my life. I never heard anybody who seemed to account for my experience.

But you didn't grow up to be a social worker, I started to say.

"Didn't I?" Morrissey said.

Dave?

Dave!

My God! Sir, he just passed out!

Nonsense! It's obviously an ill-attempted ploy to skip class!

Right?

Quotes from a Morrissey interview with *The Guardian* (Aug 2, 1997)
and a Margaret Thatcher interview with *BBC News* (Feb 11, 1975)

Recommended listening:
Morrissey's 'Margaret on the Guillotine' from his debut solo album *Viva Hate* (1988)

RED PATENT LEATHER part one

In early 1975, the young English fortune-seeker and future iconoclast Malcolm McLaren takes over the New York Dolls' management. He and his girlfriend, Vivienne Westwood, design red patent leather costumes for the band and convince them to use a Soviet-style hammer and sickle motif for their stage show as a provocative means of promotion.

McLaren took the Communist Party image further by insisting that all tables in the Little Hippodrome venue in which they performed should be draped in red fabric and even suggested that every drink sold while the Dolls were appearing should have an injection of red dye. David Johansen clutched a copy of the Maoist handbook like a Bible. Being the final year of the USA's war with Vietnam, the shows did not go down well with the audience.

Recommended listening:
New York Dolls' live album *Red Patent Leather* recorded in March 1975 (released in 1984)

RED PATENT LEATHER part two

Morrissey shouldered the burden of converting the UK into New York Dolls devotees.

As self-elected President of the UK New York Dolls Fan Club, he wrote to the music press extolling their virtues. And even produced a red badge for fans to wear.

'Wear it proudly comrade,' he instructed.

Recommended Reading:
Nina Antonia's account of the red patent leather days in her New York Dolls biography *Too Much, Too Soon* (1998)

RED PATENT LEATHER part three

In October 1975, KISS release a live version of their single 'Rock and Roll All Nite', a song considered by many rock fans to be the Rock and Roll National Anthem.

Meanwhile in Stretford, Manchester.

The song and their make-up cemented their reputation as one of the biggest party bands of their era and led to a genre known as 'pantomime' rock. Although at first they embraced the DIY ethos of the New York punks, they soon joined the established music industry and many of their OTT stage antics were adopted by subsequent heavy metal acts.

Fun fact: KISS' drummer, Peter Criss, was a childhood friend of the New York Dolls' drummer Jerry Nolan, who landed KISS their first big gigs.
If Criss' drum intro made 'Rock and Roll All Nite' one of the most recognisable rock intros ever, the fact that Nolan taught him his first drum skills makes the KISS-Dolls connection even more ironic.

Recommended listening:
KISS' live version of their single 'Rock and Roll All Nite' from their legendary live album *Alive!* (1975)

RED PATENT LEATHER part four

Following Malcolm McLaren's advice, the New York Dolls adopt the Red Patent Leather look. The band soon face great criticism for this choice.

In 1975, foundering in drug abuse and interpersonal conflicts, the band was on the brink of splitting up. The Dolls do a five-concert tour of New York's five boroughs, supported by Television, which includes Tom Verlaine and Richard Hell. They then head to Florida.

This show is in co-ordination with the Dolls' very special 'entente cordiale' with the People's Republic of China.

Later that year, Johnny Thunders and Jerry Nolan quit the New York Dolls, the same week that Richard Hell leaves Television.
Together they form The Heartbreakers, playing The Coventry in Queens soon after.

Thunders is replaced by local guitarist Blackie Goozeman for the remainder of the Florida tour. As Blackie Lawless, he would later become the singer and guitarist in '80s HM shock rockers W.A.S.P.

Even though he led the New York Dolls fan club in the UK, Morrissey would read about the collapse of his favourite band through tidbits in music magazines' news columns.

Trash

November 1975.
Granada Studios, Manchester.

Recommended listening:
Morrissey's live cover of the New York Dolls' 'Trash' from their self-titled debut album *New York Dolls* (1973), released as a b-side on the 7" re-issue of Morrissey's classic single 'Suedehead' (2010)

Recommended viewing:
Michael Winterbottom's *24 Hour Party People*, a film revolving around Tony Wilson's influence on the Manchester scene (2002)

Grunwick was a mail order film processing company. In 1976, manager Malcolm Alden sacked a young man, Devshi Budi, and three other young men then walked out in protest. That same afternoon, Jayaben Desai and her son Sunil walked out after a row with the same manager.

The following Monday morning they began picketing the gates and were joined by 50 other workers.

The Grunwick strike at its height involved thousands of trade unionists and police in confrontations outside the small film processing factory in North London, with over 500 arrests on the picket line and frequent police violence. It was also one of the first strikes to involve a group of Asian women. The worldwide publicity attracted by the dispute made it a thorny political issue for the Labour government.

Recommended listening:
Morrissey's 'Bengali in Platforms' from his debut solo album *Viva Hate* (1988)

Recommended web reading:
The Working Class Movement Library's article and resources on the Grunwick strike
www.wcml.org.uk

asleep
part one

In reference to the Grunwick strike, the leader of the Opposition, Mrs. Margaret Thatcher, asked today:

"What action does the Prime Minister propose to take to protect the right of the law-abiding citizen to go peacefully to work?"

"Leslie, how about we move onto another news report of almost equal gravitas for members of the public?"

"The Prince of Wales has just named Mike Oldfield as his favourite rock artist and mentioned that he plays Oldfield's massive hit, Tubular Bells, in the Royal Palace almost daily."

'Rock' artists and the establishment 101:
Five years later, in 1981, Mike Oldfield was asked to compose a piece for the Royal Wedding of Charles, Prince of Wales, and Lady Diana Spencer, titled 'Royal Wedding Anthem'.

Recommended listening:
The Smiths' 'The Queen is Dead' from the album *The Queen is Dead* (1986)

Recommended viewng:
BBC Four's *Timeshift* documentary on the Grunwick strike (2010)

asleep
part two

Have you thought about being in control of your death?
Have you thought about shuffling off this mortal coil at a time of your choosing?

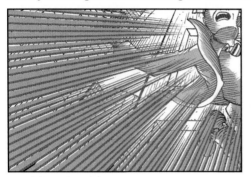

Yes I have. Yes I have.
And I think this self-destruction is honourable. I always thought it was.
It's an act of great control and I understand people who do it.

Quotes from a Morrissey interview with BBC's Kirsty Young on *Desert Island Discs* (Nov 29, 2009)

Recommended listening:
The Smiths' 'Asleep' from their final singles compilation album *The World Won't Listen* (1987)

asleep
part three

Recommended listening:
The Smiths' 'Asleep' from their final singles compilation album *The World Won't Listen* (1987)

asleep
part four

Recommended listening:
The Shangri-Las' 'Leader of the Pack' from their debut self-titled album (1965)

She was six years older, but 5,000 years wiser.

I'm sure she's very happy now, on that pavement.

Quotes from a Morrissey interview with *The Guardian* (Aug 2, 1997)

Recommended listening:
The Smiths' 'Asleep' from their final singles compilation album *The World Won't Listen* (1987)

asleep
part six

The church was thrust upon me.
Every week I would have to go to confession and sit and invent sins I hadn't committed to please the priest.

It is probably the worst thing you can do to a child, to make it feel guilty, and guilt is astonishingly embedded in Catholic children without them knowing why.

--and did ye know this lost soul that killed herself the other day?

It is a ferocious burden to carry.

We went through this routine with the Moors victims, too, I do not...

Are ye confessing to having sinned again, boy? Have ye been havin' impure thoughts?

Fuck off.

How evil can children be?

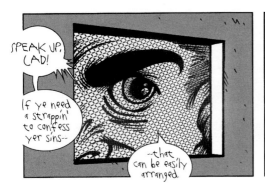

SPEAK UP, LAD!

If ye need a strappin' to confess yer sins--

--that can be easily arranged.

Fu-- Fu--

Forgive me, father--

--for I have sinned.

Quotes from a Morrissey interview with *The Guardian* (Aug 2, 1997)

Recommended listening:
The Smiths' 'Asleep' from their final singles compilation album *The World Won't Listen* (1987)

THE MODERN DANCE part one

Following in the footsteps of The Stooges and the New York Dolls, a slew of New York based bands, inspired by the stripped-down sounds of 1960s garage music, set out to challenge the overcomplicated and compromised music that '70s prog rock bands produced.

Hailing from Boston, MA, The Modern Lovers were one of the first bands to uphold these new principles. Led by Jonathan Richman, a young songwriter so obsessed with The Velvet Underground that he managed to convince them to let him open their set just before they broke up, The Modern Lovers married '60s anti-estabishment attitude with '70s sensitivities and a back-to-basics approach. On New Year's Eve 1972 they supported the New York Dolls at the Mercer Arts Center on a bill which also included Wayne County and Suicide. A new era had just begun.

Suicide was an early synthesizer/vocal duo that began gigging in 1970.
The band consisted of vocalist Alan Vega and Martin Rev on synthesizers and drum machines. Never widely popular amongst the general public, Suicide's music is today considered one of the greatest influences of synthpop, techno, the industrial dance sounds of the '80s and '90s and the new wave of electroclash.
In a November 1970 flyer, the band became the first ever to use the phrase "punk music" to advertise a concert and describe their sound.

Soon after, a new wave of musicians started performing in New York's Lower East Side and created a scene that provided a fresh and energetic outlook.
Acts like Teenage Jesus and the Jerks, The Dead Boys, Pere Ubu, Devo and many more emerged from this scene and led the way for the punk and no wave movements that would arise.

Focusing on short songs with electric guitars, strong drums, and a direct, unproduced approach, these wannabe musicians influenced a diverse group of young clubgoers who would in turn take these ideals and create their own legends, from Television's Tom Verlaine and Sonic Youth's Thurston Moore and Kim Gordon to a young unknown dancer called Madonna Ciccone.

Recommended listening:
The Modern Lovers' punk anthem 'Roadrunner' from their self-titled debut album (1976)
Suicide's 'Ghost Rider' from their long-awaited self-titled debut album (1977)
Teenage Jesus and the Jerks' 'Orphans', penned by Lydia Lunch, from their EP *Orphans/Less of Me* (1978)
Pere Ubu's 'The Modern Dance' from their debut album *The Modern Dance* (1978)

THE MODERN DANCE part two

Founded in December 1973 by Hilly Kristal on Manhattan's Bowery, CBGB became a worldwide reference point for the stripped down, back-to-basics approach that the New York punk bands brought back to rock music. Its full name was CBGB & OMFUG, which stood for 'Country Bluegrass Blues and Other Music For Uplifting Gormandizers'. Kristal's original intent was to open a club where country and blues acts could perform, but another fate awaited the venue.

In 1973, at CBGB's precursor, Hilly's On The Bowery, two locals, Bill Page and Rusty McKenna, convinced Kristal to allow them to book concerts. Although the term "punk rock" was never used, these acts laid the musical foundation for the bands which followed.

After the Mercer Arts Center collapsed in August 1973, there were few locations in New York where unsigned bands could play original music, and some of the Mercer refugees, including Suicide, The Fast, Wayne County and the Magic Tramps, all played in the very early days of CBGB.

The club soon became a haven for teenagers looking for something other than the glitter poses of the glam era and the shoegazing pompousness of the prog bands.
CBGB had only one rule: the band had to play primarily original music.

No cover bands were booked, although most of the regular bands played one or two covers during their sets. Hilly Kristal's son claims the rule was meant to help the club avoid paying ASCAP royalties for the compositions being performed. This strict policy led the bands to write original compositions.

Recommended listening:
Suicide's 'Johnny' from their long-awaited self-titled debut album (1977)
Wayne County & the Electric Chairs' single 'Fuck Off' (1977)
The Fast's single 'Boys Will Be Boys' (1976)

THE MODERN DANCE part three

At the core of the newly built New York Bowery club CBGB was Television.

Their influences ranged from the Velvet Underground to the staccato guitar work of Dr. Feelgood's Wilko Johnson, all expertly performed by Tom Verlaine. The band's bassist/singer, Richard Hell, created a distinctive look with cropped, ragged hair, ripped T-shirts held together by safety pins, and black leather jackets which formed the basis for punk rock's visual style.

In the spring of 1975, Patti Smith and Television shared a two-month weekend residency at CBGB that significantly raised the club's profile.

Television's sets included Richard Hell's 'Blank Generation', which became the scene's emblematic anthem. Soon after, Hell left Television and founded a band featuring a more stripped-down sound, The Heartbreakers, with two former New York Dolls, Johnny Thunders and Jerry Nolan.

Morrissey would watch these developments as a distant observer, by reading the sparse *NME* or *Melody Maker* features and ordering the few LP imports to reach Manchester.

Recommended listening:
Originally performed by Television and then The Heartbreakers, punk rock's first anthem, Richard Hell and the Voidoids' 'Blank Generation' (1976)
Television's landmark album *Marquee Moon* (1977)

Recommended viewing:
Ivan Kral and Amos Poe's documentary filmed during the outbreak of the first NY punk scene *The Blank Generation* (1976)

THE MODERN DANCE part four

The first wave of punk was aggressively modern, distancing itself from the bombast and sentimentality of early 1970s rock. According to Ramones drummer Tommy Ramone, "In its initial form, a lot of the 1960s stuff was innovative and exciting. Unfortunately, what happens is that people who could not hold a candle to the likes of Hendrix started noodling away. Soon you had endless solos that went nowhere. By 1973, I knew that what was needed was some pure, stripped down, no bullshit rock 'n' roll."

Drawing on sources ranging from the Stooges to The Beatles and The Beach Boys to Herman's Hermits and 1960s girl groups, the Ramones condensed rock 'n' roll to its primal level: "1-2-3-4!" which their bass player Dee Dee shouted at the start of every song, as the group had barely mastered the rudiments of rhythm. The Ramones played their first gig at CBGB in August 1974, on the same bill as another new act, Blondie. By the end of the year, the Ramones had performed 74 shows, each about 17 minutes long.

The Artistics, formed in 1974 by Rhode Island School of Design students and led by David Byrne, dissolved within a year, but its members moved to New York, eventually sharing a communal loft. Unable to find a bass player in New York City, Chris Frantz encouraged his girlfriend Tina Weymouth to learn to play by listening to Suzi Quatro albums. They played their first gig as Talking Heads, opening for the Ramones at CBGB, in June 1975. They quickly drew a following and were signed to Sire Records in 1977, releasing promptly their hit single and legendary new wave anthem, 'Psycho Killer'.

In April 1974, Patti Smith, a member of the Mercer Arts Center crowd and a friend of Richard Hell's, came to CBGB for the first time to see Television perform. A veteran of independent theatre and performance poetry, Smith was developing an intellectual,feminist take on rock 'n' roll. By June she had recorded 'Hey Joe/Piss Factory', featuring Television guitarist Tom Verlaine. Released on her own Mer Records label, it heralded the scene's do it yourself (DIY) ethic and has often been cited as the first punk rock record.

Inspired by the burgeoning new music scene at the Mercer Arts Center, Chris Stein sought to join a similar band. He joined The Stilettos in 1973 as their guitarist and formed a romantic relationship with one of the band's vocalists, Deborah Harry, a former waitress and Playboy Bunny. Settling on the band name Blondie, they became regulars at Max's Kansas City and CBGB. Their third album, *Parallel Lines*, released in September 1978, became the group's most successful effort, selling 20 million copies worldwide. It broke the final barrier between this obscure underground scene and the mainstream.

Quotes from a Tommy Ramone interview with *Uncut* magazine (Jan 2007)
Sources: *Punk* magazine and Wikipedia

Recommended listening:
The Ramones' self-titled debut album *The Ramones*. All of its 29 glorious minutes (1976)
Talking Heads' debut album *Talking Heads: 77*, featuring their hit single 'Psycho Killer' (1977)

THE MODERN DANCE part five

Having gathered a small following from the fans of their former bands, The Heartbreakers, formed by ex-NY Dolls Johnny Thunders and Jerry Nolan and ex-Television bassist Richard Hell, had the future almost set in stone for them. *A gravestone that is.*

June 1975. 430 King's Road, London.
Malcolm McLaren returns from New York to concentrate on his and Vivienne Westwood's SEX boutique.

Backstage that night...

EDUCATION IN REVERSE **PART ONE**

Spring 1976.
384 Kings Rd, Stretford, Manchester.
Young Steve Morrissey prepares for his
O-level exams.

Recommended listening:
Morrissey's debut solo album *Viva Hate* (1988). The working title for *Viva Hate* was *Education in Reverse*,
which was changed at the last minute. The Australian distributors weren't informed of the change and
the album was released as *Education in Reverse* there. Most copies were recalled, but some still exist.

EDUCATION IN REVERSE **PART TWO**

Spring 1976.
Stretford Technical School, Manchester.

Recommended listening:
Morrissey's debut solo album *Viva Hate* (1988)

Generate! Generate! part one

Johnny Marr's family lived near a store that sold all manner of cleaning aids, from brushes to mops and buckets.

I played the mop in front of my mirror until my mom and dad bought me a toy guitar.

Then, every year for Christmas, the guitar got bigger and better.

Quotes from a Johnny Marr interview with *Deseret News* (May 3, 2003)

Recommended listening:
'Generate! Generate!' from Johnny Marr's long-awaited debut solo album, *The Messenger* (2013)

Generate! Generate! part two

Can you remember the moment you fell in love with the guitar?

Yeah, I was four or five and there was a little wooden toy hanging in the window of a shop that sold mops and buckets and brooms around the corner from my house in Ardwick.

Whenever we walked past it I'd be doing that thing that you see dogs on a lead do, where they just dig into the pavement and don't move.

My mother got so sick of it that she bought it for me.

I painted it white and stuck on beer bottle tops to make it look like an electric guitar, and I carried that thing around everywhere.
I couldn't believe it when I discovered there were shops that sold real ones...

Quotes from a Johnny Marr interview with *Shortlist* magazine (Feb 14, 2013)

Recommended listening:
'The Right Thing Right' from Johnny Marr's long-awaited debut solo album, *The Messenger* (2013)

Generate! Generate! part three

Next jump was at one of my uncle's.

I picked up an acoustic at a party.

He had sideburns and Chelsea boots.

I thought he was the bee's knees.

Quotes from a Johnny Marr interview on BBC6's *Radcliffe and Maconie* (Jan 18, 2013)

Recommended listening:
'I Want the Heartbeat' from Johnny Marr's long-awaited debut solo album, *The Messenger* (2013)

Generate! Generate! part four

Then as a boy, there was an Irish showband that used to play at Stockport Road.

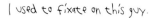
I used to fixate on this guy.

He had a red Telecaster...

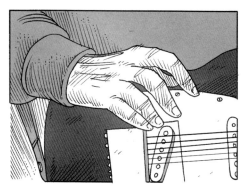

...which to me was like a rocket. Or a spaceship!

Quotes from a Johnny Marr interview on BBC6's *Radcliffe and Maconie* (Jan 18, 2013)

Recommended listening:
'Say Demesne' from Johnny Marr's long-awaited debut solo album, *The Messenger* (2013)

Generate! Generate! part five

I was sad when I was a little kid, because the area where I grew up was very heavy. Ardwick in the '60s was actually grim

It did always seem to be very rainy and there was a lot of traffic.
Women in beehives bringing up large families on not a lot of money, wearing coats on HP.

It was a young Irish community, a lot of parties, and weddings, and a lot of melancholy in the music that was around me at that age.
Old Irish ballads like 'Black Velvet Band', which I really used to love.

Even the stuff my folks were listening to, like Del Shannon, there was a dark, gothic sadness about it.
That really hooked me and seemed to resonate with my surroundings.

...a black velvet band.

Tied up with...

WC

Quotes from a Johnny Marr interview printed in Simon Goddard's *Mozipedia* (2010)

Recommended listening:
The Dubliners' 'The Black Velvet Band' from the album, *A Drop of the Hard Stuff* (1967)

Generate! Generate! part six

Johnny's family moves from Ardwick to a council estate in Wythenshawe.

It's amazing because it was one of the most notorious housing estates in the country...

...but it was only there that I was able to feel artistic and creative.

It was only then, when I got to about 12 or 13, that I started to feel a bit more outgoing.

Wythenshawe allowed me to feel all right about being a guitar player.

Nice badge, mate.

Thanks...

...your riff ain't too bad, either.

Quotes from a Johnny Marr interview printed in Simon Goddard's *Mozipedia* (2010)

Recommended listening:
Neil Young's 'Tonight's the Night' from the album *Tonight's the Night* (1975)

Generate! Generate! part seven

The first electric guitar I ever owned was bought with my own savings from my paper round and I wanted it to look like Rory's guitar... and his guitar, which everyone knows, was beaten and battered.

So while a teacher was, like, talking to a few lads, about, I don't know, making a bookshelf or something, I brought in the body of the guitar. I got a blowtorch and I started going "Fshhhh!" and I started to set fire to this guitar.

So I run up to it and I'm "FFFFUUUUUU!!" and I'm blowing it out! So of course it looked dreadful. It was just like a burnt guitar then. So I went at it again!

I must've burnt this guitar four or five times! The whole thing was going up in flames. I think it looked quite good in the end actually, but it was a pretty, pretty stupid thing to do. But that was being a fan, you know!

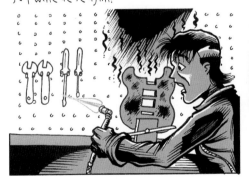

Quotes from a Johnny Marr interview for the documentary *Ghost Blues: The Story of Rory Gallagher* (2010)

Recommended viewing:
Ian Thuillier's documentary *Ghost Blues: The Story of Rory Gallagher* (2010)

Generate! Generate! part eight

Every spare minute we would spend in the soundproof rooms at school, where there were pianos and stuff like that.

Our form room was also the music class so there was a piano in the corner which we used to muck around on and we'd both bring our guitars in. We used to lock ourselves in there in the dinner hour and just play guitar and play piano and just mess about.

Just honing our skills.
We didn't want a proper job – we're nuts!
We just wanted to be musicians.

Johnny was dead keen.

I'd show him something and a week later he could play it better than me.

That's how keen he was.

Quotes from Andy Rourke interviews for the documentary *Inside The Smiths* (2007) and Simon Goddard's *Mozipedia* (2010)

Recommended viewing:
Stephen Petricco and Mark Standley's documentary dedicated to The Smiths' rhythm section, *Inside The Smiths* (2007)

HORSES part one

Just how obsessed were you, as a teenager, with Patti Smith?

I was very obsessed because I was very lonely and then therefore when I heard music that I felt was designed for me, it was so unusual that the gratitude I expressed was almost too much. With Patti Smith, when I bought that very first album, I sat up all night listening to it on a very tiny stereo, and I couldn't stop.

And I thought it was extraordinary because it was the voice of somebody who perhaps had felt unattractive all their lives, in every way.

Yet here they were, singing about it, and seemed to know a way to make the misfortune of their lives become attractive.

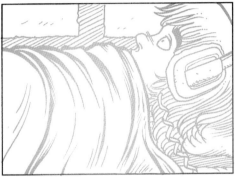 

And I felt that, well, I could therefore simply sing about my life and how I really feel...

...and perhaps it could transform itself into something acceptable.

Quotes from a Morrissey interview with *The Daily Telegraph* (June 17, 2011)

Recommended viewing:
The Patti Smith Group performing 'Horses' live on *The Old Grey Whistle Test* (1976)

HORSES part two

The boy was in the hallway drinking a glass of tea.
From the other end of the hallway
a rhythm was generating.
Another boy was sliding up the hallway.

He merged perfectly with the hallway.
He merged perfectly, the mirror in the hallway.
The boy looked at Johnny, Johnny wanted to run,
but the movie kept moving as planned.

The boy took Johnny
he pushed him against the locker.
He drove it in, he drove it home,
he drove it deep in Johnny.

The boy disappeared, Johnny fell on his knees,
started crashing his head against the locker,
started laughing hysterically.
When suddenly Johnny gets the feeling
he's being surrounded by horses.

Coming in, in all directions, white shining silver studs
with their nose in flames.
He saw horses.

Quotes from Patti Smith's 'Land' from the album *Horses* (1975)

Recommended viewing:
The Patti Smith Group performing 'Horses' live on *The Old Grey Whistle Test* (1976)
Morrissey reciting the intro to 'Horses' live at the Manchester Arena, before singing 'You Have Killed Me' (July 28, 2012)

HORSES part three

Born in 1946 to a strict, religious family in Chicago – they later moved to New Jersey – Patricia Lee Smith felt the need to rebel from a very early age.

Feeling too confined within organised religion, as a teenager Patti developed an interest in Tibetan Buddhism, a fairly obscure religious doctrine at the time.

In 1967, she left Glassboro State College and worked briefly in a factory.
She soon after moved to New York City.

Having become pregnant by a student she met in her sophomore year, Patti gave birth to her first child, a daughter, on April 26, 1967, and chose to place her for adoption.

Recommended viewing:
The Patti Smith Group performing 'Horses' live on *The Old Grey Whistle Test* (1976)

HORSES part four

New York, 1969.

I'm sorry Miss Smith, but in the state of New York you need to work two straight weeks before receiving your first paycheck.

But... but I'm starving! I can't wait another week! What am I going to do?!

Hey man... don't worry... I'll buy you some food, if you dig hangin' out!

Thus after the good Samaritan bought Patti food...

Now, how about comin' over to my place for some COCKtails?

Err, Ahh... Shit! How do I get outta this?

Holy! It's that boy I met at that party!

Please, please pretend you're my boyfriend. This guy's creepin' me out!

Dude, the girl's with me. Scram!

What the hell! You cockteasing skank!

Quotes from a Patti Smith interview with the Louisiana Museum of Modern Art on meeting and falling in love with Robert Mapplethorpe (2012)

Recommended viewing:
The Patti Smith Group performing 'Horses' live on *The Old Grey Whistle Test* (1976)
Morrissey reciting the intro to 'Horses' live at the Manchester Arena, before singing 'You Have Killed Me' (July 28, 2012)

HORSES part five

At the bookstore Patti worked in.

Hey there!
Thanks for saving my ass in the park the other day.
That guy was really creeping me out!
Whoa! You into Rimbaud?

I'm into anything
you're into, Patti!

Patti Smith and the young, unknown Robert Mapplethorpe hit it off immediately, becoming one of the most iconic couples of the early '70s.

Their intense romantic relationship was tumultuous as the pair constantly struggled with poverty and Mapplethorpe with his own sexuality. In her book *Just Kids*, Smith referred to Mapplethorpe as "the artist of my life".

Although they broke up in the mid-'70s, the two would remain friends until Robert's death in 1989 from complications due to AIDS. His photos would inform most of Patti Smith's record artwork.

Recommended listening and viewing:
Robert Mapplethorpe's iconic photo of Patti Smith,
which was used on the front cover of her debut album, *Horses* (1975)

Recommended reading:
Patti Smith's memoir *Just Kids* (2010),
detailing her relationship with photographer Robert Mapplethorpe

HORSES part six

In 1969 Patti Smith left for Paris with her sister and started busking and doing performance art. When Smith returned to New York City, she lived in the Chelsea Hotel with her lover, the photographer Robert Mapplethorpe.

It was probably around early 1970.
They had a party, they used to have several press parties for rock bands, and sometimes the rock bands would be there and they had one for The Doors. We never had enough food, so I would go to these 'cause they would have lots of food.

And I would bring a bag and just take the food, 'cause I didn't really like the parties.
So The Doors' party was really cool 'cause they had these long tables with all the food at the entrance and then you went into the party.
So I had this big bag and I was getting food for me and Robert.

So I was taking fruit and bread and all this stuff and I hear this voice go:
"The hamburgers are really good too!"
And I look and way at the end sitting all by himself was Jim Morrison. And I was like "Uhh.... caught!"
But I just went over and got a hamburger and said "Thank you" and he nodded and that was it.

Quotes from a Patti Smith interview with CBS's *Sunday Morning* (2012)

Recommended listening:
Patti Smith's cover of The Doors' 'Soul Kitchen' from her covers album *Twelve* (2007)

Recommended reading:
Patti Smith's memoir *Just Kids*, detailing her relationship with photographer Robert Mapplethorpe (2010)

HORSES part seven

In *Just Kids* there's a description of your first performance at St Mark's church on February 10th, 1971.

Right. It was on Bertolt Brecht's birthday. It was Robert Mapplethorpe who helped me get it. Robert always thought I should have a poetry reading 'cause he really liked to hear me read my poems.

I really wanted it to be special. I was seeing Sam Shepard at the time. We were doing a play together called Cowboy Mouth and I said to Sam, "I really want my poetry reading to have something special."

And he said, "Why don't you get a guitar player and maybe sing a little or something?"

"Hmmm."

Quotes from a Patti Smith interview with the Louisiana Museum of Modern Art (2012)

Recommended reading:
Patti Smith's memoir *Just Kids*, detailing her relationship with photographer Robert Mapplethorpe (2010)

HORSES part eight

So I had met Lenny Kaye,
and he was working at a record store and
I said, "I think that guy Lenny plays guitar."

So I went and visited Lenny and I said,
"You play guitar right?" and he said, "Yeah" and I said,
"Wanna play with me at St Marks and do some sonic
stuff, a couple of songs and then can you make your
guitar sound like a car crash?" and he said, "No problem!"

So we put together 18 minutes and we did our poetry
reading. Some people loved it and heralded it as a new thing.
And other people thought I should be arrested for
desecrating the church.

The first song Patti Smith ever performed
was 'Fire of Unknown Origin', in memory
of Jim Morrison who had just died.

Recommended listening:
Patti Smith's cover of The Doors' 'Soul Kitchen' from her covers album *Twelve* (2007),
as well as her cover of 'Crystal Ship'

Recommended viewing:
Patti Smith's 'Fire of Unknown Origin' in tribute to Jim Morrison,
as performed at the Louisiana Museum of Modern Art (2012)

HORSES part nine

Soon after her initial performance as a singer/
songwriter, Patti Smith started hanging out with
New York's decadent '70s scene.

John Cale Lou Reed

Patti Smith Allen Ginsberg David Byrne

Performing live with her newly-christened Patti Smith
Group at Max's Kansas City and CBGB, Patti soon
became the talk of the town. Financed by punk
curator Sam Wagstaff, the band recorded a first
single, 'Hey Joe'/'Piss Factory', in 1974.

'Hey Joe' was a version of the rock standard with the
addition of a spoken word piece about fugitive heiress
Patty Hearst. 'Piss Factory' describes the helpless anger
Smith had felt while working on a factory assembly line
and the salvation she discovered in the form of a shoplifted
book by the 19th century French poet Arthur Rimbaud.

I had devoted so much of my girlish daydreams to Rimbaud.

Rimbaud was like my boyfriend.

Quotes from a Patti Smith interview with Thurston Moore for *BOMB Magazine* (Winter 1996)

Recommended listening:
Patti Smith's first single 'Hey Joe' and its b-side 'Piss Factory' (1974)
Morrissey and Marr's all-star fave cast, Lou Reed, John Cale, Patti Smith, Mick Ronson and David Byrne
live at the Ocean Club in New York (July 21, 1976)

Recommended reading:
Arthur Rimbaud's uncompleted suite of prose poems *Illuminations* (1886)

HORSES part ten

By 1975 Patti Smith would find herself an equal in the company of all her idols, including the biggest of all, Bob Dylan, who quickly became a fan and invited her to tour with him.

The influence she had on the rising punk scene (and all the scenes that arose from it, from post-punk to no wave and beyond) would earn her the nickname Godmother of Punk.

Patti Smith would later recall the alienated teenagers and artistic misfits that looked up to her as their patron saint: They were my people. They were exactly the people I had in mind. I wrote 'Horses' for Michael Stipe. I wrote 'Horses' for Morrissey. And they found it.

Equally, Morrissey never hid his admiration for Patti. **There's a photo of you as a teenager in which you have long, messy hair. Was that in tribute to Patti Smith?** It was. Yes, it was from 1976. Yes. And it was directly because of her first album. (Pause) We do these things.

Quotes from a Patti Smith interview with *Uncut* (May 2012)
and a Morrissey interview with *The Daily Telegraph* (June 17, 2011)

Recommended viewing:
The Patti Smith Group performing 'Horses' live on *The Old Grey Whistle Test* (1976)
Morrissey reciting the intro to 'Horses' live at the Manchester Arena, before singing
'You Have Killed Me' (July 28, 2012)

In June 1976, Steven Patrick Morrissey sat his first O-level exam. Depending on his success, he would continue his studies at a university.

Recommended listening:
Morrissey's 'Because of My Poor Education'
released as a b-side to his single 'I'm Throwing My Arms Around Paris' (2009)

Recommended listening:
Morrissey's 'Because of My Poor Education'
released as a b-side to his single 'I'm Throwing My Arms Around Paris' (2009)

Because of My Poor Education part three

Outline the background to and the terms of the following treaties:
(i) Rapallo (1922);
(ii) Lausanne (1923);
(iii) Locarno (1925).

Outline the main domestic achievements of two of the following governments in Britain:
(i) Lloyd George's Coalition government of 1918–22;
(ii) Baldwin's Conservative government of 1924–29;
(iii) the National government of 1931–40.
How do you explain the dominance of the Conservative party for most of the interwar years?

Describe the part played by each of the following in Russia during the course of the year 1917:
(i) Tsar Nicholas II;
(ii) General Kornilov;
(iii) Alexander Kerensky.
Why was the Bolshevik party able to secure power in October 1917?

In June 1976, Steven Patrick Morrissey sat his final subject, history, for his O-levels and would have to wait until September for the results. It would prove the longest summer that he could remember.

Recommended listening:
Morrissey's 'Because of My Poor Education'
released as a b-side to his single 'I'm Throwing My Arms Around Paris' (2009)

Because of **My Poor Education** part four

Recommended listening:
Morrissey's 'Because of My Poor Education'
released as a b-side to his single 'I'm Throwing My Arms Around Paris' (2009)

Because of My Poor Education
part five

Recommended listening:
The New York Dolls' 'Personality Crisis' from their self-titled debut album *New York Dolls* (1973)

STANLEY KNIVES
PART ONE

Morrissey was not a fan of Aerosmith.

'… as much to offer Seventies rock as Ena Sharples,' he observed in a letter to MM, as ever shading his views with a touch of Coronation Street.

He was sticking with the New York Dolls.

Recommended reading:
The letter written by Morrissey, published in the *Melody Maker* (Sep 16, 1975)

Recommended listening:
Morrissey's 'Reader Meet Author' from the album *Southpaw Grammar* (1995)

June 1976.
Shortly after Morrissey's exams.
His last week at school.

Recommended listening:
Morrissey's 'The Teachers Are Afraid of the Pupils' from the album *Southpaw Grammar* (1995)

As well as the Dolls, Morrissey never forgot his liking for Jobriath, the overtly gay glam rock singer, also from New York.

In a letter to *Sounds* he reprimanded the media for snubbing both.

Recommended reading:
The letter written by Morrissey, published in *Sounds* (Dec 27, 1975)

Recommended listening:
Morrissey's 'Best Friend on the Payroll' from the album *Southpaw Grammar* (1995)

In another letter to *Sounds* Morrissey drew attention to a raft of acts he considered to be children of the Dolls...

...among them Kiss, the hateful Aerosmith, The Tubes, Wayne County, the Dictators and even Bruce Springsteen.

Recommended reading:
The letter written by Morrissey, published in *Sounds* (Dec 27, 1975)

Recommended listening:
KISS' self-titled debut album, *KISS*, and its follow-up, *Hotter Than Hell*, released within the same year (1974)
Bruce Springsteen's breakthrough album, *Born to Run* (1975)

STANLEY KNIVES
PART FIVE

June 1976.
Shortly after Steven Morrissey's exams.

Recommended listening:
Morrissey's 'Honey, You Know Where to Find Me' from the album *Southpaw Grammar* (1995)

NO FUTURE
part one

June 1976.

Steven!

Betty.

So, you've decided to join the land of the living.

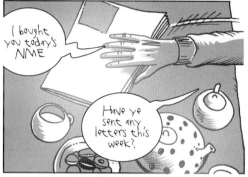

I bought you today's NME.

Have ye sent any letters this week?

Oh, you know, the usual.

What's the point anyway?

Everything's become so bland since the Dolls decided to spli....

PUNK IN ENGLAND?!

Recommended listening:
Morrissey's 'Nobody Loves Us' from the album *Southpaw Grammar* (1995)

NO FUTURE
part two

Summer 1975.
430 King's Road, London.

Recommended listening:
Sex Pistols' 'God Save the Queen' from their only album *Never Mind the Bollocks, Here's the Sex Pistols* (1977)

Recommended viewing:
Julien Temple's touching documentary, *The Filth and the Fury*,
on the history of the Sex Pistols, as told by the Pistols (2000)

NO FUTURE
part three

July 3rd, 1973.
Hammersmith Odeon Theatre, London.

Shortly after David Bowie's final concert as Ziggy Stardust all his gear was stolen by a group of burglars. Years later, Steve Jones confessed to having been involved when, still unknown, he was a petty thief.

Recommended reading:
Jon Savage's extensive interviews for his book *England's Dreaming, The England's Dreaming Tapes* (2010)

Recommended viewing:
Julien Temple's touching documentary, *The Filth and the Fury*, on the history of the Sex Pistols, as told by the Pistols (2000)

Autumn 1975.
430 King's Road, London.

Upon Malcolm McLaren's insistence, Glen Matlock, an art student who occasionally worked at McLaren and Vivienne Westwood's boutique, was recruited as the The Strand's regular bassist and songwriter.

Recommended listening:
Roxy Music's 'Do the Strand' from their second album, *For Your Pleasure* (1973)

Recommended reading:
Jon Savage's extensive interviews for his book *England's Dreaming*, *The England's Dreaming Tapes* (2010)

Recommended viewing:
Julien Temple's touching documentary, *The Filth and the Fury*,
on the history of the Sex Pistols, as told by the Pistols (2000)

Autumn 1975.
430 King's Road, London.
McLaren and Westwood's SEX boutique.

Sylvain Sylvain's white Gibson Les Paul was passed on to young Steve Jones by Malcolm McLaren in 1975. He was advised to learn how to play it within three months, otherwise it would be returned to McLaren.

Recommended listening:
Roxy Music's 'Do the Strand' from their second album, *For Your Pleasure* (1973)

Recommended reading:
Jon Savage's extensive interviews for his book *England's Dreaming*, *The England's Dreaming Tapes* (2010)

Recommended viewing:
Julien Temple's touching documentary, *The Filth and the Fury*, on the history of the Sex Pistols, as told by the Pistols (2000)

Autumn 1975.
In which we find new band
QT Jones and His Sex Pistols rehearsing.

Later on in the pub next door...

Recommended listening:
Small Faces' 'Tin Soldier' from their posthumous retrospective double album, *The Autumn Stone* (1969)

Recommended viewing:
Julien Temple's touching documentary, *The Filth and the Fury*,
on the history of the Sex Pistols, as told by the Pistols (2000)

Autumn 1975.
In the pub next to McLaren and Westwood's
SEX boutique in London.

And so, on that fateful day, Malcolm McLaren presses
the button on his jukebox that will ignite the engine
that changed the world all over.

Autumn 1975.
The Sex Pistols have finally formed
and have just begun rehearsing.

Recommended listening:
Sex Pistols' 'Pretty Vacant' from their only album *Never Mind the Bollocks, Here's the Sex Pistols* (1977)

Autumn 1975.
Following the formation of the Sex Pistols, John Lydon, now renamed Johnny Rotten by his guitarist Steve Jones, due to his dental issues, generates his own band of acolytes.

What the fuck's wrong with your hamster, mate?

That's Sid Vicious, John!

Syd Barrett called himself that (and he was the only member of Pink Floyd that mattered)!

Sid Vicious? What a silly fucked up name!

Johnny Rotten gave his best friend, John Ritchie, the nickname Sid Vicious. The two found themselves squatting with two other mates: John Wardle (later known as Jah Wobble) and John Gray.

This gang of four were always seen together and were colloquially known as The Four Johns; an almost post-apocalyptic band of no-gooders straight from the pages of *A Clockwork Orange*.

It's official then, you fucker!

From now on, your name's Sid Vicious!

Haha.

FUCK! OFF!

Recommended reading and viewing:
Stanley Kubrick's movie *A Clockwork Orange* (1971),
based on Anthony Burgess' dystopian novella of the same name (1962),
both of which influenced the look and attitude of punk.

November 6th, 1975.
St. Martin's College.

The Sex Pistols would play their first ever gig, opening for seasoned headliners Bazooka Joe, at St. Martin's College, where their bass player Glen Matlock was studying.

The Pistols barely managed to get through half their set before the plug was pulled by the hostile, conservative art school crowd.

Sensing the future happening right before his eyes, Bazooka Joe's Stuart Goddard quit the band the following day, changed his name to Adam Ant and formed punk band The B-Sides.

Recommended listening:
Sex Pistols' cover of The Stooges' 'No Fun' from the first bootleg of their music to be released, *Spunk* (1977)

WHAT DO I GET?
part one

**February 1976.
Manchester.**

After reading an *NME* review of the Sex Pistols' first performance, Peter McNeish and Howard Trafford travelled to London to see them live in February 1976. Unbeknownst to them, this trip would play a pivotal role in the worldwide explosion of indie music.

Recommended listening:
Buzzcocks' single 'What Do I Get?' (1978)

Recommended reading:
Jon Savage's extensive interviews on the first days of Punk, *The England's Dreaming Tapes* (2010)

WHAT DO I GET?
part two

February 1976.
SEX boutique.
After Peter McNeish and Howard Trafford
have seen the Sex Pistols perform live...

Quotes from a Howard Devoto interview with Jon Savage for his supplementary book
The England's Dreaming Tapes (2010)

Recommended listening:
Buzzcocks' *Spiral Scratch* EP (1977)

WHAT DO I GET?
part three

May 1976.
Stretford, Manchester.

Wow! How time passes!

Would you believe you'll be in the States next month?

Mmm... I'm just dying to see something interesting.

They said that punk would come to England, but I can't see any...

TEA

NEW MUSICAL EXPRESS NME

BOLAN TO MAKE COMEBACK?

WHAT ARE ELO UP TO?

ONE NIGHT WITH THE WHO

SEX... What on!?

SPLURCH

What is it Steven?!

THE SEX PISTOLS ARE COMING TO MANCHESTER!!

Recommended listening:
Buzzcocks' 'Boredom' from the *Spiral Scratch* EP (1977)

WHAT DO I GET?
part four

June 4th, 1976.
In the pub across from Manchester's
Free Trade Hall.

Hey there, lad! You interested in having the time of your life tonight?

C'mon now what's your name, lad?

Bugger off faggot.

Mark Smith.

What's it to you?

The Sex Pistols are in town and you're going to spend the night in a rundown ol' pub?

The SEX WHO?!

The greatest show on earth!

They are changing the world as we know it!

Sod it! Let's go... what've we got to lose?

I dunno. Whaddya reckon, Paddy?

Good lads!

Step right in, ladies an' germs!

Tonight ONLY: the Sex Pistols are playing Manchester's Lesser Free Trade Hall!

One day you'll be able to recall: "I was there TOO!"

Oh God, what're we doing??

I've only sold 30 tickets. This will barely change Manchester, let alone the world.

Years later it was revealed that it was Mark E. Smith, who would form The Fall, who had been pulled out of the pub by Malcolm McLaren himself to attend the first Sex Pistols gig in Manchester.

Recommended viewing:
BBC documentary *I Swear That I Was There* (2011),
in which all the audience members of the first Manchester gig are interviewed

384 Kings Road, Stretford, Manchester.

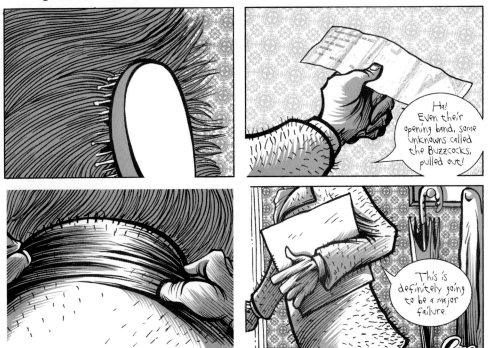

On June 4th, 1976, Steven Morrissey left his home to see the first Sex Pistols performance in his home town. His life would change forever.

Recommended listening:
Buzzcocks' 'Time's Up' from the *Spiral Scratch* EP (1977)

In a letter to *NME* he referred sardonically to their 'jumble sale attire'...

...took exception to the Pistols' denial that they were inspired by the downtown New York scene...

...likening Johnny Rotten to David Johansen...

...and drew attention to the fact that Pistols' manager Malcolm McLaren...

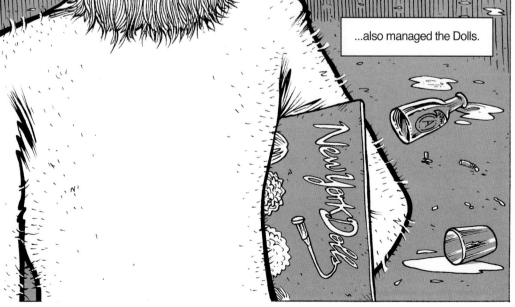

...also managed the Dolls.

Closing his letter to *NME*, Morrissey emphasised the parallels between the Sex Pistols – 'very New York' – and the Dolls.

Deep down, however, he could tell that the punk movement would snowball into something bigger...

and that the Sex Pistols would outshine his beloved New York Dolls, as the greatest band of his generation.

Recommended reading:
The letter written by Morrissey, published in the *NME* (June 16, 1976)

BODIES part one

On the evening of June 4th, 1976, history was made in the Lesser Free Trade Hall in Manchester. Although years later many more people claimed to have been at the gig, the estimated crowd is said to have been between 30 and 60 people.

Of the confirmed attendees, the undeniable ones were the members of The Buzzcocks, who also organised the gig, but couldn't open for the Pistols as they felt ill-rehearsed. Pete Shelley and Howard Devoto would become leading figures of Manchester's music scene.

Other confirmed attendees were the later *NME* scribe Paul Morley, as well as Mark E. Smith. Tony Wilson was also there, but it remains a matter of debate as to whether or not Mick Hucknall, later of Simply Red, was.

Buzzcocks/ Magazine

Stephen Morris, Peter Hook, Ian Curtis and Bernard Sumner all attended the gig. The following day Hook borrowed £35 from his mother to buy his first bass guitar. They formed their first band, Warsaw, soon after.

Art of Noise   The Fall   Factory Records   Simply Red

Morrissey's letter to the *NME*, published the very following week, remains the only true evidence of an undeniable attendance.

Joy Division/ New Order

The Smiths

It is said that every member of the audience either formed a band the following day or would influence music in a profound way.

Recommended reading:
David Nolan's research on the true attendees, *I Swear I Was There: The Gig That Changed the World* (2006)

Recommended viewing:
BBC's documentary on the legendary gig, including interviews with the attendees, *I Swear That I Was There* (2006)
Michael Winterbottom's film about the Manchester music scene, *24 Hour Party People* (2002)

BODIES part two

June 4th, 1976.
Lesser Free Trade Hall, Manchester.
The Sex Pistols' first gig in the North.

Recommended reading:
David Nolan's research on the gig's attendees, *I Swear I Was There: The Gig That Changed the World* (2006)

Recommended viewing:
Grant Gee and Jon Savage's documentary *Joy Division*, released to coincide with the Curtis biopic *Control* (2007)
Michael Winterbottom's film about the Manchester music scene, *24 Hour Party People* (2002)

BODIES part three

June 4th, 1976.
Lesser Free Trade Hall, Manchester.
The Sex Pistols' first gig in the North.

By continuously preaching The Gospel According To The New York Dolls, and by siding himself with the friendlier Buzzcocks camp, Morrissey would alienate himself from the rest of the Manchester punk scene before that adventure had even begun.

Recommended listening:
Sex Pistols' 'Bodies' from their only album *Never Mind the Bollocks, Here's the Sex Pistols* (1977)

COMBAT ROCK PART ONE

Stretford, Manchester.
Early 1976, a few months before the Sex Pistols'
legendary gig in Manchester.

Dear Steve,
I'm writing to inform you that I will no longer be
able to participate in any of the NY Dolls proceedings
since they disbanded, there's really no point, right?

The Dolls are dead. Punk is what's happening, baby!
I'm thinking of forming a band in the coming days.
You should too!

Ciao, Mick.

Ever since noticing Morrissey's address in the *Melody
Maker*'s letters column, Mick Jones corresponded with
him for years. The two wrote to each other about their
common love for the New York Dolls, as well as more
personal issues. And then punk came riding in. Jones
formed the London SS, while Steve remained stuck in
his bedroom depression, waiting for his ticket out.

Recommended reading:
John Robb's interviews from UK punk's protagonists *Punk Rock: An Oral History* (2007)

COMBAT ROCK PART TWO

Stretford, Manchester.
Early 1976, a few months before the Sex Pistols'
legendary gig in Manchester.

Taking a hint from the New York Dolls and Malcolm
McLaren's provocative tactics, Mick Jones teamed
up with Geir Wade and Tony James to create one of
the first English proto-punk bands. They chose to
switch the Communist-look shock-tactics for Nazi
regalia, aimed at provoking their parents' generation,
who fought in WWII against the Germans.

With a love of the Dolls as strong as the young Steven
Patrick Morrissey, Mick Jones essentially took all the
Dolls' lessons to heart and created one of the last glam
bands in town, complete with androgynous look, long
hair and lots of Johnny Thundersesque posing.

Unfortunately for later punks, the irony of dressing in
Nazi-wear was not really understood. It ultimately had
a negative effect on the movement, especially through
the far-right punk bands of the late '70s.

Recommended listening:
Dead Kennedys' 'Nazi Punks Fuck Off' from their EP *In God We Trust, Inc.* (1981)

COMBAT ROCK PART THREE

Stretford, Manchester.
Early 1976, a few months before the Sex Pistols'
legendary gig in Manchester.

We got this tragic letter from Manchester from Morrissey.
Manchester to us seemed like a million miles away.
It would have been really strange if it had happened.

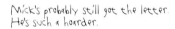

Mick's probably still got the letter.
He's such a hoarder.

Quotes from a Tony James interview for John Robb's book *Punk Rock: An Oral History* (2007)

Recommended reading:
The Clash's 'Career Opportunities' from their eponymous debut album *The Clash* (1977)

Mick Jones: I used to spend a lot of the time on the phone talking to people. You had to get past that one first. Loads of people came down, like Keith Levene, Terry Chimes, Topper Headon, Brian James.

Although they existed very briefly, London SS brought together individuals with similar musical, fashion attitude and ideas, who from that point struck friendships and formed bands. If the SEX boutique and the Sex Pistols were the yin of punk rock, then the London SS was the yang. From the London SS came the beginnings of Generation X, The Clash, The Boys and The Damned.

Disbanding the London SS shortly after Mick Jones' departure, Tony James recruited Billy Idol and created one of punk's earliest commercial success stories, Generation X.

Drifting from band to band in the '80s, James revisited his punk vision of a provocative band that would use the SS initials and out-there tactics by putting together Sigue Sigue Sputnik.

Although their debut single was produced by Giorgio Moroder, the band faced such a huge amount of media outcry (*I mean, paid commercials between tracks?!*) that they eventually broke up.

Having tried out a huge number of local artists and wannabe musicians, Mick Jones settled on the core of Keith Levene on guitars, Paul Simonon on bass, Terry Chimes on drums and Joe Strummer, singer of pub rock band The 101ers, as their frontman. Managed by Malcolm McLaren's associate, Bernie Rhodes, the band found themselves opening for the Sex Pistols just a month after Morrissey saw them in Manchester. Ditching London SS's Nazi imagery for working class and leftist lyrics, The Clash, as they would come to be known, spearheaded the advocacy of radical politics in punk rock.

Quote from a Mick Jones interview for John Robb's book, *Punk Rock: An Oral History* (2007)

Recommended listening:
The Clash's 'Know Your Rights' from the album *Combat Rock* (1982)
Sigue Sigue Sputnik's Giorgio Moroder-produced 'Love Missile F1-11' from their debut album *Flaunt It* (1986)

COMBAT ROCK PART FIVE

July 1976.
The Sex Pistols announce a second concert at Manchester's Lesser Free Trade Hall, just one month after their first gig there.

The two opening bands, the Buzzcocks and Slaughter & the Dogs began a rivalry that still goes on to this day, when both printed posters for the gig that showcased their band as the main opening act.

Punk was begining to pick up speed and by this time more and more teenagers had started dressing up and acting the role. To the people that initiated it, this second generation almost seemed like a parody.

Recommended reading:
Jon Savage's definitive history of punk music, *England's Dreaming: Sex Pistols and Punk Rock* (1991)

an unhappy birthday

May 22nd, 1976.
384 Kings Road, Stretford, Manchester.

Recommended listening:
The Smiths' 'Unhappy Birthday' from their final album *Strangeways, Here We Come* (1987)

holidays in the sun
part one

July 20th, 1976.
Lesser Free Trade Hall.
The Sex Pistols are about to perform for the second time in Manchester.

Due to the hype surrounding the Pistol's performances, this time round the crowd is twice as big as their first concert.

holidays in the sun
part two

July 20th, 1976.
Lesser Free Trade Hall.
The Sex Pistols perform for the second time in
Manchester.

People were unwilling to respond to the Sex Pistols.
The audience was very slim. It was a front-parlour affair.

The Sex Pistols still had slightly capped sleeves,
and flares were not entirely taboo at that point.
Their jeans were somewhere in the middle.

I liked them, but they seemed like a clued-in singer
and three patched musicians.

Quotes from a Morrissey interview regarding the first Sex Pistols concert in Manchester,
for Jon Savage's definitive history of punk music, *England's Dreaming: Sex Pistols and
Punk Rock* (1991)

Sex Pistols' 'Problems' from the album *Never Mind the Bollocks, Here's the Sex Pistols* (1977)

holidays in the sun
part three

July 20th, 1976.
Lesser Free Trade Hall.
Slaughter & the Dogs are the first band to open for
the Sex Pistols' second performance in Manchester.

Performing after Slaughter & the Dogs, Buzzcocks
played for the very first time in front of an audience,
blowing young Morrissey's mind (and his expectations
of a Northern band actually sounding terrific).

By the time the Sex Pistols appeared another peculiar,
fateful event would take place at the concert. Johnny Marr's
circle of friends from Wythenshawe, including Stephen
Pomfret, recognised Morrissey from his haircut and the
New York Dolls record he was holding throughout the gig.

Recommended listening:
Slaughter & the Dogs' first single 'Cranked Up Really High' (1977)
Buzzcocks' 'Breakdown' from their debut EP, *Spiral Scratch* (1977)

holidays in the sun
part four

July 20th, 1976.
Wythenshawe, Manchester.
The council estate home of 13 year-old Johnny Maher.

And so, two spliffs later...

Recommended listening:
Sex Pistols' 'No Feelings' from the album *Never Mind the Bollocks, Here's the Sex Pistols* (1977)

holidays in the sun
part five

Late July 1976.
384 Kings Road, Stretford, Manchester.

Recommended listening:
The New York Dolls' 'Jet Boy' from their self-titled debut album *New York Dolls* (1973)

holidays in the sun
part six

Late July 1976.
Coach depot, Manchester.

Manchester-London coach.

Heathrow Airport, London.

London-New York flight.

Recommended listening:
The New York Dolls' 'Private World' from their self-titled debut album *New York Dolls* (1973)

holidays in the sun
part seven

Late July 1976.
John F. Kennedy International Airport, New York.

Recommended listening:
The New York Dolls' 'Vietnamese Baby' from their self-titled debut album *New York Dolls* (1973)

holidays in the sun
part eight

August 1976.
New Jersey, USA.
In which we find a hairdresser on fire...

...and a very lazy sunbather.

Recommended listening:
Morrissey's 'Hairdresser on Fire', b-side to his first solo single 'Suedehead' (1988)
Morrissey's 'The Lazy Sunbathers' from the album *Vauxhall and I* (1994)

holidays in the sun
part nine

August 1976.
New York, USA.

Recommended listening:
The New York Dolls' 'Jet Boy' from their self-titled debut album *New York Dolls* (1973)

August 1976.
New York, USA.

I was always fascinated by glamour but I wasn't surrounded by it. I used to avidly seek out American GQ magazines, which was very difficult to find in Central Manchester in the '70s. It was quite expensive too. But I would seek out this magazine almost religiously and I would write to the editor and send them photos of myself...

Morrissey laid claim to being the next Michael Schoeffling, another hero of his: he was this astonishingly good-looking model who was on the cover of many of those old GQ issues. He tried to become an actor, made about three films in Hollywood, then went off and had loads of children

(The aesthetic of The Smiths) really emerged from all the photographs I'd collected and all the books I'd found and kept and taken back to my bedroom for many years.
All of those Smiths sleeves had literally been stuck on my bedroom walls during the '70s.

The sleeve of 'William, It Was Really Nothing', for example, was of a male figure sitting on a bed next to a huge amplifier and that was a picture I'd ripped from American GQ years earlier. It was actually an advertisement for a sound system and I got caught out for that later on. But that's an example of how much of an impact fashion photography and fashion magazines had on me.

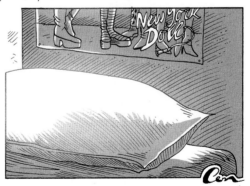

In 2005 Morrissey was presented with the Solo Artist of the Year Award by *GQ* magazine for his 2004 comeback.

Quotes from a Morrissey interview with *i-D* magazine (May 2004)

Recommended viewing:
Michael Schoeffling in John Hughes' classic coming-of-age comedy, *Sixteen Candles* (1984)

Recommended listening:
The Smiths' 'William, It Was Really Nothing' from their compilation *Hatful of Hollow* (1984)

America is not the world
part two

August 2nd, 1976.
The Runaways live at CBGB.

August 17th, 1976.
Talking Heads live at the Ocean Club.

In August 1976 the cream of the crop of the new wave of artists performed in New York, at the time when Morrissey was visiting his mother's sisters. To this day it remains a mystery whether he attended any of these gigs.

August 31st, 1976.
The Patti Smith Group live at the Ocean Club.

Recommended listening:
Morrissey's 'America is Not the World' from the album *You Are the Quarry* (2004)
The Runaways' 'Cherry Bomb' live at CBGB, NY (August 2nd, 1976)
Talking Heads' 'The Book I Read' live at the Ocean Club, NY (August 17th, 1976)
Patti Smith's 'Rock n Roll Nigger' live at the Ocean Club, NY (August 31st, 1976)

August 1976.
New York City.

Prior to Morrissey's first trip to New York, his idols, the New York Dolls, had disbanded after disagreeing about the direction that they would to take.

Briefly managing the band in 1975, Malcolm McLaren had laid the seeds for their new controversial Red Patent Leather look, which wasn't received well by the public. By the end of that year Johnny Thunders, Arthur 'Killer' Kane and Jerry Nolan had left the group.

After trying out musicians to replace their fan favourite guitarist Johnny Thunders, including future W.A.S.P. legend Blackie Lawless, David Johansen and Sylvain Sylvain decided to carry on simply as The Dolls.

Their venture lasted no more than a year. By the end of 1976 The Dolls had officially disbanded. As Morrissey's luck would have it, The Dolls had played four bills at Max's Kansas City in July 1976, just a month before he arrived.

The Dolls would play another four shows in New York that following September. It's more than likely, being a hardcore fan and president of their UK fan club, that he visited the landmarks associated with the band, possibly in a vain effort to bump into one of his idols. Yet the irony cannot be missed that he came so close to seeing them perform live.

Twenty-eight years later Morrissey played a pivotal role in reuniting the surviving members of the New York Dolls, when he curated the 2004 Meltdown festival.

He finally got to see them perform.

Recommended listening:
David Johansen's 'She Knew She Was Falling in Love' from the album *In Style* (1979)

Recommended web reading:
A meticulously researched chronology of The New York Dolls' live performances at
www.fromthearchives.com/nyd/chronology.html

America is not the world
part four

August 1976.
New Jersey, USA.

Recommended listening:
Morrissey's 'America is Not the World' from the album *You Are the Quarry* (2004)

August 1976.
New York City.
Celebrations for the Bicentennial Anniversary of
the American Revolution ran throughout the States
in 1976, which culminated in massive parades held
in New York in the summer.

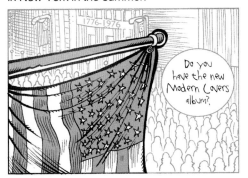

Recommended listening:
David Johansen's 'Big City' from the album *In Style* (1979)

America is not the world
part six

September 1976.
New York, USA.

In early September 1976, Steve Morrissey travelled from New York to the UK, returning back home where his O-level results and an unknown future awaited him. He would obsess about returning to live in the States.

Recommended listening:
Morrissey's 'I Will See You in Far-Off Places' from the album *Ringleader of the Tormentors* (2006)

Staircase at the University
part one

September 1976.
Kings Road, Stretford, Manchester.

Recommended listening:
Morrissey's 'Staircase at the University' from the album *World Peace is None of Your Business* (2014)

Staircase at the University
part two

What did you want to be when you grew up?
Oh, I'm afraid I always wanted to be a librarian.

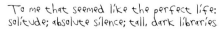

Quotes from 'Morrissey Answers 20 Questions', *Star Hits* (1985)

Recommended listening:
The Smiths' 'How Soon is Now?' from their first compilation *Hatful of Hollow* (1984)

**September 1976.
384 Kings Rd,
Stretford, Manchester,
M32 8GW.**

Having spent a year preparing at the Stretford Technical School, and all summer waiting for the results, Steve Morrissey returned home from his holiday in the States to discover that he had failed his O-level exams.

Morrissey managed to get three O-levels, passing English literature, sociology and the general paper, but received a U in history, failing the subject he was never fond of.

Staying true to his working class roots, he quickly dispelled any further notions of receiving a higher education and set out to find his place among the country's workforce.

Recommended listening:
The Smiths' 'I Started Something I Couldn't Finish' from the album
Strangeways, Here We Come (1987)

Staircase at the University
part four

September 1976.
Stretford Civic Centre,
Manchester.

Recommended listening:
The Smiths' 'Heaven Knows I'm Miserable Now' from their first compilation *Hatful of Hollow* (1984)

Staircase at the University
part five

September 1976.
Stretford Civic Centre,
Manchester.

NEXT!

Uhh, hullo.

I... I just failed my O-levels and I...

I need to find a job so I can support my... my family.

How old are you?

Seventeen going eighteen.

Ha! I know your type!

Just out of school and here already to collect the dole!

Well, you're gonna have to wait in THAT queue, if you came here for cash!

Bloody leeches!

C'mooon! 'urry up! Ain't got all day!

Staircase at the University
part six

September 1976.
Stretford Civic Centre,
Manchester.

Recommended listening:
The Smiths' 'That Joke Isn't Funny Anymore' from the album *Meat is Murder* (1985)

September 1976.
Not very far away from Stretford's Civic Centre, Manchester.

Five minutes later...

Recommended listening:
The Patti Smith Group's second album, *Radio Ethiopia* (1976)

Staircase at the University
part eight

On his return from America Morrissey sought to renew his friendship with Julie Porter, writing to her on September 8 and asking her if she knew the address of another mutual friend, Ann-Marie McVeigh.

Morrissey wanted Ann-Marie to return some paperwork of his that he had lent her.

He told Julie he wouldn't be returning to college, and mentioned his 'terrific' trip to America.

He also informed Julie that he was unemployed and had plenty of time on his hands.

This letter was circulated on the internet in the mid '00s but was never verified as authentic.

Recommended listening:
The Smiths' 'Ask' from the live album *Rank* (1988)

Staircase at the University
part nine

September 1976.
384 Kings Rd,
Stretford, Manchester,
M32 8GW.

NME – done!
Melody Maker – done!
Sounds – done!

Record Mirror – done!
Rolling Stone – done!
GQ – done!

Having failed his O-levels, Morrissey next tried writing for the music press.
Now with some money guaranteed from the dole, he had both the free time and the stamp money to write letters to the different magazines on a regular basis.

Recommended listening:
The Patti Smith Group's 'Ask the Angels' from the album *Radio Ethiopia* (1976)

GLAMOROUS GLUE
PART ONE

1976.
In a drug-fuelled frenzy, David Bowie becomes his Thin White Duke character, his final fictional persona of the '70s and one created for his 1976 *Station to Station* album.

His personality during interviews of this period seemed more alarming than ever before.

He later said he had been living on "red peppers, cocaine and milk".

With his drug habit impacting on his physical and mental health, Bowie decided to move from Los Angeles to Paris and then West Berlin, where he lived with Iggy Pop and began recording his Berlin Trilogy.

Now a mainstream star, punk represented the cutting edge of alternative music which had once been the province of Bowie. Yet Steve Morrissey faithfully stood by his childhood hero, following his every career change.

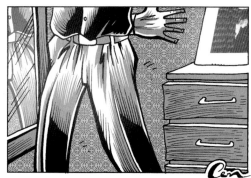

Recommended listening:
David Bowie's 'TVC 15' from the album *Station to Station* (1976)

Recommended viewing:
BBC's documentary *Cracked Actor* on David Bowie, which depicted his fragile mental state during this time (1975)

GLAMOROUS GLUE
PART TWO

September 25th, 1976.
Stretford, Manchester.

By constantly bombarding the letter columns of all the music press with New York Dolls-related fanboy witticisms, young Steve Morrissey found himself on a blacklist of sorts.

He managed to overcome this predicament by submitting multiple letters to the magazines under different aliases, sometimes as Steven, others as Steve, other times as Steve Morrissey or even plain Morrissey. On September 25th, 1976, two of his letters, written under two different names, were published in a single issue of *Sounds*. An undoubtable moment of triumph.

Recommended listening:
Morrissey's 'Glamorous Glue' from his Mick Ronson-produced, glam-influenced album, *Your Arsenal* (1992)

Morrissey fell for Patti Smith, declaring *Horses* to be the most exciting rock album of the year in a letter to *Sounds* that also drew attention to her 'sardonic humour'.

But he still loved the Dolls, wearily dismissing 'incompetent no-talents' like the Ramones and even the Pistols, in another letter printed in the very same issue.

Recommended reading:
The two letters written by Morrissey and published in *Sounds* (Sep 25, 1976)

Recommended listening:
The Patti Smith Group's groundbreaking debut album, *Horses* (1975)

GLAMOROUS GLUE
PART FOUR

October 1976.
Stretford Civic Centre,
Manchester.

Later at home...

And so at the ticket vendor...

Recommended listening:
The Patti Smith Group's 'Free Money' from their debut album, *Horses* (1975)

GLAMOROUS GLUE
PART FIVE

ODEON THEATRE
BIRMINGHAM
STRAIGHT MUSIC presents
PATTI SMITH + The Stranglers
EVENING 7-30 p.m.
SUNDAY **24**
OCTOBER
REAR STALLS
£1-50
JJ21
NO TICKET EXCHANGED NOR MONEY REFUNDED
THIS PORTION TO BE RETAINED   [P.T.O.]

October 24th, 1976.
Manchester-Birmingham coach.

Odeon Theatre, Birmingham.

Patti Smith's groundbreaking debut album, *Horses*, had such an impact on young Steve Morrissey that, years later when he formed The Smiths with fellow Pattiphiliac Johnny Marr, their very first composition would be 'The Hand That Rocks the Cradle', a song directly inspired by Patti Smith's 'Kimberly'.

Furthermore, in 2005 Morrissey would cover and release her song 'Redondo Beach' and even opened his 2012 Manchester gig by chanting the opening lines from *Horses*' title track.

Recommended listening:
Morrissey's cover of Patti Smith's 'Redondo Beach' from his album, *Live at Earls Court* (2005)
Patti Smith's 'Kimberly' from her debut album, *Horses* (1975)
The Smiths' 'The Hand That Rocks the Cradle' from their self-titled debut album, *The Smiths* (1984)

October 1976.
Within a fortnight of Patti Smith's Birmingham concert and bankrolled by his unemployment allowance, Morrissey went on a gig spree and attended, as far as we know, at least three gigs in the Manchester area by up-and-coming punk bands.

Deaf School from Liverpool, who would influence the late '70s Northern art-rock scene.

Split Enz, one of the most successful New Zealand acts, featuring brothers Tim and Neil Finn. Their musical style was eclectic, incorporating influences from art rock, vaudeville, swing, rock, and pop. They established a reputation for a highly distinctive visual style, thanks to their colourful, offbeat costumes and hairstyles. Various band members went on to form and perform in a variety of groups, including Crowded House, Schnell Fenster and Citizen Band.

Roogalator, a pub rock band formed in London in 1972 by the US born guitarist Danny Adler, bass guitarist Giorgi Dionisiev and drummer Malcolm Mortimer. Adler had previously recorded demos with 10cc's Graham Gouldman and played with Smooth Loser. After they disbanded Mortimer joined Ian Dury in Kilburn & the High Roads.

By displaying a more expressive art rock attitude, these bands acted as trailblazers for the outrageous look of early '80s new wave and New Romantics groups.

They also enabled fans to expand beyond the limitations of punk.

Recommended listening:
Roogalator's 'Love and the Single Girl' (1977)

Recommended viewing:
Deaf School performing 'Taxi' live on Granada TV (1977)
Split Enz's promo-video for 'Sweet Dreams' (1976)
Crowded House's music videos 'Don't Dream It's Over' and 'Weather with You' (1986/1991)

September 4th, 1976.

The last episode in the first series of Granada Television's late night magazine programme *So It Goes* presented by Tony Wilson (broadcast only in the Manchester area) featured the debut TV appearance of the Sex Pistols. Opening with a shout of *"Get off your arse"*, Rotten and co delivered a furious, brutally intense rendition of 'Anarchy in the UK'.

Prior to their appearance, there was a lot of tension in the studio between the band and the producers.

Tony Wilson remembered: There were terrible scenes in the dining room all afternoon, like when I had to tell Jordan she couldn't wear her swastika armband on TV. And then they had their huge row with Clive James He disliked them intensely. After that day, Clive and alternative culture went their separate ways.

Jordan, Malcolm McLaren's assistant in his SEX store, recalled: You've got Clive James, who is a terrible Australian straightie, being huffy and shocked, so we just waded in. I called him a baldy old Sheila. John just called him Bruce for an hour.

NME journalist Charles Shaar Murray described it as: the most utterly immediate thing I've ever seen on television.

As he viewed the show on a regular basis, Morrissey would bear witness to the rise of the Sex Pistols from unknown misfits to revolutionary punk figure-heads.

Quotes from Jon Savage's definitive history of punk music *England's Dreaming: Sex Pistols and Punk Rock* (1991)

Recommended viewing:
Sex Pistols performing 'Anarchy in the UK' live on Tony Wilson's *So It Goes* (1976)

GLAMOROUS GLUE
PART EIGHT

Malcolm McLaren on the New York Dolls versus the Sex Pistols:

Maybe it's because they're so close to the media, but they're all so scared by them I used to talk to journalist Lisa Robinson and David Johansen would pull me into the toilet and say, 'Don't you know who you're talking to? Don't say those things!'

My God, if you worry about what you say to her...

The trouble with the Dolls was that their hype was so much bigger than they were. They really had an opportunity to change it all around, but instead of ignoring all that bullshit about signing up with a company and a big advance, they got sucked in. There's no mystery about the New York scene.

Pretty soon Richard Hell is going to leave the Heartbreakers and Sire Records will dangle a contract in front of him and he knows it won't help and won't do any good but he'll sign it because it's what's expected of him

The trouble with the pubs is that they're free, and people come for that reason If you're at a Sex Pistols gig you wanted to go, because you spent money to get in. I opened the shop because I wanted people to make a certain statement and they were my clothes The Sex Pistols are another extension of that.

The New York scene has absolutely nothing to do with us, sneers John.
All anyone talks about is the image.
No-one's ever mentioned the music.
Steve and Paul deliver the fatal blows:
They're not like us.
They all have long hair.
Yeah, Anglophiles with Brian Jones mop heads.

Quotes from Malcolm McLaren's interview with *Sounds'* Jonh Ingham (April 24, 1976)
The article featured the first extensive interview with the Sex Pistols and their manifesto.

Recommended listening:
Sex Pistols' 'Bodies' from their only album *Never Mind the Bollocks, Here's the Sex Pistols* (1977)

GLAMOROUS GLUE
PART NINE

When a man is able to connect with his feelings, he is able to care more.
Warren Farrell

If more men were homosexual, there would be no wars, because homosexual men would never kill other men, whereas heterosexual men love killing other men. Wars and armies and nuclear weapons are essentially heterosexual hobbies.
Morrissey

November 1976.
With his parents' marriage having virtually disintegrated before his eyes, Steve Morrissey delved more and more into men's liberation and feminist literature, attempting to define his own place as a 20th Century Boy.

In the mid '70s macho culture still held sway and, despite the promise held by the glam icons of just a few years earlier, sexual emancipation seemed a long way off.
In late 1975 British Home Stores sacked openly gay trainee Tony Whitehead and a national campaign subsequently picketed their stores.

Some of the first men's lib books he mentioned after forming The Smiths were Warren Farrell's *The Liberated Man* and Jack Nichols' *Men's Liberation*. These type of readings would prove prophetic, to say the least.

Even worse, despite the inital hope produced by the outburst of punk, a movement based on free expression, homophobic and racist attacks were increasing at an alarming degree in the UK.

Quotes from a Morrissey interview with Amy Rose of *Rookie Mag* (Feb 26, 2013)

Recommended listening:
T. Rex's '20th Century Boy' from the 1994 reissue of their album *Tanx* (1973)

Recommended reading:
Warren Farrell's *The Liberated Man* (1974)
Jack Nichols' *Men's Liberation: A New Definition of Masculinity* (1975)

GLAMOROUS GLUE
PART TEN

From evening soaps to preteen romances, the message is that inner values are for losers.

Warren Farrell

By November 1976 Morrissey was finally free of the burden of school and, while trying to save money to return to the States, spent most of his unemployment allowance on new records and men's liberation books.

It's at this stage of his life that he also confirmed his stance against compulsory participation in sporting events and any behaviour typically expected of a male in western society.

"Today, violence against women is rightly abhorred. But we call violence against men entertainment. Think of football, boxing, wrestling... All are games used to sugarcoat violence against men, originally in need of sugarcoating so 'our team' – or 'our society' – could bribe its best protectors to sacrifice themselves."

There are many ways in which a woman experiences a greater sense of powerlessness than her male counterpart; the fears of pregnancy, aging, rape, date rape and being physically overpowered; less socialisation to take a career that pays enough to support a husband and children...

Fortunately, almost all industrialised nations have acknowledged these female experiences.
Unfortunately, they have acknowledged only the female experience.

Warren Farrell's *The Myth of Male Power*

Steven! I'm home!

You comin' down for dinner, honey?

Yes, mother...

God, I have to find a job ASAP...

and emancipate myself from this nuclear family unit!

It is also in his late teens that he told his close circle about trying to live a celibate life.

Recommended listening:
Morrissey's 'Glamorous Glue' from his Mick Ronson-produced, glam-influenced album, *Your Arsenal* (1992)

Recommended reading:
Warren Farrell's *The Liberated Man* (1974)
Warren Farrell's *The Myth of Male Power: Why Men are the Disposable Sex* (2000)

Heaven Knows
I'm Miserable Now
part one

November 15th, 1976.
384 Kings Rd,
Stretford, Manchester,
M32 8GW.

In order to keep receiving his unemployment allowance, Steve Morrissey's local job centre offered him a job as a civil servant. It was an offer he could not refuse.

Recommended listening:
The Smiths' 'Heaven Knows I'm Miserable Now' from their first compilation album, *Hatful of Hollow* (1984)

Heaven Knows I'm Miserable Now
part two

November 21st, 1976.
Department of Health and Social Security,
Manchester.

Recommended listening:
The Smiths' 'Nowhere Fast' from the album *Meat is Murder* (1985)

Heaven Knows
I'm Miserable Now
part three

November 23rd, 1976.
Department of Health and Social Security,
Manchester.

Ian Curtis worked as a civil servant around the time
that Steve Morrissey worked for the DHSS.
Curtis was responsible for the payment of unemployment
benefits and for helping unemployed Mancs find work.
He left to become an assistant disablement resettlement
officer at Macclesfield's Job Centre.

Recommended listening:
Joy Division's 'She's Lost Control' from their debut studio album *Unknown Pleasures* (1979)

Hard work is simply the refuge of people who have nothing whatever to do.

Oscar Wilde

**November 27th, 1976.
Department of Health and Social Security,
Manchester.**

Back home at Kings Rd, Stretford.

With a joint income of £50 a week, 1976 looked like a grim year for Steve Morrissey and his mother, especially if he were to lose his unemployment allowance.

Recommended reading:
Oscar Wilde's *The Remarkable Rocket* from his collection of children's stories,
The Happy Prince and Other Tales (1888)

Heaven Knows
I'm Miserable Now
part five

There is no work so delightful as the
work one does for others.

Oscar Wilde

**November 30th, 1976.
Stretford Civic Centre,
Manchester.**

Recommended reading:
Oscar Wilde's *The Devoted Friend* from his collection of children's stories,
The Happy Prince and Other Tales (1888)

shoplifters of the world unite part one

December 1976.
384 Kings Rd,
Stretford, Manchester,
M32 8GW.

5:38pm

6:41pm

9:23pm

11:54pm

In December 1976 Betty Dwyer filed for divorce from Steven Morrissey's father, Peter. The proceedings would last for the whole month, turning the already dim festive spirit into a nightmare.

Recommended listening:
The Smiths' 'Shoplifters of the World Unite'
from their second compilation album, *The World Won't Listen* (1987)

shoplifters of the world unite part two

100 Club, London.

Encouraged by Malcolm McLaren, *NME* journalist Nick Kent is attacked by two Sex Pistols fans after writing a scathing review of their latest gig.

I went over to Malcolm and, for the first time ever, he was quite cold. I just thought, "Well, he's in a bad mood," and sloped off to the very back where I waited for the group to perform.

I started noticing that this guy, Sid Vicious, would, whenever he walked past, kick me in the shins. At first, it seemed like a clumsy mistake; the second time, this was on purpose.

Lydon goes on-stage, and Sid decides to stand directly in front of me. I tapped him on the shoulder and I said, very careful, "Could you move over?"

Sid immediately pulled this chain out.

He made some remark which he thought was insulting, like, "I don't like your trousers."

The guy next to me immediately makes a motion towards Vicious and then pulls his knife out, and he really wants to cut my face. Years later, I find his name is Wobble.

This was a real speed freak, and this is when it got very unhealthy.

I remember putting my hands up and not moving a muscle, and then Vicious tapped him on the shoulder and he disappeared immediately. It was all set up.

Vicious then had a clear aim and got me with the bike chain. It wasn't painful. The main thing was that it drew a lot of blood, which was just pouring down my face and my chest.

Vivien Westwood, McLaren's wife, ran behind apologising profusely and remonstrating "That guy who attacked you was just a nutter... a psychopath. We've told the band not to have him around."

Quotes from a Nick Kent interview for Jon Savage's definitive history of punk music, *England's Dreaming: Sex Pistols and Punk Rock* (1991)

shoplifters of the world unite part three

**384 Kings Rd,
Stretford, Manchester,
M32 8GW.**

Morrissey came to the rescue of his beloved New York Dolls again in November, penning a letter to *NME* in response to comments by their star writer Nick Kent.

He particularly liked Dolls singer David Johansen's comment: 'Who cares about music when one has such a sense of drama?'

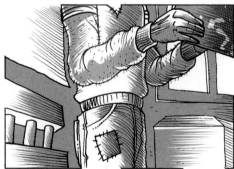
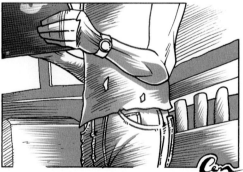

He saw an echo of the Dolls in all the emerging UK punk bands.

And suggested it was time for NME to 'break the office rules' and publish an article on them.

Recommended reading:
The letter written by Morrissey, published in the *NME*, in which he attacked their journalist, Nick Kent, over his comments on the New York Dolls (Nov 19, 1976)

Recommended listening:
The New York Dolls' self-titled debut album, *New York Dolls* (1973)
The New York Dolls' second and final album with the original lineup, *Too Much Too Soon* (1974)

shoplifters of the world unite part four

Meanwhile, Nick Kent receives medical treatment following his assault by Sid Vicious at the 100 Club. He opts to keep a low profile for a while.

Morrissey is less than sympathetic to Kent's plight. At least the hatemonger will stop attacking the Dolls in the press for a while!

And Kent is less than enamoured with Morrissey.

While Morrissey enjoys his penmanship.

Fuckin' little prick!

Pure genius, Steve!

Morrissey and Nick Kent would form a love-hate relationship through the pages of the British music press, lasting even after The Smiths formed, a band which Kent praised at every opportunity.
Their relationship crash-landed in May 1985 when Kent published an extensive exposé in *The Face* revealing a plethora of unknown facts from Morrissey's shady past to the public for the very first time.
The exposé remains the core basis for most biographies written after the demise of The Smiths.

Recommended reading:
The letter written by Morrissey, published in the *NME* (Nov 19, 1976) and a Nick Kent *NME* article (Dec 17, 1977)
Nick Kent's exposé on Morrissey's past, *Dreamer in the Real World*, from *The Face* (May 1985)

shoplifters of the world unite part five

December 1st, 1976.
Thames Television, London.

After Queen cancelled their appearance on Bill Grundy's *Today* show, the producers invited the Sex Pistols to take their place, in order to cash in on the new punk fad. The interview began with Grundy introducing the band, but he then started provoking his guests. Grundy jokingly made advances to Siouxsie Sioux, who appeared as part of the band's entourage. Annoyed with Grundy's sleazy demeanour, Steve Jones responded by slagging off the interviewer on TV.

The interview destroyed Grundy's career, elevated the Sex Pistols to notoriety, and signalled the arrival of punk rock to the nation at large.

Morrissey would use the same provocative tactics employed by the Pistols. when writing the lyrics/manifestos for The Smiths' most notorious songs, created especially to provoke the media and conservative public. The most notable example is 'Shoplifters of the World Unite' in which Moz declared that he was "bored before he even began" and "my only weakness is, well, never mind". A subliminal reference to Pistols' staple Stooges cover 'No Fun' and their only studio album, *Never Mind the Bollocks*? Who knows...

Recommended viewing:
The Sex Pistols' legendary appearance on Bill Grundy's *Today* show (Dec 1,1976)
Julien Temple's documentary, *The Filth and the Fury*, on the history of the Sex Pistols (2000)

December 2nd, 1976.

Following their appearance on Bill Grundy's *Today* show, the Sex Pistols became household names. Moral outrage was splashed across tabloid front pages the morning after. *The Daily Mirror*'s response was its classic 'The Filth and the Fury' headline.

Following a campaign waged in the south Wales press, a crowd including carol singers and a Pentecostal preacher, protested against the group outside a show in Caerphilly.

Bernard Brook-Partridge, a Conservative member of the Greater London Council and its chairman of the arts committee, declared:

Most of these groups would be vastly improved by sudden death. The worst of the punk rock groups I suppose currently are the Sex Pistols.

They are unbelievably nauseating. They are the antithesis of humankind. I would like to see somebody dig a very, very large, exceedingly deep hole and drop the whole bloody lot down it.

Sure, they suck, but "Filth"?

Watch where you're going, punk!

Punk?! Me?

The divide between Britain's punk youth an the morally conservative adults would continue to grow throughout the late-'70s.

Recommended listening:
The Smiths' 'These Things Take Time' from their first compilation, *Hatful of Hollow* (1984)

Recommended viewing:
The Sex Pistols' legendary appearance on Bill Grundy's *Today* show (Dec 1,1976)

1976. Birmingham, UK.

During a concert in Birmingham, a heavily drunk Eric Clapton allegedly made a long speech on stage in which he slagged off immigrants and referred to British anti-immigration Conservative MP, Enoch Powell. The speech was recorded and highly-publicised by the *NME, Melody Maker,* the *Guardian* and *Times.*

Author Caryl Philips, who was a witness to the event, said: *Nobody cheered, but after he played another song, he did the same again. It was extraordinary, but he stood there being overtly offensive and racist. I was completely mystified as to why this man playing black music would behave this way.*

Do we have any foreigners in the audience tonight? If so, please put up your hands.

I think you should all just leave. Not just leave the hall, leave our country. Get the foreigners out. Get the wogs out. Get the coons out.

I used to be into dope, now I'm into racism. It's much heavier, man. Fucking wogs, man. Bastard wogs. Britain is becoming overcrowded and Enoch will send them all back.

Enoch for Prime Minister! Throw the wogs out!

Britain's becoming a black colony. Keep Britain white!

This is a white country... THIS IS ENGLAND!

To make matters worse, the recession which had hit Britain in the '70s started taking its toll on the working classes. Influenced by the ultra-conservative claims of former Tory MP and far-right propagandist, Enoch Powell, some started taking up these racist views.

Of course it didn't help that David Bowie, earlier in the year at Victoria Station, had made a Nazi salute to his fans, who would respond with the same salute. He would also suggest that a fascist dictator and the extreme right was needed in Britain and that Hitler was a proto-rock star of sorts.

I see the River Tiber foaming with much blood.

Oi!

Therefore, when the first punks wore swastikas as a tongue-in-cheek statement aimed at their WWII veteran parents, the new generation found this distorted display of the hate symbol appealing. Likewise when the '60s skinhead movement resurfaced as Oi on the heels of punk, it took everyone by surprise that their once open-minded views, influenced by the Jamaican rude boy styles and culture, now welcomed white-power, racist ideologies.

Recommended viewing:
Shane Meadows' *This is England*, which centres on early '80s young English skinheads (2006)

the filth and the fury
part three

November 11th, 1976.
Through his letter-writing strategy, Morrissey manages to have two letters published within the same issue of *Melody Maker* under two aliases. In the first letter he once more trashes the Sex Pistols for having the audacity to lift the sound and look of the New York Dolls and in the second he accuses the new British punk movement of being inferior to its New York counterpart. In this second letter he also preaches the gospel New York Dolls/Jobriath/Patti Smith, who at this moment have become the focal point of his influences and his very being; he'll never stop praising them for the rest of his life.

His first letter suggests the Sex Pistols are only worthy of inclusion in fashion magazines.

The second letter compares UK punk unfavourably with its US counterpart, and he's reversed his opinion of the Ramones, bracketing them with the Dolls, Patti Smith and Jobriath.

The two letters written by Morrissey and published in *Melody Maker* (Nov 11, 1976)

Recommended listening:
Jobriath's 'Inside' from his self-titled debut album, *Jobriath* (1973)

December 5th, 1976.
Outside The Electric Circus, Manchester.

Amidst the furore created by their appearance on Bill Grundy's *Today* show, the Sex Pistols set off on their Anarchy Tour, which would see them perform alongside The Damned, The Clash and Johnny Thunders & The Heartbreakers.

On December 9th, 1976, The Heartbreakers were to perform at Manchester's Electric Circus. Morrissey would at last have the chance to see a Doll live on stage.

Recommended listening:
The Heartbreakers' 'Born to Lose' from their only studio album, *L.A.M.F.* (1977)

the filth and the fury
part five

December 7th, 1976.
Manchester Royal Infirmary.

According to biographer, Johnny Rogan, Morrissey lost one of his dearest friends and fellow concert-goers, Angie, to leukemia in the same week that their beloved New York Dolls, Johnny Thunders and Jerry Nolan, toured Manchester as The Heatbreakers alongside the Sex Pistols and The Clash on the ill-fated 1976 Anarchy Tour.

Recommended listening:
The Smiths' 'I Know It's Over' from the album, *The Queen is Dead* (1986)

Recommended reading:
Oscar Wilde's short story *The Canterville Ghost* from his collection
Lord Arthur Savile's Crime and Other Stories (1891)

CHINESE ROCKS
PART ONE

December 1976.

With Johnny Thunders leading the band, The Heartbreakers travel to Britain to join the Sex Pistols, The Clash and The Damned on the now legendary Anarchy Tour, replacing The Ramones, who had quit the tour due to a lack of organisation.

Heralded by all the UK punk rockers, who had been inspired by the New York Dolls, The Heartbreakers stayed in England for over a year, recording their debut album, *L.A.M.F.*

To the young punks, Thunders was essentially the first legit 'star' who they got to meet. To Steve Jones, who was already apeing most of his moves and riffs, he seemed like the perfect role model.

Fellow Heartbreaker and ex-Doll, Jerry Nolan, later claimed that he and Thunders first introduced much of the British punk scene to heroin during this time.

Recommended listening:
The Heartbreakers' heroin anthem 'Chinese Rocks' from their only studio album, *L.A.M.F.* (1977)

CHINESE ROCKS
PART TWO

December 9th, 1976.
Back entrance to The Electric Circus, Manchester, where we find guitarist Mick Jones sneaking in Morrissey to check out The Heartbreakers' soundcheck.

A New York Dolls fanatic himself, Mick Jones of The Clash had struck a friendship with Steven via correspondence, as Morrissey was the President of the Dolls' UK fan club.
Jones would find himself in the centre of the storm as part of the notorious Anarchy Tour.

Recommended listening:
The Clash's 'White Riot' from their self-titled debut album, *The Clash* (1977)

CHINESE ROCKS
PART THREE

December 9th, 1976.
Inside The Electric Circus, Manchester, in which Morrissey bumps into The Heartbreakers just before their soundcheck.

Johnny?

Je... Jerry?

How can I help you, man?

The Hear...

I touched you at the soundcheck In my heart, I begged "take me with you"

I... I've been the... the President of the New York Dolls' fan club for the past three years and...

Oh God, I'd rehearsed all this at home and now I'm just blabbering away.

Johnny, I'm on a mission to get David, Sylvain and you back together as the Dolls!

THE DOLLS? seriously?

Johansen can go fuck himself as far as I'm concerned.

But to you I was faceless I was fawning, I was boring

Do me a favour and beat it, kiddo.

Beat... but... but Johnny... Jerry... all I...

You heard him. SCRAM!

Even though Johnny Thunders and Jerry Nolan rebuffed young Steven Morrissey when he tried to meet them by sneaking into their soundcheck before their Anarchy Tour gig in Manchester, his blind devotion to the New York Dolls would lead him years later to downplay their behaviour:

They weren't friendly and why should they be? Who was I, anyway?

Most biographers consider the encounter was depicted in The Smiths' 'Paint a Vulgar Picture'.

Recommended listening:
The Smiths' 'Paint a Vulgar Picture' from their final album, *Strangeways, Here We Come* (1987)

December 9th, 1976.

The Heartbreakers soundcheck at The Electric Circus, just as Morrissey contemplates his disastrous meeting with his idol, Johnny Thunders, former guitarist of the New York Dolls.

Morrissey first saw Linder in Manchester, 1976, when she introduced the Buzzcocks at the Lesser Trade Hall. He next caught sight of her at a soundcheck for a Sex Pistol's gig.

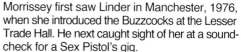

Linder was slightly older than Morrissey's 17 years. She had formidable hair. Morrissey decided to approach her.

They were mentally in tune, thoughts aligned, perfectly matched.

In the midst of the greatest disaster of his life, Steven Morrissey met Linder Sterling. She would become his best friend from that day onwards.

Recommended listening:
The Smiths' 'Wonderful Woman', allegedly written about Linder, released as a b-side to 'This Charming Man' (1983)

CHINESE ROCKS
PART FIVE

December 9th, 1976.
As Morrissey recovers from his disastrous meeting with his idol, the Anarchy Tour gig at last commences at Manchester's The Electric Circus when Johnny Thunders and The Heartbreakers perform one of their most intense sets.

December 9th, 1976.

When the Anarchy Tour reached Manchester it would be the Sex Pistols' third gig in the city. By then the local punk community was well acquainted with one another as new bands emerged daily.

Ian Curtis thought Pete Shelley very approachable, even though he felt they had made it.

Beyond Johnny Thunders and The Heartbreakers, Manchester staple, the Buzzcocks also opened for the Sex Pistols' third gig, replacing The Damned at the last minute.

The gig would be one of frontman Howard Devoto's last performances with the band.

The Clash performed before the Pistols and their politically charged lyrics, competitiveness with the headliners and raw energy would bring the house down.

It was the Sex Pistols, however, that everyone came to see. The band, that night at its peak, would not be out-performed by any other punk band on that legendary bill.

Recommended listening:
Buzzcocks' 'Love Battery' from the album, *Another Music in a Different Kitchen* (1987)

CHINESE ROCKS
PART SEVEN

December 9th, 1976.
The Electric Circus, Manchester.
Immediately after the Sex Pistols'
third Manchester gig.

WONDERFUL WOMAN
part one

Linder Sterling grew up in Wigan, a town which in the '70s had its own rich and distinctive musical scene based around the legendary Wigan Casino.

My dad was a bricklayer, and my mum used to work in a biscuit factory. I longed for the exotic things in life from an early age and never got them. Shoes. Still have the same problem.

I got interested in everything I couldn't have. I got interested in classical music, 'cos we never had any in the house, so I'd get these old 78s from my aunties and dress up in old scarves and dance around the living room. Not so much pop music, 'cos everybody liked it.

Everybody at school would go to the Casino. At the time it was always Northern Soul. I went a couple of times but when you grow up with something, it becomes a bit boring. I was more into folk music, listening mainly to Joan Baez, but also Bob Dylan. I also learned to play guitar and sing songs.

There was a family that lived down the road, and they gave singing lessons for 50p an hour, and I would stay all night. They would tell me to write my own words, because in the folk tradition it was very normal to write your own songs.

come you masters of war.

Quotes from Linder Sterling interviews given to Jon Savage for *The England's Dreaming Tapes* (2009), his companion book to his critically acclaimed history of UK punk rock, *England's Dreaming* (1991), and *Nude Magazine* #9 (2011)

Recommended viewing:
Elaine Constantine's *Northern Soul* (2014) regarding Wigan Casino's soul music scene

By 1964 Linder found herself raiding the school library. Because I went to a poor school, all we had to read were lots of books on Greek and Roman mythology. So I became an expert on the Classics when I was about ten!

She also found that she was good at drawing; so good in fact that she let it slip, bored by the easiness of it. But she picked it up again a couple of years later and qualified for art college in Manchester, where she studied graphic design & illustration at the Manchester Polytechnic from 1974 until 1977.

I was doing a combination of feminist statements and looking at things like pornography which was very hidden away. A lot of people thought my early work was done by a man. They seemed to think only a man would work with that kind of imagery, and were genuinely shocked to discover it was created by a woman.

Peter Saville and Malcolm Garrett were at the same college as me at the same time. At the end of the '60s here was a pretty amazing art education to be had in Britain, and we came in at the tail end of it

Manchester Polytechnic students at the time that punk broke, Saville, Sterling and Garrett (together with Sex Pistols' designer Jamie Reid) would become the most influential graphic designers of their generation.

Quotes from a Linder Sterling interview with *Nude Magazine* #9 (2011) and from Ludus' biography on LTM Recording's website

Recommended listening:
The Smiths' 'Wonderful Woman', allegedly written about Linder, released as a b-side to 'This Charming Man' (1983)

WONDERFUL WOMAN
part three

Once I arrived in Manchester in 1973 I realised that it was just like a slightly bigger version of Wigan. There wasn't a lot going on in Manchester at the time. The poly disco every Wednesday was the highlight.

Otherwise, there was nowhere to hear Bowie and Roxy Music stuff, or the Philadelphia sound. On the other hand the scene at art school before punk broke out was all Roxy Music, quiffs and gels.

And there weren't many good bands around... just Deaf School... and they were from Liverpool like me.

I remember when punk came along, suddenly all the nice shirts that had been worn were being painted and crayoned on. The same shirts I'd seen earlier. And the tuxedos were being ripped up.

Quotes from Linder Sterling interviews given to Jon Savage for *The England's Dreaming Tapes* (2009), his companion book to his critically acclaimed history of UK punk rock, *England's Dreaming* (1991), and *Nude Magazine #9* (2011)

Recommended viewing:
Deaf School performing 'Taxi' live on Granada TV (1977)
Elaine Constantine's *Northern Soul* (2014) regarding Wigan Casino's soul music scene

WONDERFUL WOMAN
part four

June 1976.

I was sitting in Manchester's Southern Cemetery sketching one day, walked out, and this van was parked outside with a poster tacked on, saying:

Malcolm McLaren presents the Sex Pistols' ...and the names McLaren sounded tartan, and tartan and sex and pistols and guns, so I suggested to this friend that we go.

Then in the afternoon I was tidying my room, and I kept finding safety pins, and I was pinning them on my clothes...

I remember going into the Lesser Free Trade Hall, and I think it was Johnny Rotten who took my money, and I saw Vivienne and Malcolm, and I just knew that something strange was going to happen. I just knew it. These people looked so separate and apart and so different.

Quotes from Linder Sterling interviews given to Jon Savage for *The England's Dreaming Tapes* (2009), his companion book to his critically acclaimed history of UK punk rock, *England's Dreaming* (1991), and *Nude Magazine #9* (2011)

Recommended listening:
Sex Pistols' 'God Save the Queen' from their only album
Never Mind the Bollocks, Here's the Sex Pistols (1977)

WONDERFUL WOMAN
part five

I went to the Sex Pistols, Buzzcocks, Slaughter & the Dogs concert. The first time ever. The girl I was with fell in love with Howard Devoto and said, Please, can we stay and talk to the singer! So we stayed, but then the singer took more to me!

I talked to Pete Shelley first, who was very friendly straight away and then Howard. We went for a drink afterwards at the Conti club.

As well as collaborating closely with the band, Linder became romantically involved with Howard Devoto. Taking inspiration from Andy Warhol's Factory collective, Linder provided the band with artwork for flyers and record covers.

Howard and I lived in the same house. Pete Shelley lived next door. It was very close knit and fairly intense. But at the same time we had to keep our focus and our absolute integrity.

Unbeknownst to her, Pete Shelley would also become infatuated with Linder and his unfulfilled love for his best friend's girlfriend would inspire him to write Buzzcocks' first punk rock love songs.

Quotes from Linder Sterling interviews given to Jon Savage for *The England's Dreaming Tapes* (2009), his companion book to his critically acclaimed history of UK punk rock, *England's Dreaming* (1991), and *Nude Magazine* #9 (2011)

Recommended listening:
Buzzcocks' classic single 'Ever Fallen in Love (With Someone You Shouldn't've)?' (1978)

Recommended reading:
Susan Brownmiller's feminist classic *Against Our Will: Men, Women, and Rape* (1975)

June 4th, 1976.
Lesser Free Trade Hall, Manchester.
Johnny was wearing this big mohair jumper that seemed to be growing all the time...

...the fluff getting longer, and arms growing out, like an octapus. It was a shimmery night. All energy and light.

It was just fascinating... me longing as usual for something different. Exotic. And these strange leather trousers and mohair jumpers. It was just so strange...

When did you become Linder?
I was born in 1976.

Before you were Linda?
Yes, punk allowed you to re-christen yourself and be re-born. Proclaiming Cinderland then gave me a psychic territory, a home and a landscape.

Quotes from Linder Sterling interviews given to Jon Savage for *The England's Dreaming Tapes* (2009), his companion book to his critically acclaimed history of UK punk rock, *England's Dreaming* (1991), and *32c magazine* #11 (2006)

Recommended listening:
Sex Pistols' only studio album *Never Mind the Bollocks, Here's the Sex Pistols* (1977)

WONDERFUL WOMAN
part seven

Linder: I did my foundation and first-year graphics, and then went off to London in the summer holidays, met Howard, came back dressed in PVC and my life changed.

I did my whole college course. I remember having my bondage trousers as part of the degree show.

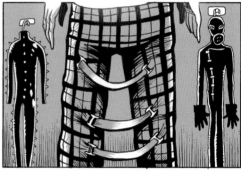

Morrissey first saw Linder when she introduced Buzzcocks onstage at the Lesser Free Trade Hall in the summer of 1976.

In an article about her written for *Frieze* magazine in June 2004, Morrissey suggested Linder's life was a docudrama, 'potent and therefore lethal'.

As muse to both Pete Shelley and Howard Devoto, Linder Sterling's appartment in Salford would become the meeting point of the Buzzcocks camp and Manchester's first punk community.

Quotes from Linder Sterling interviews given to Jon Savage for *The England's Dreaming Tapes* (2009), his companion book to his critically acclaimed history of UK punk rock, *England's Dreaming* (1991), and from an article written by Morrissey himself about his friendship with Linder Sterling for *Frieze* magazine (June 2004)

Recommended listening:
Buzzcocks' classic single 'What Do I Get?' (1977)

WONDERFUL WOMAN
part eight

August 29th, 1976.
Screen on the Green cinema, Islington, North London.
The Screen on the Green was an adventure. We hired the van and all went down to London in that. Borrowed a camera for the night.

I remember being in the bar with Vivienne and somebody else. They came up and said, "Who are you a fan of?" At the time I thought, what a daft thing to say, and I said, "I'm a fan of me." How dare you presume, you know?

I remember Vivienne standing at one side, jumping up and down and screaming. I thought she was wonderful. Wasn't The Clash on that night? They had these badges, like smashed mirrors, and I thought it was a strange thing to wear. I didn't really approve of the Tommy badges. It was a bit off-putting, it didn't tally with my idea of what was happening. I thought, no.

I wore gel on the hair, pots of eyeliner, red lips. It was tight and black. I remember Pete not knowing what to wear, so he wore two pairs of my footless tights. I think a cleaning woman's pink smock. And his hair was bleached blond. He was wonderful that night, so full of energy.

Quotes from Linder Sterling interviews given to Jon Savage for *The England's Dreaming Tapes* (2009), his companion book to his critically acclaimed history of UK punk rock, *England's Dreaming* (1991)

Recommended listening:
Buzzcocks' 'Breakdown' from their debut EP, *Spiral Scratch* (1977)

WONDERFUL WOMAN
part nine

August 29th, 1976.
Screen on the Green cinema, Islington, North London.

I did photography for a very short period, until my camera got stolen.

I took pictures of Siouxsie and the girl who died, Tracie. And Simon Barker.

I remember asking a boy I didn't know to come outside, so I could take his picture.
He had this chain through his nose.
Then the next week the same boy was on the cover of the *News of the World*.

It really began to happen then, shock horror:
"THIS BOY HAS HIS NOSE PIERCED AND WEARS LEATHER"
He was from Wales.

Quotes from Linder Sterling interviews given to Jon Savage for *The England's Dreaming Tapes* (2009), his companion book to his critically acclaimed history of UK punk rock, *England's Dreaming* (1991), and *Nude Magazine* #9 (2011)

Recommended reading:
Linder Sterling's career retrospective, *Linder: Works 1976–2006*, which contains a compilation of her graphics and photos of the early punk scene (including a young pre-fame Ian Curtis in leather, Siouxsie Sioux et al) (2006)

WONDERFUL WOMAN
part ten

December 9th, 1976.
Morrissey remembers noticing Linder Sterling at the Anarchy Tour soundcheck in Manchester's Electric Circus and promptly approached her, after which they soon struck up a friendship. However, Linder's account of the meeting differs.

He wanted to speak to Howard and Peter, but they were sound-checking so he spoke to me and we hit it off pretty quickly.

A couple of days later in some Salfordian greasy spoon.

We were both really into the America of Andy Warhol and Factory, and we both had a fascination with British cinema and that notion of the recent past... the past of our childhood and our formative years.

It was a fascinating, dynamic and intense relationship.

Dedicated to Steve Silverwood, guitarist extraordinaire/slang orthographer

Quotes from Linder Sterling interview for *Nude Magazine* #9 (2011)

Recommended reading:
Linder Sterling's photographic portrait of Morrissey's life on the road, *Morrissey Shot* (1992)

December 1976.
Across the road from Johnny Maher's home in Wythenshawe, south Manchester, we find his friends Billy Duffy and Rob Allman rehearsing with their teen band, Eye Routine.
Johnny realised that Rob and Billy were very clued up on music for such a young age.

Johnny was only 13 when they met but this didn't matter because he was so keen to learn. He and Billy Duffy have been friends ever since.

Billy remembers that Johnny lived across the street and just started turning up. He didn't mind the age gap and, in any case, there was no awkwardness because Johnny fitted in well.

Billy remembers Johnny's insatiable appetite for all things rock and roll and how he always asked the right questions. He became quite paternal towards Johnny and even sold him the first amplifier he had owned.

Entering Johnny Marr's life in 1976, Billy Duffy would not only play a crucial role as both his mentor and role model, but would also make the first connection with Morrissey.

Recommended reading:
Johnny Marr's and Billy Duffy's interview for BillyDuffy.com's Stories (2013)

Recommended listening:
The Smiths' 'William, It Was Really Nothing' from the compilation album *Hatful of Hollow* (1984)

Johnny loved hanging out with Billy at Rob's house because the musicians who met there were all into different bands and guitarists. They liked to analyse the playing styles of their favourites, both UK and American. The scene there was both encouraging and competitive and everyone was very serious about music.

Johnny liked Rory Gallagher and James Williamson from the Stooges.

Billy was into Mick Ronson, Paul Kossoff of Free, The Who and Johnny Thunders of the New York Dolls.

Rob was seriously into Neil Young and then he discovered Tom Verlaine of Television from New York.

Others who caught their eye were Nils Lofgren who'd played with Neil Young and Nile Rodgers, the guitarist with Chic.

Recommended reading:
Johnny Marr's and Billy Duffy's interview for BillyDuffy.com's Stories (2013)

Recommended listening:
Rory Gallagher's 'Moon Child' from the album *Calling Card* (1976)
The Stooges' 'Search and Destroy' from their-Bowie produced album, *Raw Power* (1973)

1976. Wythenshawe.

Billy Duffy retains fond memories of the Wythenshawe gang of guitarists. It reflected the social mix of Brookway High School, kids from middle-class families who lived in semi-detached houses with cars in the drive and others who were working-class. Billy and Johnny, both of Irish descent, came from the latter and for them music seemed like the only way out.

Billy recognised that punk was a lifeline for boys like him because it showed that anyone could form a band and become famous.

Johnny would bunk off school to head into Manchester and hang out. He became a Perry Boy and credits Billy more for giving him good shoewear advice, rather than any guitar mentoring.

Billy turned Johnny on to the Stooges *Raw Power* album and the New York Dolls. They were never together in any band.

Billy and Johnny are still friends to this day.

This is it, Johnny... This is our ticket outta here!

Punk? Dunno, Billy... Sounds kinda awful... amateur

Riding on the new wave of Manchester punk, Billy Duffy played guitar in a series of minor bands, like The Nosebleeds and Studio Sweethearts before joining Theatre of Hate and, later on, Southern Death Cult, which would soon be renamed The Cult. It is with The Cult that he finally achieved the success he so longed for.
His riffs for songs like 'She Sells Sanctuary' and his iconic pose for the cover of their album *Sonic Temple* would ensure him the guitar hero status.

Recommended reading:
Johnny Marr's interviews for Consequence of Sound.net (Feb 2013), TheArtsDesk.com (Aug 2013) and a Johnny Marr's and Billy Duffy's interview for BillyDuffy.com's Stories (2013)

Recommended listening:
The Cult's 'She Sells Sanctuary' from the album *Love* (1985)

December 1976. Manchester.
Mike Joyce on his infatuation with Buzzcocks' drummer, John Maher.

Meanwhile at the same gig is a young guitarist from Wythenshawe, also named Johnny Maher, with best friend Andy Rourke. They bear witness to his namesake's deification.

Mike Joyce managed to fulfill his teenage dream when, after the demise of The Smiths and John Maher's departure from the Buzzcocks, he became their official drummer from 1990 until 1992.

Quotes from a Mike Joyce interview in the *Q Classic* special
Morrissey & the Story of Manchester (2006)

Recommended listening:
The drum intro to The Smiths' 'The Queen is Dead' from the album *The Queen is Dead* (1986)
Joyce's pounding drums from The Smiths' 'Death of a Disco Dancer'
from their final album *Strangeways, Here We Come* (1987)

THE BOY WITH THE
THORN IN HIS SIDE PART ONE

Late December 1976.
384 Kings Road, Stretford, Manchester.
In another letter to his friend Julie from Stretford Tech Morrissey tells her, perhaps tongue-in-cheek, that he is desperate to get a job and doesn't care what it is, so long as it is illegal.

He explains that he wants to go swimming but can't because he has an ear infection.

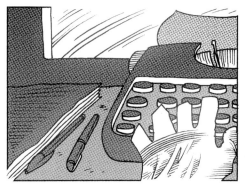

During Christmas 1976 the Buzzcocks recorded their debut EP, *Spiral Scratch*, in three hours.
Produced by Martin Hannett, who would soon become legendary for his work with Joy Division, the record was a vital step for the Manchester scene.

Having no record label support, the band had to borrow £500 from their friends to finance the EP. Released on the Buzzcocks' New Hormones label, *Spiral Scratch* was the first record from an independent label and sparked the UK indie scene.

The record sold out its initial 1000 printing and went on to sell 16,000 copies, firstly by mail order and later with the help of the Manchester branch of music chain store Virgin, whose manager also persuaded other regional branch managers to follow suit.

Recommended reading:
Unverified letter to Julie allegedly attributed to Morrissey, which circulated on the net in the mid '00s

Recommended listening:
The Smiths' 'The Boy with the Thorn in His Side' from the album *The Queen is Dead* (1986)
Buzzcocks' seminal EP *Spiral Scratch* (1977)

Late December 1976.
384 Kings Road, Stretford, Manchester.

Totally broke and living off one £5 a week DHSS unemployment allowance, Steven Morrissey had no other choice but to start looking for a regular job in order to help his family out with the bills.

In an effort to mess with society's gender expectations, he applied for a job as an au pair boy.
Christmas Eve also found him placing an ad in *Sounds*, looking for musicians to form a punk group. It seemed as if all his peers had by this stage formed bands.

His domestic life took a turn for the worse, as his parents' divorce was imminent and the tension between them would often rise to an alarming level.

Morrissey was rejected for the au pair boy position, but 12 years later was credited on the 'Interesting Drug' promo disc, cut especially for his 29th birthday, as 'Motorcycle Au Pair Boy'.

Details of Morrissey's activities during this period were exclusively revealed in Johnny Rogan's biography *Morrissey & Marr: The Severed Alliance* (1992).

Recommended reading:
The limited 12" etched promo disc of Morrissey's 'Interesting Drug',
cut as a gift for his 29th birthday, with the catalogue number SPM29 (1989)

THE BOY WITH THE
THORN IN HIS SIDE **PART THREE**

Christmas 1976. Manchester.
The divorce procedures for Peter Morrissey and
Elizabeth Dwyer's marriage are finally completed.
My parents got divorced when I was 17, though
they were working towards it for many years.

Realising that your parents aren't compatible, I think,
gives you a premature sense of wisdom that life isn't
easy and it isn't simple to be happy.

Happiness is something...

...you're very lucky to find.

Twenty years of my life...

...gone with the simple stroke of a pen.

Betty?

Need a lift, lass?

I'll... we'll be fine, Peter.

M-Merry Christmas, Betty.

The unhappy marriage of Morrissey's parents would
inspire a plethora of songs, especially immediately
after the breakup of his own 'marriage' with The Smiths;
songs like 'Break Up the Family', 'Will Never Marry'
and '(I'm) The End of The Family Line' were conceived
just as he was going through his own legal proceedings
with his former band, causing the memories of his
own deteriorating family life to come rushing back.

Quotes from a Morrissey interview with *The Face* (July 1984)

Recommended listening:
Morrissey's 'Break Up the Family' from his debut solo album *Viva Hate* (1988)
Morrissey's 'Will Never Marry' from his early singles compilation *Bona Drag* (1990)
Morrissey's '(I'm) The End of the Family Line' from the album *Kill Uncle* (1991)

December 31st, 1976. New Year's Eve. Manchester.
Facing a bleak future, Steven Morrissey found himself on a £5 a week allowance and with absolutely no prospects of finding a job.

Furthermore, during the past six months he had witnessed the creation of a series of punk bands which rose from obscurity. It seemed he was destined to be stranded for another year in the family life he longed to escape.

Recommended listening:
Morrissey's 'Such a Little Thing Makes Such a Big Difference'
from his from his early solo singles compilation *Bona Drag* (1990)

CEMETRY GATES
part one

January 1977.
Whalley Range, Manchester.

In 1977 Linder teamed up with journalist Jon Savage and published the art fanzine *The Secret Public*. It was the second New Hormones product after the Buzzcocks' already iconic *Spiral Scratch* EP and was distributed through Rough Trade and other independent outlets.

Recommended listening:
The Smiths' 'Cemetry Gates' from the album *The Queen is Dead* (1986)

January 1977.
Stretford, Manchester.

Whaah! The CJs from my St Mary's Secondary days are looking for a new bass player!

They actually weren't that bad... for a covers band! But they can probably use some original material i.e. my lyrics!

Bad thing is I can't play any instruments. Then again all the punk bands have been raving on and on about not needing to know how to actually play. It's all about the attitude!!!

I mean, how hard can it be? All I need is to strike an Arthur 'Killer' Kane pose and I've already landed the gig!

Melody Maker
SEX PISTOLS
Record Mirror
BUZZCOCKS
NME
BLANK GENERATION
1977

And on the bass guitar:

Steven 'Killer' Morrissey!

Recommended listening:
The New York Dolls' debut album *New York Dolls* (1973)

CEMETRY GATES
part three

January 1977.
Stretford, Manchester.
CJs bass player auditions.

According to his former schoolmates, Jim Verrechia and Chris Power, in Johnny Rogan's *Morrissey & Marr: The Severed Alliance* (1992), Morrissey failed to pass the bass player audition for their band, The CJs, who had began amassing a small audience playing the local pub and hotel circuit.

Recommended listening:
The Kingsmen's 'Louie Louie' (1963)

January 1977. Manchester.
I think our experience was of just absolutely no confidence in ourselves. Morrissey was totally unemployable.

And we'd look in through people's windows.

One of Morrissey's questions, more than mine, was:

And he'd say:

Quotes from a Linder Sterling interview for the Channel 4 documentary, *The Importance of Being Morrissey* (2003)

Recommended listening:
The Smiths' 'There Is a Light That Never Goes Out' from the album *The Queen is Dead* (1986)

CEMETRY GATES
part five

**Southern Cemetery,
Chorlton-cum-Hardy, Manchester.**

Quotes from a Linder Sterling interview on *The South Bank Show* (Oct 18, 1987) and from Tony Fletcher's *A Light That Never Goes Out* (2012)

Recommended listening:
The Smiths' 'Cemetry Gates' from the live album *Rank* (1988)

BORN TO LOSE
part one

In his *Autobiography*, Morrissey confessed that his love for the New York Dolls extended beyond his obsession with their primal sound.

Jerry Nolan on the front of the Dolls debut album is the first woman I ever fall in love with; the positioning of the legs is playmate call-girl.

From the moment he laid eyes on the cover of their debut album in 1973, the Dolls would become Steve Morrissey's major fixation. *I always liked the Dolls because they seemed like the kind of group the industry couldn't wait to get rid of. And that pleased me tremendously. I mean there wasn't anybody around then with any dangerous qualities so I welcomed them completely.*

Years later a bittersweet encounter with his idols, Jerry Nolan and Johnny Thunders, who toured as The Heartbreakers opening for the Sex Pistols, led him to a love/hate relationship with the former Dolls' solo output.

Sadly their solo permutations simply crushed whatever image I had of them as individuals.
Now I think they're absolute stenchers!

When The Smiths launched in the early '80s, Morrissey would denounce his love for the New York Dolls in the British press in an effort to distance his band from his teen obsession (quotes he would later regret making):

If any of it is really examined intellectually it was probably totally dim It was just a teenage fascination and I was laughably young at the time.

Quotes from a Morrissey interview with *Melody Maker* (Nov 3rd, 1984)

Recommended listening:
The Smiths' 'Sheila Take a Bow' from their latter compilation album, *Louder Than Bombs* (1987)
The Heartbreakers' 'Born to Lose' from their only studio album, *L.A.M.F.* (1977)

Recommended reading:
Morrissey's *Autobiography* (2013)

BORN TO LOSE
part two

January 1977.
New York-London flight.
Ladies restroom.

Having had sex with all members of the Ramones and the New York Dolls – except their drummer Jerry Nolan – notorious junkie groupie Nancy Spungen travelled from New York to London on a mission to add the last remaining Doll to her screw list.
Jerry Nolan was touring the UK, opening for the Sex Pistols with fellow ex-Doll Johnny Thunders in their post-Dolls proto-punk band, The Heartbreakers.

Recommended listening:
The Heartbreakers' 'Goin' Steady' from their only studio album, *L.A.M.F.* (1977)

BORN TO LOSE
part three

January 1977.
The Heartbreakers open for the Sex Pistols on
their Anarchy Tour.

Dissed by Jerry Nolan and unable to fulfill her mission of
getting into bed with all the New York Dolls, Nancy Spugen
settled for hardcore Heartbreakers fan, Sid Vicious.
From that day on they would be inseparable. *Till death
did them part.*

Recommended listening:
The Heartbreakers' 'Born to Lose' from their only studio album, *L.A.M.F.* (1977)

Recommended viewing:
Alex Cox's biopic *Sid and Nancy* (1986)

BORN TO LOSE
part four

When the New York Dolls performed their song 'Looking for a Kiss' on *The Old Grey Whistle Test*, instantly turning a young Steve Morrissey into a life-long fan, little did they know that the song would spark off one of the first diss track feuds in recording history.

Furious about Sid Vicious' addiction to heroin and blaming it on Johnny Thunders, who was touring with the Sex Pistols, Johnny Rotten penned 'New York', a homophobic rant that dissed the Dolls' legacy.

By the time Johnny Thunders made a comeback, penning the Pistols-thrashing 'London Boys', The Heartbreakers had quit the Anarchy in the UK tour and returned to New York.

Clearly siding with the ex-Doll, Morrissey wrote a barrage of letters to the musical press, slamming the Pistols and praising The Heartbreakers. Perhaps inspired by the recorded diss feud, he would use his lyrics in the future to settle scores with former friends or bandmates, most notably on 'Sorrow Will Come in the End' from his album *Maladjusted* (1997).

Recommended listening:
The Sex Pistols' 'New York' from the album, *Never Mind the Bollocks, Here's the Sex Pistols* (1977)
The Heartbreakers' 'London Boys' from the outtakes compilation, *L.A.M.F.: The Lost '77 Mixes* (1994)

Recommended viewing:
The New York Dolls performing 'Looking for a Kiss' live on *The Old Grey Whistle Test* (1973)

Manchester 1977.
Following the Sparks concert.

Morrissey was lurking around the breakfast rooms the morning after our shows.

Grabbing little bits of the bread rolls that we hadn't finished.

And he would take them home...

...and enshrine them in some sort of way.

Quotes from a Sparks interview for the Channel 4 documentary,
The Importance of Being Morrissey (2003)

Recommended viewing:
Sparks performing 'Lighten Up, Morrissey' on *The Culture Show* (2008)
Sparks performing 'This Town Ain't Big Enough for Both of Us' on *Top of the Pops* (1975)

sound and vision part one

1977 found David Bowie sharing an appartment with Iggy Pop in Berlin, writing new material shaping his own projects and for a new direction in Iggy's career, following his departure from The Stooges.

Bowie would focus on a minimalist, ambient sound, using lyrics sparingly and teaming up with ex Roxy Music synth genius Brian Eno, whilst also harnessing the skills of producer and former T Rex associate Tony Visconti.

The three albums that he recorded within this period would be later dubbed the Berlin Trilogy.

At a time when punk demanded new heroes, Bowie might have fallen out of favour with Morrissey.

Yet, many of Bowie's associates on the Berlin Trilogy were past favourites of Morrissey and so he followed this bold new direction.

Save for Eno, Morrissey has since collaborated or appeared on stage with several of Bowie's '70s associates, having had records produced both by Mick Ronson and Toni Visconti.

Recommended listening:
David Bowie's 'Sound and Vision' from his Tony Visconti-produced album, *Low* (1977)
Morrissey's 'You Have Killed Me' from his Tony Visconti-produced album, *Ringleader of the Tormentors* (2008)
The entirety of Morrissey's Mick Ronson-produced glam-fest album, *Your Arsenal* (1992)

sound and vision part two

Early 1977.
Stretford, Manchester.
Beset by financial problems, Steven Morrissey had to decide promptly whether to try passing O-levels again or help his family with the growing bills and expenses.

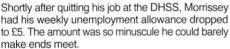

Shortly after quitting his job at the DHSS, Morrissey had his weekly unemployment allowance dropped to £5. The amount was so minuscule he could barely make ends meet.

He had no choice, but to join the endless queue at the Stretford Civic Centre in search of a permanent job.

Quotes from the Margaret Thatcher speech to the Zurich Economic Society (Mar 14th, 1977)

Recommended listening:
Morrissey's 'Margaret on the Guillotine' from his debut solo album, *Viva Hate* (1988)

sound and vision part three

By early 1977 the Sex Pistols were at the epicentre of punk and the focus of the UK tabloids, having sworn repeatedly on Bill Grundy's *Today* television show.

Soon after, the band began falling apart. Encouraged by Malcolm McLaren, the Pistols would make the ill-judged decision to kick out their bass player (and main songwriter) Glen Matlock.

The uproar caused by the Pistols' appearance on *Today* led to the band being dropped by their record company, EMI. Ever the agent provocateur, McLaren staged a freakshow for the press, having the band sign a contract with new label, A&M Records right in front of Buckingham Palace.

Matlock's replacement was Pistols fanatic Sid Vicious, who despite not knowing how to play a single note would one day be revered as one of the most famous bass players of all time. Egged on by his new girlfriend, Nancy Spungen, Sid's erratic behaviour and Punk Ken looks would become both a stereotype and the template for future generations of punk rockers.

Following their rejection from EMI, on March 16th, 1977 A&M Records also broke their contract with the Pistols. Twenty-five thousand copies of the planned 'God Save the Queen' single had already been pressed, yet all the copies were destroyed in order to avoid any controversy due to the Queen's upcoming Silver Jubilee.

Recommended listening:
Sex Pistols taking the piss out of EMI on their album
Never Mind the Bollocks, Here's the Sex Pistols (1977)

sound and vision part four

January 26th, 1977.
The Patti Smith Group's Radio Ethiopia tour.

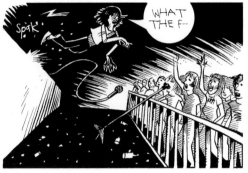

Whilst performing in front of a rabid crowd in Florida, Patti Smith tripped over her monitor and fell off the stage, crashing 15 feet below into the orchestra pit. Cracking two vertebrae in her neck as well as bones in her face, she would require 22 stitches to close the gashes on her head.

It would take months of painstaking physical therapy for her to regain the ability to walk, let alone sing.

Morrissey would not see her perform for at least another year. When she re-emerged, she had become a new person, a new performer.

Recommended listening:
The Patti Smith Group's 'Pissing in a River' from the album, *Radio Ethiopia* (1976)

sound and vision part five

1977.
Rob Allman's house, Wythenshawe.
So what's happening with Johnny in early '77?

18:32

23:19

In 1977 Johnny continued hanging out with his Wythenshawe Gang, getting tighter with the older Billy Duffy, who would share with him his guitar tips, punk wisdom and one day even his singer.
Billy would later find fame as the guitarist of The Cult.

Recommended listening:
The Cult's 'She Sells Sanctuary' from the album *Love* (1985)
Neil Young's 'Heart of Gold' from the album *Harvest* (1972)

the naked civil servant
part one

May 22nd, 1977.
384 Kings Road, Stretford, Manchester.

Recommended listening:
The Smiths' 'Still Ill' from their eponymous debut album *The Smiths* (1984)
The Smiths' 'Unhappy Birthday' from their final album *Strangeways, Here We Come* (1987)

the naked civil servant
part two

May 1977.
Inland Revenue, Manchester.

Having been appointed by the Stretford Civic Centre to a position in HM Inland Revenue for a wage of £22.50 per week, Steven Morrissey would spend the foreseeable future doing tedious office work for the British Government department responsible for the collection of direct taxation.

A far cry from the TV film *The Naked Civil Servant*, based on Quentin Crisp's life and which put a flamboyant twist on work as a civil employee.

Morrissey's weekly wage details from correspondence cited in Johnny Rogan's biography *Morrissey & Marr: The Severed Alliance* (1992).

Recommended viewing:
The ITV telemovie *The Naked Civil Servant* starring John Hurt as Quentin Crisp, in the role that turned both Hurt and Crisp into stars (1975)

the naked civil servant
part three

**17:09
Inland Revenue, Manchester.**

**21:53
35 Mayfield Road, Whalley Range.**
Linder and Morrissey would spend countless evenings at Linder's flat in Whalley Range reading and discussing feminist and men's liberation literature.

Years later, when asked if he liked strong women, Morrissey replied:

Yes, I do... Germaine Greer, for instance. I would like to eventually turn into Germaine Greer.

Quotes from a Morrissey interview with *Melody Maker* (Sep 27, 1986)

Recommended reading:
Germaine Greer's *The Female Eunuch* (1970)
Molly Haskell's *From Reverence to Rape: The Treatment of Women in the Movies* (1974)
Susan Brownmiller's *Against Our Will* (1975)
Nancy Friday's *My Mother, My Self* (1977)

the naked civil servant
part four

May 1977.
Following Glen Matlock's departure from the Sex Pistols, their manager, Malcolm McLaren, rechristened 'No Future', a Matlock written song. It was now called 'God Save the Queen' and released in order to provoke the middle class, who were about to celebrate her Silver Jubilee.

Punks, republicans and anti-monarchists from all over the country used this heightened tension as an opportunity to stage anti-Jubilee marches, aiming to question and protest against the classist, sexist and racist system that the medieval monarchy represented.

Meanwhile, the Teddy Boy and punk rivalry had begun in earnest, escalating into an urban youth war. Feeling disgruntled that Malcolm McLaren had misused and appropriated their style, Teds would randomly attack punks just for wearing brothel creepers or drainpipes.

Just after the release of 'God Save the Queen', Teddy Boys attacked most members of the Sex Pistols with an intent to kill. Johnny Rotten was cornered alone in an alley and severely attacked with a razor to the face, incapacitating him for months.

Recommended listening:
Sex Pistols' 'God Save the Queen' from their only studio album
Never Mind the Bollocks, Here's the Sex Pistols (1977)

Recommended viewing:
Julien Temple's documentary, *The Filth and The Fury* (2000)

Summer 1977.
Trapped in the daily routine of his job at the Inland Revenue, 1977 would prove to be the beginning of the truly miserable years in Steven Morrissey's life.

During this period, his hero David Bowie was experiencing one of his most prolific periods, releasing the acclaimed album *"Heroes"* and co-writing his Berlin flatmate Iggy Pop's greatest album, *Lust for Life*.

The previous year, Martins Scorsese's masterpiece, *Taxi Driver*, was released, expertly capturing the grime of '70s New York, the city Morrissey still dreamt of moving to.

According to biographer, Johnny Rogan, Morrissey considered changing his name to Byron De Niro, an amalgam of the name of political revolutionary and Romantic poet, Lord Byron, and *Taxi Driver*'s lead actor, Robert De Niro.

Recommended listening:
David Bowie's "Heroes" from the album *"Heroes"* (1977)
Iggy Pop's 'Lust for Life' (music written by Bowie) from the album *Lust for Life* (1977)

Recommended viewing:
Martin Scorsese's classic vigilante motion picture, *Taxi Driver* (1976)

Recommended reading:
Lord Byron's *Selected Prose*, published by Penguin (1972)
Johnny Rogan's *Morrissey & Marr: The Severed Alliance*, published by Omnibus Press (1992)

May 1977.
Andy Rourke's home.
Although Andy taught Johnny the basics on guitar, a couple of years later Johnny had not only surpassed his skills but could now give Andy tips.

Riding on the rush of punk, but still heavily influenced by the American rock scene, in 1977 they decided it was time to get a band together. Sensing Andy's natural groove, Johnny's only requirement was that Andy switch to the bass guitar.

Andy initially felt that he had been demoted to a lesser instrument. It was only when they got the rhythm section together that Andy realised his true calling.

Gathering the other band members from their expanding Wythernshawe clique, Johnny and Andy recruited their friend Bobby Durkin on drums and fellow Man City fan Kevin Kennedy on guitar. Kennedy would later find fame as 'Curly' Watts on Morrissey's TV obsession *Coronation Street*. Just another of the strange coincidences in Johnny and Moz's lives.

From that day forth Johnny and Andy's friendship manifested itself in their inseparable guitar-bass combo. They would perform together for the next 10 years.

Recommended listening:
Morrissey's 'I'm Throwing My Arms Around Paris' from the album, *Years of Refusal* (2009)
Tom Petty and The Heartbreakers' 'American Girl' from their self-titled debut album (1977)

June 1977.
Greenwood Road, Benchill.
Johnny and Andy's band, The Paris Valentinos, perform for the very first time in front of a live audience at a street party in Benchill, which was organised for the Queen's Silver Jubilee.

With an average age of 13, The Paris Valentinos were unaware of the anti-Jubilee marches which were spreading across the country; marches which the politically more aware Steven Morrissey would attend with friends from the Buzzcocks camp.

Johnny's ever-expanding Wythenshawe circle of friends, including Billy Duffy, Rob Allman, Steve Pomfret and Phil Fletcher, attended Johnny and Andy's first gig, which consisted mostly of Tom Petty, Thin Lizzy, Neil Young and Rory Gallagher covers.

They tried to get their friends to gather money to cover the cost of renting the equipment, but it all ended up being spent on cheap booze, helping to fuel the street party and an all-night free binge.

Source:
Johnny Rogan's biography *Morrissey & Marr: The Severed Alliance* (1992)

Recommended listening:
Thin Lizzy's 'The Boys Are Back in Town' from the album, *Jailbreak* (1976)

Exactly one month later, Marc Bolan died when the Mini Cooper in which he was a passenger ran into a tree close to his home in South West London. Nine days prior to the accident David Bowie had appeared on Marc's TV show, this first ever TV appearance together patching up some long-standing differences between them. Bolan was just 29.

The tabloids had stalked Elvis, following him every time he visited a hospital after a health scare. They had a field day when Presley and Bolan died, speculating on every aspect of their tragically short lives and deaths.

August 1977.

Within the span of a month the world mourned the loss of two pioneering musical spirits: the kings of rock 'n' roll and glam rock were dead.

Elvis Presley died on August 16th, 1977, at the age of 42, after a series of health issues following years of chronic barbiturate abuse and horrific dieting.

He was found kneeling in front of his toilet reading *The Scientific Search for the Face of Jesus*.

In Morrissey's *Autobiography*, he would show an unpublished photograph of his father during his youth in the mid-50s holding onto his prize collection of Elvis records and singles. Upon Elvis's death, the *NME* reminded their young punk readers of Presley's early rebellious years and Morrissey returned to his father's record collection to re-evaluate his fallen hero.

In 1987, going full circle on the tenth anniversary of his heroes' deaths, Morrissey donned heavy mascara and was photographed for 'Shoplifters of the World Unite' press shoot in a back-to-roots effort to recall Elvis Presley's early days (in combination with his love for the all things glam rock). He thus honoured them and also reminded his fans of his earlier idols' importance with one simple gesture.

Recommended listening:
The Smiths' cover of Elvis' 'His Latest Flame', in a medley with 'Rusholme Ruffians', from their only live album, *Rank* (1988)

Recommended viewing:
Ringo Starr's concert film of Marc Bolan and T. Rex in their prime, *Born to Boogie* (1972)

August 1977.
Virgin Records, Manchester.

Two days later.

A former actress at Andy Warhol's Factory, Wayne County was a transsexual rock'n'roll singer from Georgia, also known as Jayne County, who was part of the New York musical underground. Morrissey had arranged to meet friends at Wayne County's Manchester show but never showed up.

Autumn 1977.
Virgin Records.
Steven Morrissey discovers a fateful card on the record store's wall and decides that his destiny lies within the message it carries.

After calling Billy Duffy, who had written the card requesting a singer for his non-existent band, Morrissey journeyed from Stretford to Wythenshawe in order to meet the guitarist face to face. According to Morrissey, Billy at the time was living with his mother...

...and was dating an impressive, buxom girl called Karen Concannon!

Based on their mutual love for the Dolls, Billy and Steven hit it off right off the bat.

Recommended listening:
The Smiths' 'William, It Was Really Nothing'
from their early singles compilation album *Hatful of Hollow* (1984)

Summer 1977.
Manchester.
Not content with working a nine-to-five job at the Inland Revenue, Steven Morrissey's dream to either join a band or write about music is partially realised when he begins collaborating with the *Kid's Stuff* punk fanzine, covering his favourite groups and the new wave of Manchester bands.

In *Kids Stuff* #7 he would write an appraisal of Manchester darlings, and his personal friends, the Buzzcocks, as well as make one of the first press mentions of the pre-Joy Division band, Warsaw.

Originally called Stiff Kittens, Ian Curtis would rename the band Warsaw inspired by David Bowie's recent song, 'Warszawa'. In order to avoid confusion with the London punk band Warsaw Pakt, they renamed themselves Joy Division in early 1978. In keeping with the misguided Nazi chic of the time, they borrowed their new name from the prostitution wing of a Nazi concentration camp mentioned in the 1955 novel *House of Dolls*.

Recommended listening:
The Drones' 'Lookalikes' from the album, *Further Temptations* (1977)
Warsaw's 'The Kill' from their scrapped self-titled debut album recorded in 1977 (1994)
David Bowie and Brian Eno's 'Warzawa' from Bowie's album *Low* (1977)

No One Can Hold a Candle to You **part two**

Summer 1977.

In the summer of 1977 Morrissey placed an ad in *Sounds* asking for New York Dolls acetates in exchange for a substantial amount of 'concrete sacks'.
The ad was fatefully replied by James Maker, who would become his lifelong friend and confidant.

Recommended listening:
Raymonde's (James Maker's band) 'No One Can Hold a Candle to You'
from their album, *Babelogue* (1987)
Morrissey's cover of Raymonde's 'No One Can Hold a Candle to You'
offered as a b-side to his single 'I Have Forgiven Jesus' (2004)

Recommended reading:
Morrissey's account of the day from his *Autobiography* (2013)

No One Can Hold a Candle to You **part three**

The gay scene in Manchester was always atrocious. Do you remember Bernard's Bar, now Stuffed Olives? If one wanted peace and to sit without being called a parade of names then that was the only hope. Bernard's Bar was fine for a while but what I was really into was the music.

Once, in a night out in Manchester, Morrissey and his friend James Maker were heading to Devilles after drinking at the Thompson's Arms.

They were set upon by a gang of late twenty-something, drunken beer monsters.

So they ran.

Unfortunately, they caught James and began kicking him.

Quotes from a Morrissey interview with *Melody Maker* (Sep 27, 1986)

Recommended viewing:
Morrissey's cover of Raymonde's 'No One Can Hold a Candle to You'
from his live concert film, *Who Put the M in Manchester?* (2005)

No One Can Hold a Candle to You part four

James somehow made himself get up and they ran to find a bus to take them back to Stretford, the beer monsters chasing them.

Morrissey and James made the mistake of jumping on an empty bus, with no hope of escape from the louts outside.

We had all these coins and we just threw them in their faces and flew out of the bus.

We ran across the road to a bus going to God-knows-where.

Quotes from a Morrissey interview with *Melody Maker* (Sep 27, 1986)

Recommended listening:
Raymonde's 'Been Too Many Years' from their album, *Babelogue* (1987)

We slammed four fares down and ran to the back seat and the bus begins to move and we end up in Lower Broughton.

Suddenly the emergency doors swing open and these tattooed arms fly in — it was like Clockwork Orange. The bus is packed, nobody gives a damn.

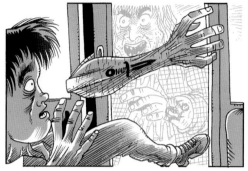

We get out and we're in the middle of nowhere — just hills. On top of this hill we could see a light from this manor house.
We went up these dark lanes to the manor house and knocked on the door.
It was opened by this old senile, decrepid Teddy Boy, no younger than 63, with blue suede shoes on.

We had to walk back to Manchester. It took us seven days. We came back home to my place, finally, at something like 5am and listened to 'Horses' by Patti Smith and wept on the bed.

That's my youth for you in a nutshell.

Quotes from a Morrissey interview with *Melody Maker* (Sep 27, 1986)

Recommended listening:
Patti Smith's 'Land Part I: Horses' from her debut album, *Horses* (1975)

Recommended viewing:
Stanley Kubrick's *A Clockwork Orange* (1971)

Inland Revenue.
Wythenshawe.

Meeting regularly at Steve Pomfret's home in Wythenshawe, Morrissey, Bill Duffy and Pomfret would begin rehearsing in an effort to form a new Manchester punk band. Unbeknownst to the rest of the group, it was the first time Morrissey had sung to a microphone with a band backing him up.

In his *Autobiography* he would describe that instant as an almost revelatory moment, when singing gave him voice and an identity bereft of others' expectations.

Singing about his own life was long overdue. Years later, Morrissey would relate the experience in his single 'Sing Your Life'.

Recommended listening:
Morrissey's 'Sing Your Life' from his second solo album, *Kill Uncle* (1991)
New York Dolls' 'Teenage News' from their live album, *Red Patent Leather*, recorded in 1975 (1984)

Steve Pomfret's house, Wythenshawe.

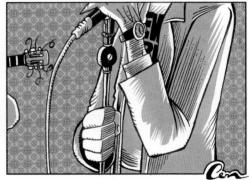

In Autumn 1977, Steven Morrissey, Billy Duffy and Steven Pomfret settled on the name T-Shirt for their new punk band.

Recommended listening:
Loudon Wainwright III's 'Reciprocity' from his album, *T Shirt* (1976)

sing your life part three

Steven Morrissey takes a break from his workload at the Inland Revenue and pens another epistle to the *NME* about Johnny Thunders' and Jerry Nolan's Heartbreakers and the disillusionment of punk.

Having experienced Johnny and his Heartbreakers live, Morrissey has cast aside albums by Carly Simon, Loudon Wainwright, Jefferson Airplane, Buffy Sainte-Marie, Phil Ochs and even Patti Smith and his beloved New York Dolls.

His newfound fondness for the Heartbreakers knows no limit and, what's more, he's doubly impressed that they can actually play their instruments.

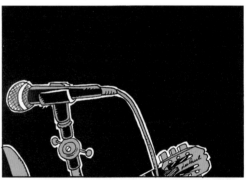

Recommended reading:
The letter written by Morrissey, published in the *NME* (Apr 2, 1977)

Recommended listening:
The Heartbreakers' only studio album *L.A.M.F.* (1977)

Steve Pomfret's house, Wythenshawe.
Morrissey, Billy Duffy and Pommy continue rehearsing after forming T-Shirt.

Pomfret would confess to biographer Johnny Rogan that he constantly felt intimidated by the peculiar questions quietly posed, solely to him, by Morrissey.

Later on, when Duffy and Pomfret decided that the band needed some money to upgrade their equipment, if they were to play a show in front of a crowd...

...Morrissey turned up with a cheap microphone.

Recommended listening:
Morrissey's 'Sing Your Life' from the album, *Kill Uncle* (1991)

Recommended reading:
Johnny Rogan's *Morrissey & Marr: The Severed Alliance*, published by Omnibus Press (1992)

Steve Morrissey writes a letter to the editor of the *NME* imploring them to focus on his favourite local band (and friends), the Buzzcocks.

In his unusual pompous fashion, Morrissey extols Buzzcocks for their originality...

...while reproaching Radio 1 for not playing Patti Smith, Loudon Wainright or the Dolls...

...and concluding that Buzzcocks are the 'best kick-ass rock band in the country'.

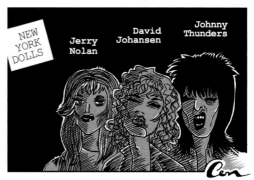

Recommended listening:
The letter written by Morrissey, published in the *NME* (Oct 4, 1977)

Recommended listening:
Buzzcocks' *Spiral Scratch* EP (1977)

**Autumn 1977.
Manchester's Inland Revenue.**

Demoted to the position of filing clerk in the damp, dark basement of the Inland Revenue, Morrissey spent his final tenure as a public servant contemplating what he considered a living death.

It would be the last time that he would work for the government.

Recommended listening:
The Smiths' 'You've Got Everything Now' from their debut album, *The Smiths* (1984)

Late 1977.
Feeling trapped within the punk rock limitations of the Buzzcocks, Howard Devoto leaves the band and forms Magazine. Parting company from his recent past meant he would also break up with Linder Sterling; Morrissey and Linder would comfort themselves by discovering the operatic melancholy of Klaus Nomi.

Morrissey considered Nomi's 'Death' to be his dying speech. It seemed prescient of Nomi's fate, when he died a victim of AIDS.

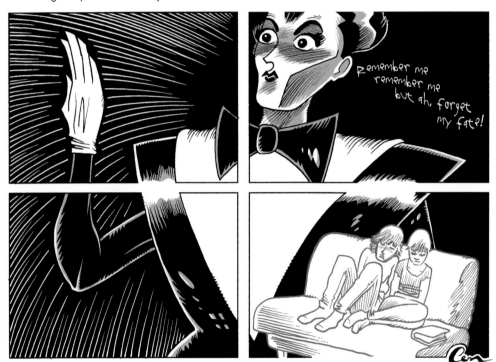

Recommended listening:
Klaus Nomi's 'Death' from Morrissey's favourite artists compilation album, *Under the Influence* (2003)

Late 1977. Manchester.

Trying to escape the threatening beer monsters, Morrissey, Linder and James Maker would hang out in the decadent gay scene clubs in order to blend in and to listen to anything but classic or prog rock.

Morrissey: The gay scene in Manchester was a little bit heavy for me. I was a delicate bloom Do you remember the Union? Too heavy for me, as was Dickens. The Rembrandt I could take. It was a bit kind of craggy. There was no place, at that time, in Manchester, in the very early stages, that one could be surrounded by fascinating, healthy people. Fascinating, healthy bikers for example.

James Maker: Sexually? I lived in the Kalahari. What consumed me was style, music, literature and being as adolescently self-absorbed as possible. Nothing of a sexual nature happened to me for years – which was astonishing since I had more than a passing resemblance to James Dean. I never went to gay clubs because I couldn't identify with the gay culture that prevailed at the time: disco-divas and clones. Frustration led me to throw myself into path of oncoming motorcyclists – which isn't really dating.

Quotes from a Morrissey interview with *Melody Maker* (Sep 27, 1986) and a James Maker interview from Pat Reid's *Morrissey* (2004)

Recommended listening:
David Bowie's 'Five Years' from his concept album
The Rise and Fall of Ziggy Stardust and the Spiders from Mars (1975)

Early 1978. Manchester.

Morrissey and Billy Duffy begin collaborating seriously for the first time, co-writing many original songs based on Morrissey's lyrics. Considering their mutual love for the New York Dolls, it's almost certain that their songs featured similar melodies and lyrical themes.

Some of the song titles that have survived are: 'I Get Nervous', 'The Living Jukebox', 'Peppermint Heaven' and '(I Think) I'm Ready for the Electric Chair'.

I first began to sing with a guitarist you may know of, called Billy Duffy (most prominently known as the guitarist for The Cult). I wrote songs with him and we tried these songs out with the rhythm section that had once belonged to the Nosebleeds

In 1978 Billy managed to gather a rhythm section for their band, T-Shirt, in the form of two fellow Wythenshawe musicians, namely bass player Peter Crookes and drummer Philip Tomanov. The musicians had previously tasted some small success as part of local punk band Ed Banger & The Nosebleeds, who had just disbanded.

I tried it with Billy, and I was just too shy. I was too closed up. I'm glad that I didn't record in those years because it would have been absolutely appalling.

Quotes from a Morrissey interview with the Japanese-based magazine, *Tokion* (March/April 2004)

Recommended listening:
The New York Dolls' 'Personality Crisis' from their self-titled debut album *New York Dolls* (1973)

Early 1978.
Between his job at the Inland Revenue and rehearsing with T-Shirt, Morrissey manages to pen a long article regarding Manchester's thriving punk scene for *Kid's Stuff* fanzine.

He railed against those who thought they were cool because they were on the dole or sported a swastika on a torn t-shirt.

Ever supportive of Manchester, he mocked mascara-wearing Londoners but did concede that since the Sex Pistols appeared in Manchester a slew of home grown bands were emerging.

...among them, his old band, the Nosebleeds...

...not to mention Buzzcocks.

Recommended reading:
The article written by Morrissey for *Kid's Stuff* fanzine (Jan 1978)

Recommended listening:
Buzzcocks' 'Breakdown' from their debut EP, *Spiral Scratch* (1977)

What do you owe the people who follow your music?

The communication or "the transaction", if you like, has taken place. I'm confused by people who want to meet me and find it rarely works when we do meet because people have such strong notions about me, and their view of me is invariably inaccurate. Nonetheless, I haven't forgotten that when I was growing up and I idolised Patti Smith. I certainly wanted to meet her. I did meet her too, and it was hugely disappointing.

Early 1978.
Patti Smith Fanzine Conference, London.

Morrissey travels to London with Phil Fletcher on behalf of *Kid's Stuff* fanzine to cover Patti Smith's press conference exclusively for British punk fanzine publications.

Following her freak accident exactly one year prior to the conference, Patti Smith spent the whole year in agonising physiotherapy, contemplating past mistakes and spiraling into a quasi-religious phase.

She farted four times. It was at a fanzine conference in London around the time of the release of Easter and the room was crowded with young, impressionable people. There was one boy at the front who was no more than 17 and she walked up to him in this crowded, quiet room and loudly asked him an extremely vulgar question about how sexually endowed he was.

I think she was completely mad at the time.

The lesson here is that sometimes it's better to cherish your illusions about people you admire than it is to meet them.

Quotes from a Morrissey interview with *LA Times* (June 16, 1991) and a Patti Smith interview with *Melody Maker* (Mar 18, 1978)

Recommended listening:
Morrissey's Pasolini reference in 'You Have Killed Me' from the album *Ringleader of the Tormentors* (2006)
Patti Smith's first mainstream hit single, 'Because the Night', which she co-wrote with Bruce Springsteen, from her album *Easter* (1978)

Years after the event that scarred him forever, Morrissey looked back at Patti Smith's defiant attitude with admiration, dismissing his initial public denunciation.

Yes, she did do that, and I was shocked. She was on the verge of 'Because the Night' and Arista had a gathering at Upper Brook Street in West London, where they were at the time, invited lots of people who ran fanzines etc, and she was brusque and she was rude, and it was horrific. But that's who she was. And later I was inclined to think, "Well, why should she be other than who she is? Why should I expect her to be anything else?" She didn't ever pretend to be a benevolent and gentle person. That's who she was.

March 1978.
The Inland Revenue's basement repository.

Quickly forgiving his idol, Steve Morrissey found himself fuming over his friend Phil Fletcher's letter in *Sounds* which lambasted Patti Smith's recent concerts as "a sad excuse for a gig".

Phil Fletcher's home, Wythenshawe.

Have you got to know her better since?

Yes, yes. As far as I can tell she's a very different person now. Much more approachable and gentle. But initially she was quite hostile, and that's how she was, and that's how her music was. She wasn't pretending to be anything otherwise. But now, to me, she's very gentle. And the age factor, passing time, the shock of having such a remarkable legacy and realising that for her, Patti, she has done and achieved what she wanted to do. Which is very gratifying for her.

Would you call yourselves friends?

As much as one can, yes. She is very friendly to me. And I to her. But we don't go playing snooker or anything.

Quotes from a Morrissey interview with *The Daily Telegraph* (Jun 17, 2011)

Recommended listening:
Patti Smith's 'Till Victory' from the album, *Easter* (1978)

March 1978.
The Inland Revenue's basement repository.
Exactly one year after Morrissey was hired by the
Inland Revenue as a filing clerk.

Recommended listening:
The Ramones' faultless '70s albums: *Ramones* (1976), *Leave Home* (1977), *Rocket to Russia*
(1977) and *Road to Ruin* (1978)

Rabid Records
FOR MOSS SIDE PEOPLE'S CENTRE

present

SLAUGHTER
& THE DOGS

GYRO | **JILTED JOHN**

ED BANGER

THE PRIME TIME SUCKERS

SPECIAL GUEST
JOHN COOPER CLARKE

Manchester Polytechnic Students Union
All Games
SATURDAY, 15th APRIL, 1978

April 15th, 1978.
Manchester Polytechnic.
T-Shirt play their first gig at Manchester University opening for Manchester punk darlings, Slaughter & The Dogs and the movement's official poet, John Cooper Clarke, on a bill hosted by Rabid Records.

Featuring the former rhythm section of Ed Banger & The Nosebleeds in their line-up, the band was advertised on the bill as ED BANGER. Morrissey has since had to constantly deny being part of any band called Ed Banger or The Nosebleeds.

In his *Autobiography* Morrissey mentioned wearing a dark green nylon shirt and feeling that he had just been fired from a cannon, which he equated with his own sexual release.

Even though Morrissey had praised Slaughter & The Dogs in articles for fanzines and letters to the British UK press, a series of misunderstandings led to a strain in their relationships and, years later, even public put downs when The Smiths hit the spotlight.

sing your life part fifteen

Harvey Goldsmith Entertainments
with the
New Manchester Review
present

MAGAZINE

PLUS SPECIAL GUEST
JOHN COOPER CLARKE
AND
THE NOSE BLEEDS

THE NEW RITZ
Whitworth Street, Manchester
Monday 8th May 1978

May 8th, 1978.
The New Ritz, Manchester.
Billed as The Nose Bleeds, Steve Morrissey, Billy Duffy, Steve Pomfret and the Nosebleeds' rhythm section perform together for the second (and final) time at The Ritz in Manchester, opening for Morrissey's good friend, and personal hero, Howard Devoto, who had just formed the post-punk outfit Magazine after leaving the Buzzcocks.

In his *Autobiography*, Morrissey would praise Duffy for motivating him to pursue his ultimate purpose in life.

Strangely enough, even though most of Billy and Pommy's Wythenshawe mates attended the gig, young Johnny Maher wasn't able to make it on the night; from Morrissey's side, Linder and his Buzzcocks camp of friends cheered him on.

The *NME* journalist Paul Morley would also fatefully attend the gig in order to review it for Morrissey's favourite music publication. He was instantly infatuated and later on would become one of The Smiths greatest advocates. Managing Manchester punk band, The Drones, Morley was in constant search for new talent; years later he would oversee Frankie Goes to Hollywood's rise to success.

Recommended listening:
Magazine's post-punk anthem, 'Shot by Both Sides', from their debut album, *Real Life* (1978)
New York Dolls' 'Teenage News' from their live album, *Red Patent Leather*, recorded in 1975 (1984)

The Nosebleeds have also noticeably metamorphosed, though probably due more to personnel changes than anything else.

Last year they were the entirely forgettable Ed Banger and the Nosebleeds (who 'created' the dirge-like single 'Ain't Bin to No Music School' for Rabid Records); now Banger has gone his own so-called eccentric way.

384 Kings Road,
Stretford, Manchester.

The Nosebleeds re-surface boasting A Front Man with Charisma, always an advantage. Lead singer is now minor local legend Steve Morrisson, who, in his own way, is at least aware that rock'n'roll is about magic, and inspiration.

Just when Paul Morley's rave review is published in the *NME*, Billy Duffy quits the band.

So The Nosebleeds are now a more obvious rock'n'roll group than they've ever been. Only their name can prevent them being this year's surprise.

Paul Morley

Following the band's breakup, Morrissey would focus his attention again on feminist and men's lib literature, sending Linder cryptic messages through the press (like the 'spare ribs' announcement, which referenced the British second-wave feminist magazine).

Quotes from a Paul Morley review, published in the *NME* (May 12, 1978)

Recommended viewing:
Morrissey performing 'Sing Your Life' live on *The Tonight Show* (1991)

NOW WE ARE
HEROES
part one

Autumn 1978.
Church of the Sacred Heart, Wythenshawe.
Johnny and Andy's first band, the Paris Valentinos break up almost at the same time that Morrissey and Billy Duffy's group disbanded.

Following Kevin Kennedy's departure from the Paris Valentinos Johnny decides to try his luck elsewhere. According to Andy Rourke, who was left without a band:
I think Johnny got itchy feet and he was like:

And where do we find young Mike Joyce in these pivotal band forming times?
First band I joined was a band called The Hoax and they were based in Manchester.

Once I started working with them, that was my first introduction, really, into being in a proper band.
The Hoax would prove to be the most consistent (and long-running) of all the pre-Smiths bands, releasing two singles in the late '70s.

Quotes from Andy Rourke and Mike Joyce interviews for the documentary *Inside The Smiths* (2007)

Recommended listening:
The Hoax's 'Now We Are Heroes' from the Manchester punk compilation *Ten from the Madhouse* (1981)

NOW WE ARE HEROES
part two

In an article for *Kid's Stuff* fanzine number 8 that was headlined "POOR LITTLE FAGGOT... SEALED WITH A KISS", Morrissey condemned the Dolls for their hedonism.

He suggested that David Johansen, the focal point of the group, was perhaps too intelligent for the others in the band, notably Jerry Nolan and Johnny Thunders. Johansen, he declared, was responsible for their best songs and the all the publicity, 'good and bad'.

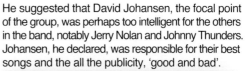

He rated 'Teenage News', Johansen's solo single and thought this captured the spirit of the Dolls, something Thunders and Nolan were unable to do in the Heartbreakers.

He predicted a new beginning for David Johansen. "I wouldn't dare get in his way – would you?' he concluded.

Cut it all off, hairdresser.

Just like that album cover I just gave you.

Shortly after the release of David Johansen's self-titled debut album, Steven Morrissey cut off his lengthy Dolls-styled mane, mimicking Johansen's own first steps towards a new mature lifestyle. He would never grow his hair long again.

Recommended reading:
The article written by Morrissey for *Kid's Stuff* fanzine #8 (Sep 1977)

Recommended listening:
David Johansen's 'She Knew She Was Falling in Love' from his second solo album *In Style* (1979)

NOW WE ARE HEROES
part three

1978. Punk Against Racism.

Following Eric Clapton's drunken declaration of support for former Conservative minister Enoch Powell in 1976 and his onstage racist remarks about British minorities, Rock Against Racism, an initiative bent on campaigning against racism in the UK, was formed. If celebrity endorsement of fascism wasn't enough, 1977 saw a widespread increase in racial conflict and the growth of white nationalist groups such as the National Front.

In spring 1978, 100,000 people marched six miles from Trafalgar Square to the East End of London, a National Front hotspot, for an open-air music festival at Victoria Park in Hackney organised by Rock Against Racism and the Anti-Nazi League, to counteract the growing wave of racist attacks in the UK. The concert featured The Clash, Steel Pulse, X-Ray Spex and the Tom Robinson Band.

A second march and concert at Brockwell Park in south London, featured Stiff Little Fingers, Aswad and Elvis Costello.

In autumn of the same year, an audience of 25,000 came to the Northern Carnival in Manchester for a concert featuring Buzzcocks, Graham Parker and the Rumour and Misty in Roots.

Meanwhile, whatever happened to the Sex Pistols?

In January 1978, the Sex Pistols embarked on a US tour, consisting mainly of dates in America's deep south. McLaren later admitted that he purposely booked redneck bars to provoke hostile situations.

Over the course of the two weeks, Sid Vicious, by now heavily addicted to heroin, began to live up to his stage name by constantly provoking the audience.

On January 14th, 1978, during the tour's final date at the Winterland Ballroom in San Francisco, a disillusioned Rotten introduced the band's encore saying:

You'll get one number and one number only 'cause I'm a lazy bastard.

That one number was a Stooges cover, 'No Fun'. At the end of the song, Rotten addressed the audience directly:

The band soon split up. It was the last time that Johnny, Steve, Paul and Sid would perform live together.

Recommended listening:
The Clash's 'White Riot' from their eponymous debut album *The Clash* (1977)
Sex Pistols' cover of The Stooges' 'No Fun', offered as a b-side to their single 'Pretty Vacant' (1977)

The Strange Case of Nancy Spungen's Death.
On the morning of October 12th, 1978, Sid Vicious claimed to have awoken from a drugged stupor to find Nancy Spungen dead on the bathroom floor of their room in the Hotel Chelsea in Manhattan, New York. She had suffered a single stab wound to her abdomen and bled to death. The knife used had been bought by Vicious after seeing Stiv of the Dead Boys brandishing a similar one.

Vicious was arrested and charged with her murder. He said they had fought that night but gave conflicting versions of what happened next, saying, I stabbed her, but I never meant to kill her and then changing his tale to Spungen accidentally falling onto the knife during their heated argument

Vicious was arrested on December 9th, 1978 and sent to Rikers Island jail. During his incarceration Sid was beaten and raped repeatedly. He had also gone through a cold-turkey withdrawal from heroin. He was released on bail two months later. Malcolm McLaren worked to raise money and the bond was eventually covered by Virgin Records. John Lydon has stated that Mick Jagger stepped in and paid for the lawyers for Vicious and has praised Jagger for never seeking any publicity for this.

On October 22nd, 10 days after Spungen's death, Vicious attempted suicide by slitting his wrist with a smashed light bulb and was subsequently hospitalised at Bellevue Hospital. He was charged with assault after breaking a bottle on Todd Smith's (Patti Smith's brother) face at a Skafish concert.

In celebration of Vicious's release from prison, his mother hosted a party at his new girlfriend's home in Greenwich Village. He died on the same night in his sleep, having overdosed on heroin his mother had obtained. Right before her death in 1996, she admitted that she gave a fatal heroin dose to her son in order to save him from going back to prison.
Vicious was not Jewish and could not be buried with Nancy, so his mother and Jerry Only of Misfits scattered his ashes over Spungen's grave.

Recommended viewing:
Sid Vicious covering Frank Sinatra's 'My Way'
from the Sex Pistols' mockumentary, *The Great Rock 'n' Roll Swindle* (1980)

I WON'T SHARE YOU

PART ONE

So when did you hear about this man Steven Morrissey?

Johnny: A couple of mates had bumped into him in Virgin Records on Market Street, which was the place to hang out. These friends of mine were keen readers of the music press, and Morrissey was getting a bit of a name for himself for writing pestering letters about the New York Dolls. This guy that we knew, Phil Fletcher, was kind of on the same trip, although he wasn't a musician so he approached Morrissey in the Virgin shop and hooked him up with our mates, one of which was Billy. I was hanging out with Billy and they were trying to get a band together. Billy would tell me how the rehearsals were going, so I got to understand that this was someone that was quite serious about singing and quite serious about writing words.

August 31st, 1978.
The foyer of the Ardwick Apollo.
Where the seldomly mentioned true first meeting of
Morrissey and Marr takes place.

Billy introduced me to Morrissey at the Patti Smith show in Manchester. I met up with him and Mick Rossi from Slaughter & The Dogs and Howard Bates, who played bass with Slaughter. It was a pretty brief hello.

I was only fourteen. There was utter non-interest, disinterest, on Morrissey's part, and a reserved curiosity on my part because he didn't look exactly as I'd pictured him. I knew he was the only guy around that really took himself seriously.

Quotes from Johnny Marr interviews from Billy Duffy.com's Stories (2013) and Q Classic's *Morrissey & The Story of Manchester* (2006)

Recommended listening:
The Smiths' 'I Won't Share You', the final track from their final album, *Strangeways, Here We Come* (1987)
Patti Smith's 'Land part I: Horses' from her debut album, *Horses* (1975)

I WON'T SHARE YOU   PART TWO

September 1978.
Wythenshawe, Manchester.
Following singer Wayne Barrett's departure from Manchester punk darlings Slaughter & The Dogs, their new guitarist Billy Duffy recommended his recent bandmate Steven Morrissey as a replacement.

Mick Rossi: I thought Morrissey was incredibly talented as a lyric writer, but then he was introvert, he was this shy man, who you know, you had to prise him out of his shell. He didn't have a lot to say. There was a lot going on upstairs, obviously. Being exposed to Morrissey at his early stage before he blossomed to what he is today was interesting too.

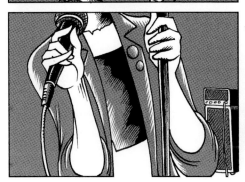

Quotes from a Mick Rossi interview for the Granada TV documentary *These Things Take Time: The Story of The Smiths* (2002)

Recommended listening:
Slaughter & The Dogs' 'Where Have All the Boot Boys Gone?' from their debut album, *Do It Dog Style* (1978)
Morrissey's 'Now My Heart Is Full' from the album *Vauxhall and I* (1994)

I WON'T SHARE YOU   PART THREE

Mick Rossi: By the time we did the second Pistols gig we already had a following. We were trying to be a street glam band. We get overlooked all the time when the history gets said, like in the movie 24 Hour Party People - we weren't mentioned in there. Tony Wilson turned up in clogs and with a handbag. When Slaughter & The Dogs did the album Do It Dog Style, we got Mick Ronson in to play on it.

Ronson was David Bowie's co-writer and lead guitarist in his glam heyday and his debut solo album, *Slaughter on Tenth Avenue*, along with Bowie's *Diamond Dogs*, went on to inspire Slaughter & The Dogs' bandname. He would later produce Morrissey's finest solo album, 1992's *Your Arsenal*.

October 1978.
Manchester-London M6 motorway.

Billy Duffy, Mick Rossi, Howard Bates and Steve Morrissey head for an audition with a renowned record company in hope of securing a recording deal for Slaughter & The Dogs.

Mick Rossi: The album came out and we toured Europe, and Wayne, (the singer) met this girl in France and moved there. Wayne left, so we were on the lookout for a new singer and Morrissey came down. This was a long time before he was famous. We got four demo tracks that I recorded with Morrissey on vocals round at my man's house, songs that have never come out.

He was very shy, very introverted, not like he is now. He was singing more conventionally than he would do later on in The Smiths, when he tended to sing and flow into the chorus. You could tell he was very talented.

It didn't really work out, although we were in the same sort of area musically. We got Eddie (the creator of) Ed Banger & The Nosebleeds in to do the vocals. He had roadied for us and was an old mate.

Quotes from a Mick Rossi interview for the essential resource on UK punk history, John Robb's *Punk Rock: An Oral History* (2006)

Recommended listening:
Slaughter & The Dogs' 'Victims of the Vampire' from their debut album, *Do It Dog Style* (1978)
Morrissey's 'Jack the Ripper' from his live album *Beethoven Was Deaf*, recorded during the *Your Arsenal* tour (1992)

I WON'T SHARE YOU   PART FOUR

October 1978.
384 Kings Rd, Stretford, Manchester.
Following Slaughter & The Dogs' unsuccesful audition with a new lineup, Morrissey is paid a final visit from his first writing partner, Billy Duffy.

I have no understanding why my name has has been linked with Slaughter & The Dogs, about whom I know absolutely nothing. But I've read several times that I was either in Slaughter & The Dogs or I auditioned for them and was rejected.

As far as The Nosebleeds are concerned, I wasn't in The Nosebleeds. Most people will say I was. But I first began to sing with a guitarist you many know of, called Billy Duffy.

I wrote songs with him and we tried these songs out with the rhythm section that had once belonged to the Nosebleeds. Because of that it seems that I was a member of The Nosebleeds and I was a member of Slaughter & The Dogs, which is news to me.

Disheartened by the politics involved in forming a band, Morrissey was not associated with another group until The Smiths. He would spend the rest of his life publicly denying any involvement with The Nosebleeds and Slaughter & The Dogs.

Quotes from a Morrissey interview with the Japanese-based magazine, *Tokion* (March/April 2004)

Recommended listening:
Morrissey's 'Speedway', his take on the rumours and lies surrounding him, from the album
Vauxhall and I (1994)

October 1978.
384 Kings Rd, Stretford, Manchester.
Following a quite harsh year, which saw constant cutbacks to the public sector and therefore Betty Dwyer's wage as a librarian, autumn finds the Morrisseys planning their permanent immigration to the US, where Betty's sister Mary and her family live.

Two weeks later.
Manchester airport.

Recommended listening:
The Smiths' 'Suffer Little Children' from their eponymous debut album (1984)

**November 1978.
Denver, Colorado.**

According to biographer Johnny Rogan, Steve Morrissey and his sister Jackie move to the US where their Aunt Mary resides in hope of securing jobs and permanently emigrating from the bleak times that Britain's been facing.

Although initially disappointed that his aunt had moved from New York to Colorado, Morrissey would find some small karmic comfort in the fact that his hero Oscar Wilde had once visited the state.

As I became a Smith, I used flowers because Oscar Wilde always used flowers. He once went to the Colorado salt mines and addressed a mass of miners there. He started the speech with: "Let me tell you why we worship the daffodil."

Meanwhile, Morrissey's best friend, James Maker, finds himself stranded in Dallas after losing a connecting flight from London. Similarly planning to move permanently to the States, the land of his ultimate hero, James Dean, it is unknown whether Maker and Morrissey ever met whilst there.

My first real sexual experience took place within hours of first touching-down at Dallas-Ft Worth airport. I was stranded there overnight en route to another city and a ranch-hand offered to rent an Eldorado and drive me downtown.

Quotes from a James Maker interview for Pat Reid's *Morrissey* (2004)

Recommended listening:
Raymonde's (James Maker's band) 'No One Can Hold a Candle to You'
from their album *Babelogue* (1987)
Morrissey's cover of Raymonde's 'No One Can Hold a Candle to You',
offered as a b-side to his single 'I Have Forgiven Jesus' (2004)

December 1978.
Arvada, Denver, Colorado.
Steve Morrissey passes on his CV to every local store hoping to secure a job and live permanently in the States. Still unconvinced that he doesn't have a future in music, he even places ads searching for musicians to form a band, but to no avail.
He applied for a job at Pathmark, but was turned down.

He met for a job interview at Target, but is again unsuccessful in this quest.

Recommended listening:
The Smiths' 'Heaven Knows I'm Miserable Now' from their first compilation album,
Hatful of Hollow (1984)

January 1979.
Denver, Colorado.

According to Morrissey's father in *The Severed Alliance*, Morrissey's mother gathers her last savings and pays for her homesick son's return flight to England. Having found a job in Denver, his sister opts to stay there and start a new life.

Needless to say, his first stop once back in Manchester would be Linder Sterling's pad in Whalley Range, which she shared with the Buzzcocks and various Mancunian artists.

Having progressed since Morrissey moved to the States, Linder was designing the covers for both Buzzcocks' and Magazine's albums, discovering her signature mass-media collage strategy which adorned and violated the classical nude female torso with household objects.

At this point, men's magazines were either DIY, cars or porn. Women's magazines were fashion or domestic stuff. So, guess the common denominator: the female body.

I took the female form from both sets of magazines and made these peculiar jigsaws highlighting these various cultural monstrosities that I felt there were at the time.
Well, the iron came from an Argos catalogue and the female torso came from a photographic magazine called Photo.
I never cleared the copyright but no one noticed, so it was alright It was made in a Salford bedroom I had a sheet of glass, a scalpel and piles of women's mags.

Originally created by Linder in colour, Buzzcocks' sleeve designer Malcolm Garrett changed the cover colour to its iconic blue monotone.

Quotes from a Linder Sterling interview with ShotByBothSides.com

Recommended viewing (and listening):
Linder Sterling's iconic artwork for the covers of:
Buzzcocks' album *Orgasm Addict* (1977)
Magazine's album *Real Life* (1978)

In 1978, Linder Sterling co-founded the post-punk group Ludus. Ludus produced material ranging from experimental avantgarde jazz to melodic pop and cocktail jazz, characterised by Linder's voice and unorthodox vocal techniques (which occasionally included screaming, crying, hysterical laughter and other unusual sounds), as well as her uncompromising lyrics, centred around themes of gender roles, love and sexuality, female desire and cultural alienation.

Linder designed many of the band's covers and posed for artistic photographs taken by Birrer thus becoming the focal point for the band's visual identity.
Although critically acclaimed, they never achieved any significant commercial success.
Morrissey proved their greatest fan, championing his friend's group at every opportunity, even many years after Ludus' untimely demise.

Simultaneously, Morrissey would begin a love-hate friendship with *Sounds* scribe Jon Savage, who collaborated with Linder on the punk fanzine, *Secret Public.*

Extracts from a letter Morrissey sent to *Sounds* entitled: "Ooo, Bitch!"

The age of romance is upon us again. Jon Savage tips Manchester as the place to be in '78.

You remember Manchester - the kids don't think you're tough if you pronounce your T's, and a gig at the Circus was always like guerrilla warfare. Too late, too late, Mr Savage.
Save your enthusiasm for the intense drama at the Vortex, but watch you don't smudge your lipstick.
Strangely, in his *Autobiography* Morrissey revealed a much warmer friendship, positioning Savage in his pre-fame inner sanctum (without neglecting any tongue-in-cheek references to Savage's middle class upbringing).

Quotes from a letter written by Morrissey, published by *Sounds* (Jan 21, 1978)

Recommended listening:
Ludus' 'My Cherry is in Sherry' from their first full length LP, *The Seduction* (1982)

Recommended reading:
Jon Savage's definitive history of punk music. *England's Dreaming: Sex Pistols and Punk Rock* (1991)

Early 1979.
As the Winter of Discontent hits Britain, massive union strikes bring the country to the brink of collapse. Having previously quit a job at the Inland Revenue, appointed to him by his local Job Centre, Steven Morrissey returns in hope of securing a new job, or at least some sort of unemployment benefit.

Yanks Records, 3 Chepstow St. Manchester.
He would soon reply to an ad placed by a local record store searching for employees. A seemingly ideal vocation.

Morrissey spent several months in the damp and chilly cellar, wrapped in a warm overcoat and ringing the till.

Recommended listening:
Ludus' 'Mouthpiece' from their cassette *Pickpocket* (1981)

Winter of Discontent, 1979.
Yanks Records, Manchester.
Morrissey had no idea what a credit card was, never having seen one before.

At the end of one of his shifts, Morrissey climbed out of the cellar to be beaten up by a gang of waiting youths.

He somehow made his was to Piccadilly Bus Station, blood streaming down his face, no one in the rush hour traffic coming to his aid.

Recommended listening:
The Smiths' 'Nowhere Fast' from the album *Meat is Murder* (1985)

PART ONE

After witnessing The Cramps perform live at the Free Trade Hall, Morrissey immediately wrote two separate letters, one to *Sounds* and the other one to the *NME*, championing the one single band that would dethrone the New York Dolls from his teenage shrine. Furthermore, he would give headliners, The Police, who had signed The Cramps to their own label, a hard time.

He described The Police as a 'farcical imitation of their "Rock Goes To College" thing' and a 'great big sloppy bowl of mush'. His disdain for The Police would continue onto the '80s when The Smiths would adamantly refuse to open for them.
But his admiration for the Cramps knew no bounds, especially for their drummer Nick Knox whom he felt was 'the most compelling in rock history'.

Recommended reading:
The letter written by Morrissey, published in *Sounds* (June 30, 1979)

Recommended listening:
The Cramps' 'Human Fly' from their debut EP, *Gravest Hits* (1979)

PART TWO

The Cramps gained a reputation as one of the most unpredictable acts to come out of New York's punk scene, practically creating psychobilly, a punk meets rockabilly genre which they performed in S&M attire utilising camp humour and retro horror/sci-fi b-movie iconography.

Their landmark free concert for patients at the California State Mental Hospital in Napa, in which they almost brought the hospital down through a full out rock 'n' roll insurrection, was almost the stuff of legend.

Soon after penning the letter, and feeling a great void left by the recent official disbandment of the New York Dolls, Morrissey went on to form another fan club, this time for The Cramps: the legendary Legion of The Cramped. It was co-run with Lindsay Hutton, his editor on the fanzine *Next Big Thing*. In 1980 they would co-release the first official Cramps fanzine, *Rockin' Bones*.

Recommended reading:
The letter written by Morrissey, published in *NME* (July 7, 1979)

Recommended viewing:
The Cramps' legendary live concert at the Napa State Mental Hospital (1978)

PART THREE

Just like New York Doll/Heartbreaker Jerry Nolan, Steve Morrissey fixated on the The Cramps' drummer Nick Knox and he appeared in at least three of his Cramps-related letters to the press.

As the former drummer of protopunk legends Electric Eels with an almost perfect quiff, his appeal to Morrissey was obvious.

Lux Interior's infamous stage antics as The Cramps' lead singer provided the band cult notoriety, while their b-movie aesthetics and outrageous demeanour became a template for all future psychobilly and shock rock acts. Lux sometimes entertained his audience by masturbating on stage, others by giving his microphone a blowjob, all whilst singing by vixen wife and guitar hero, Poison Ivy Rorschach.

In February 2009, Lux suddenly died of an aortic dissection, thus ending the 35-year husband-wife band. The next day, Morrissey would pay tribute to his hero by raising his left hand and shouting at the end of his *Jimmy Kimmel Live* TV appearance: "LUX INTERIOR!"

Recommended reading:
The letter written by Morrissey, published in *Sounds* (June 30, 1979) and a Cramps gig review written by Morrissey, published in *Record Mirror* (Apr 4, 1980)

Recommended viewing:
Lux Interior's outrageous stage performances after The Cramps' cover of The Trashmen's 'Surfin Bird'
The finalé of Morrissey's performance of 'Something is Squeezing My Skull' live at the *Jimmy Kimmel Live* TV show (2009)

SUN AND MOON PART ONE

Meeting Angie was without doubt the best luck I've ever had. How we met was that there was a bus strike in Manchester in 1979, and it also happened to be snowing, and on a Friday night.

I had to walk miles to go to a part-time job that I hated stacking shelves in the Co-op, in order to get enough money to buy records every week, and when I'd walked all that way to this job, this witch of a boss fired me.

FIRED?! What for?

For being lazy and cocky and distracted.

Part of the tradition of being fired was that you had to go out the back to the loading bay, where the entire staff of this supermarket were waiting for you with an endless arsenal, palettes and palettes of eggs. And you're stuck like a trapped animal in the loading bay...

...and you get completely pelted, and you're supposed to enjoy the jollity of this.
Now I did mention that it was snowing, and freezing, and there was a bus strike. So I had to walk back seven or eight miles, as a human omelette, to my house.

It's tradition, lad.

Now just stay still.

This lad's had it coming!

What the?!

What the FUCK!?

Quotes from a Johnny Marr interview with *The Arts Desk* (Aug 17, 2013)

Recommended listening:
Johnny Marr's 'Sun and Moon' from his debut solo album, *The Messenger* (2013)

SUN AND MOON PART TWO

Amazingly, a friend of mine who came from a really cool family lived en route, and I was in so much discomfort, I nipped into his house, to have a shower and get changed, and he went to Angie's school, and told me about this party that was going on.
And not wanting to lose face, I pretended that I knew all about this party, so we just piled down there.

From the first minute I saw her I wanted to be with her all my life.

And she was like, "Hey, I like Johnny Thunders and Iggy Pop and the good bits of the Rolling Stones a lot." Of course we're still together! I'm not an idiot.

Quotes from Johnny Marr interviews with *The Arts Desk* (Aug 17, 2013) and for Tony Fletcher's biography *A Light That Never Goes Out* (2012)

Recommended listening:
Johnny Marr's 'Upstarts' from his debut solo album, *The Messenger* (2013)

SUN AND MOON PART THREE

Angie was vegetarian when we met. I was 15 and she was 14. She was clued up.
I probably would have become vegetarian even without the song (Meat Is Murder) I suppose. The vibe was, I am a guitar player and that is what I am going to do for the rest of my life, and she was like:

Those noises I was making on a guitar, it wasn't some lonely kid sat in a bedroom on his own. I was sat there with a very beautiful 14-year-old girl, keeping quiet, flicking through magazines and looking at New York Dolls covers, sitting there two feet away listening to me doing it, her in her own world and me in mine.

Hawthorn Lane, Ashton-upon-Mersey, Manchester.
Where Andy Rourke is alone again, as his father is away for work.
Johnny: It was the three of us. All the time. We were all into the same clothes. The same music.

Andy: We were all just really good friends. Every waking hour we'd spend together. The three of us.

Quotes from Johnny Marr interviews with *The Arts Desk* (Aug 17, 2013), *Vegan* magazine (Winter 2011) and for Tony Fletcher's biography *A Light That Never Goes Out* (2012)

Recommended listening:
The Smiths' instrumental tracks:
'Oscillate Wildly' from their later singles and b-sides compilation, *The World Won't Listen* (1987)
'The Draize Train' from their only live album, *Rank* (1988)

SUN AND MOON PART FOUR

Johnny and Andy were about to sit their O-levels when they discovered that Andy was barred, having skipped too many classes during the previous year.

Our principal was such a drunk. He used to wander around the corridors, banging off the walls.

Johnny decided to press ahead with his music O-level, but the maths element proved beyond his capabilities. In the end, he took English and art, but his passion for his guitar meant he ultimately failed his exams, leaving him in the same position as Andy.

Still seeking a lucky break whilst disenchanted with both his exam results and the failure of his band the Paris Valentinos, Johnny went for the guitarist slot with local Wythanshawe band (and biker gang) Sister Ray.

Quotes from Johnny Marr interviews with *Vive Le Rock!* #6 (2012)
and for Tony Fletcher's biography *A Light That Never Goes Out* (2012)

Recommended listening:
Sister Ray's 'Suicide' from TJM Records' compilation *Identity Parade* (1980)

SUN AND MOON PART FIVE

They were a bunch of vagrant biker nasties. The guys were a lot older than me and had a bit of a history. They'd had a couple of records out and a few gigs that had got them a bit of notoriety because the singer was crazy.

Playing his first gig with biker gang/band, Sister Ray, Johnny Maher found himself performing alongside an unpredictable vocalist who suddenly donned a pig's head on stage.

After I left school at 14 I started experimenting with drugs and fell in with an older crowd. Looking back now I can't actually believe that I was enlisted into a situation with such reprobates. These fellas were nasty men and I was just 15.

Thus, the following day...

Quotes from Johnny Marr interviews with *The Daily Mail* (Aug 31, 2009), *Vive Le Rock!* #6 (2012) and for Johnny Rogan's biography *Morrissey & Marr: The Severed Alliance* (Omnibus Press, 1992)

Recommended listening:
The Velvet Underground's 'Sister Ray' from their second album *White Light/White Heat* (1968)

SUN AND MOON PART SIX

Were you ever arrested?

Yes. A couple of times.

Did that scare you?

It did the last time because it looked like it was really serious. The big trouble I got into was not because I stole something; it was because one of my friends stole some art. I had introduced him to this dodgy guy and I got caught in the middle of it...

But that was just me being a nice guy. This guy was just bothering me so much. His friend had acquired some stolen art. He thought I would have some contacts in the underworld... which I kind of didn't (smiles).

But I'm quite resourceful, so I found out who the local contact was in the underworld who specialised in these kinds of matters and put Mr. X with Mr. Y and all shit broke loose.

At 14 I started coming out of myself, pushing things to the limit. I was an idiot to get involved with stolen goods, but I suppose I liked the idea of being a bit of a Jack the Lad.

Years later I can say that I do have the honour of having been busted with my guitar plugged into my amp, so several million rock 'n' roll points to me (Johnny smiles).

Quotes from from Johnny Marr interviews with *The Daily Mail* (Aug 31, 2009) and AskMeAskMeAsk.me (May/July 2012)

Recommended listening:
Johnny Marr + the Healers' 'The Last Ride' from their album, *Boomslang* (2003)
The Smiths' 'Shoplifters of the World Unite' from their second b-sides and singles compilation album, *The World Won't Listen* (1987)

SUN AND MOON PART SEVEN

Locked up for three days in HM Prison Manchester, also known to the locals as Strangeways, Johnny contemplates his brief career as an art thief.

I was once arrested for possession of stolen LS Lowry prints. If there's one thing I'm certain about, it's that I'd have made a terrible criminal.

When I was younger I was always around people who were much crazier, but I was able to draw a line and not go too far with things... whether it was drugs or any kind of recklessness. I always wanted to experience a lot of things.

I was never a bad person. I was never not a nice person, I don't think I would never do stuff like stealing from a person or anything like that I liked a bit of devilment and a little bit of being dangerous and pushing the limits, but I have a good survival instinct as well. I was just a little wild and very daring. I wasn't scared of anything. But I always liked people and I was never violent.

Johnny is finally released from jail after getting busted for stealing art prints. As always, Angie is there to console him.

It was really quite serious. It was kind of a learning curve. It sort of toughened me up.

Hell-bent on changing his lifestyle, Johnny returns to school.

He enrolled at the West Wythenshawe College of Further Education and attended drama and music courses, freely expressing himself for the first time within an educational institution. He would also soon become president of the student union. Intending to get away from the Wythenshawe crowd that had got him into so much trouble, Johnny made plans to relocate with Angie to central Manchester and begin his life anew.

Quotes from Johnny Marr interviews with *The Daily Mail* (Aug 31, 2009), AskMeAskMeAsk.me (May/July 2012) and for Tony Fletcher's biography *A Light That Never Goes Out* (2012)

Recommended listening:
The Rolling Stones' 'Angie' from the album *Goats Head Soup* (1973)

YOU'VE GOT EVERYTHING NOW///PART ONE

Bupa Hospital, Whalley Range.
Morrissey's father manages to get his son hired in the hospital where he has been working as a porter for many years.

Morrissey sincerely hopes he will be in the sluice room for only a few weeks, ashamed to find himself brought to this pass: shaking bits of human guts from the uniforms of post-op doctors, prior to their going to the laundry.

With the small wage that he earns from the hospital, Morrissey rents a room in the nearby Whalley Range flats where the New Hormones camp have set up their headquarters. He leaves his home for the first time and follows in the artistic footsteps of his best friend, Linder.

A lyric from one of the first Smiths songs, 'Miserable Lie', seems to be inspired by this period, as it references Whalley Range.

35 Mayfield Road, Whalley Range.
Morrissey realises that Nico, the singer whose music he's been obsessing about for years, is living with Manc punk poet John Cooper Clarke in the apartment complex he is sharing with the New Hormones crowd.

Morrissey met Nico twice, in the night clubs of Manchester, her youthful beauty having been scourged by a lifelong heroin addiction.

One night, at Rafters, Nico sat centre-stage in front of her harmonium.

Her voice was frozen cold, message indecipherable, all hope lost. Morrissey treasured her four studio albums.

Nico died at the age of 49.

Recommended listening:
Nico's cover of Gordon Lightfoot's single 'I'm Not Saying' (1965)

YOU'VE GOT EVERYTHING **NOW**///PART THREE

January 1980.
Bupa Hospital, Whalley Range.
Morrissey gets a job cleaning the innards-covered surgeon's uniforms at the hospital where his father works. It's pointless to say that his life does not improve...

In fact, it only gets worse.

'You've Got Everything Now' is a throwback to when I was at school. I was quite advanced at school and when I left it seemed that all these really oafish clods were making tremendous progress and had wonderfully large cars and lots of money.

I seemed to be constantly waiting for a bus that never came.
It seemed as though although I had the brains, I didn't really have anything else.

Quotes from a Morrissey interview with BBC2's *Oxford Road Show* (1985)

Recommended listening:
The Smiths' 'You've Got Everything Now' from their self-titled debut album, *The Smiths* (1983)

JEANE /// part one

The currency of ideas in the houses I shared — as you well know, given you were there — was, in retrospect, the most memorable education in intellectual imagination. Not that anyone would use those terms, but you and Howard Devoto and Pete Shelley and others were so very, very smart.
Linder Sterling

Having just quit his gruesome job at the hospital, Steven Morrissey finds himself in an even worse financial situation, as he has just rented a room in the New Hormones flat complex in Whalley Range.

Quotes from a Linder Sterling interview conducted by Morrissey for *Interview* (March 15, 2010)

Recommended listening:
The Smiths' 'Jeane', offered as a b-side to their single 'This Charming Man' (1983)

JEANE /// part two

You and Howard Devoto and Pete Shelley and others were so very, very smart. All finding different ways of saying, "Yes, but..." It had less to do with talent than with genius — musicians and singers, but with the minds and eyes of novelists.
Linder Sterling

Amidst the huge financial issues he is facing, Steven Morrissey finds that he has to share Linder's attention with the growing crowd of artists and intellectuals in the New Hormones communal complex that he has just moved into.

Quotes from a Linder Sterling interview conducted by Morrissey for *Interview* (March 15, 2010)

Recommended listening:
The Smiths' 'Jeane', offered as a b-side to their single 'This Charming Man' (1983)

JEANE /// part three

Nowadays, boys with enormous ...record collections describe me as the "muse" to this circle in Manchester. Perhaps, perhaps, perhaps... But you were my muses, too.
Linder Sterling

He hung around a lot and eavesdropped on conversations with people and picked stuff up. He had talent but hadn't found an outlet. Morrissey was somebody who had this crush on Linder. He was a smart guy but he was... kind of one of the crowd in Manchester. Didn't seem like anything was going to happen.
Richard Boon and Peter Wright of the New Hormones label

 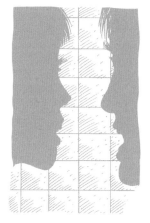 

  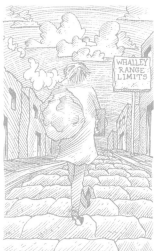

Quotes from a Linder Sterling interview conducted by Morrissey for *Interview* (March 15, 2010) and Richard Boon and Peter Wright interviews by Tony Fletcher for his book *A Light That Never Goes Out* (2012)

Recommended listening:
The Smiths' 'Jeane', offered as a b-side to their single 'This Charming Man' (1983)

MOTORCYCLE AU PAIR BOY PART ONE

Donning a "Dana Andrews smile", local lad Simon Topping befriends Steven Morrissey and they soon start hanging out, regularly.

Although his motorbike rolls up at Kings Road frequently, Simon becomes distant due to his mother's concerns about the nature of their friendship.

The pair become inseparable, quarrelling routinely on petty matters like Bette Davis' acting skills as Simon puts up with Steven's sarcastic remarks.

Years later, in 1989, on the occasion of his 29th birthday, a promo disc of his single 'Interesting Drug' credited Morrissey as Motorcycle Au Pair Boy, perhaps alluding to his fleeting friendship with Simon Topping, whilst the catalogue number was SPM29, the initials of the full name he once used.

Recommended listening:
Nico's debut solo album, *Chelsea Girl* (1967)
The limited edition 12" etched promo disc of Morrissey's 'Interesting Drug', cut to commemorate his 29th birthday with the catalogue number SPM29, crediting Morrissey as Motorcycle Au Pair Boy (1989)

MOTORCYCLE AU PAIR BOY PART TWO

Soon after bumping into Simon Topping, and disappointed that his own music career wasn't going anywhere, Steven Morrissey found himself somehow managing his friend's new band, A Certain Ratio, who were opening for Manchester's post-punk icons, Joy Division.

As with most rumours surrounding his pre-Smiths life, Morrissey would vehemently deny ever taking up such a role.

In his *Autobiography* Morrissey confessed to associating with the band, but only in an informal capacity.

Recommended listening:
A Certain Ratio's single 'All Night Party' (one of the earliest Factory Records releases, with the code FAC 5) (1979)

MOTORCYCLE AU PAIR BOY PART THREE

Morrissey travels with A Certain Ratio to Liverpool, for their debut at Eric's…

…but he can't quite love anything not of his own making – whatever their style.

Soon after their initial success, A Certain Ratio changed their management to Factory Records' Tony Wilson and immediately gained a loyal following in and out of Manchester.

In the Manchester-based film *24 Hour Party People*, which had music supervision by ACR's Martin Moscrop, Tony Wilson describes them as having all the energy of Joy Division, but better clothes.

Quote from Michael Winterbottom's *24 Hour Party People* (2002)

Recommended listening:
Brian Eno's 'The True Wheel', the lyrics of which inspired the name A Certain Ratio, from his album *Taking Tiger Mountain (By Strategy)* (1974)

MOTORCYCLE AU PAIR BOY PART FOUR

When Simon Topping appears on the cover of the NME…

…Morrissey dies inside at the thought of his old friend's success, and the lack of his own.

With the backing and contacts of Factory Records' Tony Wilson, A Certain Ratio managed to appear on the Sept 6, 1980 cover of the *NME*. Having seen success slip through his fingers once more, Morrissey buried himself in his bedroom prison.

Morrissey would focus anew on his writing, submitting articles to fanzines and getting band reviews published regularly in the *Record Mirror*. Having also renewed his interest in his movie icon, James Dean, he began writing a book on his life and times.

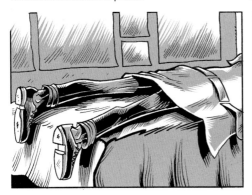

Recommended listening:
Morrissey's 'We Hate It When Our Friends Become Successful' from the album *Your Arsenal* (1992)
A Certain Ratio's debut cassette *The Graveyard and the Ballroom* (1980)

MOTORCYCLE AU PAIR BOY PART FIVE

1979.
John Muir's office, Babylon Books, Manchester.

1980.
384 Kings Road, Stretford, Manchester.

Morrissey's book, driven entirely by his enthusiasm for the New York Dolls, was taken on by a small press in Manchester.

In 1981, when his book was finally published, Morrissey had outgrown the Dolls. He dedicated it to his best friend, James Maker, with whom he had shared an obsession with both the band and James Dean.

Recommended listening:
The New York Dolls' 'Frankenstein' from their self-titled debut album, *New York Dolls* (1973)

Recommended reading:
New York Dolls by Steven Morrissey, published by Babylon Books (1981)

BABYLON///PART ONE

Comprised mostly of ultra-rare news clippings that Steven Morrissey had amassed through the '70s, when his passion for all things New York Dolls reached its peak, his book *New York Dolls*, published by Manchester's Babylon Books, was a small achievement amidst his unending series of failed ventures.

Quotes from detractors of the band, especially from other groups who had hit the big time by aping the Dolls' schtick, were spread throughout Morrissey's book.

"The Dolls failed because they lived their rock & roll fantasy. They were *supposed* to be drunk, and they were."

Gene Simmons (KISS)

Furthermore, Morrissey's ambiguous stance on his own sexual preferences was made public for the time through the titillating chapter titles ('How to Tear Pantyhose on One Easy Lesson', 'How to Get to the Sex of Your Choice', 'Would You Let YOUR Son Room with a Doll?') peppered throughout the book. By the time he formed The Smiths, this practice, combined with his intense study of the men's lib movement, would make his sexuality one of music's great mysteries.

Babylon Books' publisher John Muir informed Johnny Rogan that the book sold more than 3,000 copies, partly because it was the only book devoted to the band and partly because it was sold in record stores on the same shelves as the growing fanzine movement.

The publisher's preface noted: "Many thanks to Steven Morrissey – watch out for his James Dean book." They would not publish the Dean book until after The Smiths' success.

Recommended reading:
New York Dolls by Steven Morrissey, published by Babylon Books (1981)

Recommended listening:
The New York Dolls' 'Babylon' from their second album, *Too Much Too Soon* (1974)

BABYLON///PART TWO

Unemployed and with nothing to lose, Morrissey submitted numerous letters and reviews to the press, in hope of securing a job as a music journalist.

Unaware of Jobriath's fall from grace, he – anonymously – requested that *Sounds* run a feature on him.

He also issued a plea to Elektra Records to rerelease Jobriath's two albums *Jobriath* and *Creatures Of The Street*, pointing out that he was better looking than Sonja Kristina of Curved Air.

1980 proved a fruitful year because, even though the *NME* and *Sounds* turned down his reviews and articles, *Record Mirror* hired him to professionally review local gigs. In their March 29th, 1980 issue, he reviewed The Photos' and their support band Mark Andrews & The Gents' gig at the Manchester Polytechnic. He praised The Photos for their smoothness – 'so smooth they almost slip off stage' – and drew a comparison between their singer Wendy Woo and Debbie Harry of Blondie.

Taking a small break from co-organising The Legion of The Cramped fan club, Morrissey writes a passionate article on the return of Sparks, who had just employed the services of electrogenius producer Giorgio Moroder, to revamp their sound.

His fondness for the Mael Brothers hadn't waned during the two year hiatus between the albums *Introducing Sparks* and *Number 1 In Heaven*. 'God bless Sparks', he concluded.

Talking of The Cramps, his review of their Manchester Polytechnic gig for the Apr 4th, 1980 issue of *Record Mirror* reconfirmed that they had replaced the Dolls as his favourite band.

What he admired the most was their commitment beyond a motive for financial gain, not to mention their 'deathly white' faces. 'God forbid they don't suffer the Doll's fate,' he implored.

Recommended reading:
The reviews written by Morrissey, published in *Record Mirror* (Mar 29 and Apr 4, 1980)

Recommended listening:
Jobriath's 'Inside' from his Eddie Kramer-produced self-titled debut album (1973)
The Photos' 'Do You Wanna Dance?' from their self titled debut album (1980)
Sparks' Giorgio Moroder-produced album *No. 1 in Heaven* (1979)
The Cramps' 'I Was a Teenage Werewolf' from their debut album, *Songs the Lord Taught Us* (1980)

BABYLON///PART THREE

Despite the untimely demise of their band, Paris Valentinos, Johnny and Andy continued rehearsing at Andy's home, as his father was constantly away on business trips.

Joined by Rob Allman, a legendary guitar player from their Wythenshawe clique who used to play in Billy Duffy's early bands, the trio soon decided to form a new group.

Recruiting Wythenshawe mate Bobby Durkin on the drums, who they performed with in their Paris Valentinos days, and classically trained pianist Paul Whittall on keyboards, the newly christened White Dice were a soft rock unit leaning heavily on their American influences namely Tom Petty, Bruce Springsteen and Neil Young.

As Billy Duffy had by now moved to London to pursue his career as a guitarist with Studio Sweethearts and with Lonesome No More, Rob Allman would replace him as Johnny's father figure. A photo exclusively published in *The Severed Alliance* from this era depicts them trying to replicate the cover of Springsteen's *Born to Run*, on which he is leaning on his saxophonist and friend, Clarence Clemons.

Recommended listening:
Bruce Springsteen and the E Street Band's 'Thunder Road' from the album, *Born to Run* (1975)

BABYLON///PART FOUR

Morrissey reviewed Lonesome No More for *Record Mirror* (May 31, 1980), complementing them on their professionalism and Koulla Kakoulli's strong vocals. He mentioned three songs, 'Turn Insane', 'Forget My Past' and 'Lonesome No More' and though their set 'oozed with great possibilities'.

Even though Morrissey reviewed Billy Duffy's band, Lonesome No More, favourably and crashed at his flat whenever he visited London, he strangely enough never bumped into young Johnny Maher, who would also occasionally visit Billy. Coincidentally Johnny's band, White Dice, which he formed with Andy Rourke and Rob Allman, had just won a competition to record a demo via Elvis Costello's F-Beat Records and possibly sign a contract with the company.

Crashing at Billy Duffy's flat whilst recording the White Dice demo, Johnny and his girlfriend Angie, would listen for hours to tales of Billy's new adventures as a professional musician in the capital city.

Billy's advice, as well as his persistent praise of his ex-band mate Morrissey's skills, would prove influential in the near future.

Recommended reading:
The Morrissey review of Lonesome No More, published in *Record Mirror* (May 31, 1980)

Recommended listening:
Lonesome No More's single 'Turned Insane' (1981)
Tom Petty and the Heartbreakers' 'American Girl' from their eponymous debut album (1976)

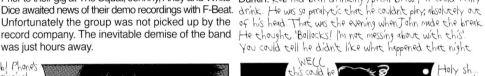

Johnny: The band I was in now was White Dice and we rehearsed underneath Joy Division in TJ Davidson's. That's where the scene was I had to sleep in the rehearsal room a couple of times because the landlord was going to nick our stuff, because we couldn't pay the rent. Luckily for me that's how devoted I was!

Andy: We were a great band, we had like harmonies and keyboards. We only ever did, again, one gig, at this place called The Squat on Offs Road, slightly partly university. Yeah, good times, exciting times.

Prior to their gig at The Squat, Johnny, Andy and White Dice awaited news of their demo recordings with F-Beat. Unfortunately the group was not picked up by the record company. The inevitable demise of the band was just hours away.

Durkin: Rob had been drinking Special Brew. He could really drink. He was so paralytic that he couldn't play; absolutely out of his head. That was the evening when John made the break. He thought, 'Bollocks! I'm not messing about with this.' You could tell he didn't like what happened that night.

Following the breakup of White Dice, Johnny's hero, Rob Allman, fell into a downward spiral of alcohol and substance abuse, whilst he witnessed his former bandmates, Billy Duffy and Johnny Marr, become global stars with The Cult and The Smiths respectively. Throughout the '80s he would continue performing with former White Dice keyboardist, Paul Whittall.

Rob Allman died suddenly in 1993 of a brain hemorrhage. Johnny, Billy, Paul Whittall, Steve Pomfret and their Wythenshawe circle of friends reunited one final time to bid farewell to the wasted talent of a man who could've been a contender. Johnny said of his friend:
It was an unfulfilled life that killed Rob.

Quotes from interviews for the documentary *These Things Take Time: The Story of The Smiths* (2002), for John Robb's book *The North Will Rise Again: Manchester Music City 1976–1996* (2009), for Tony Fletcher's biography *A Light That Never Goes Out* (2012) and Johnny Rogan's Omnibus Press classic *Morrissey & Marr: The Severed Alliance* (1992)

Recommended listening:
The Rolling Stones' 'The Last Time' from the album *Out of Our Heads* (1965)

SIGHTSEEING PART ONE

Steven Morrissey and his circle of friends, which consisted mostly of acts signed to Richard Boon's New Hormones label, tended to frequent The Beach Club, which essentially became an unoffical hang out point for the label. Morrissey was at the Beach Club to review Linder's band Ludus for *Record Mirror* (May 10, 1980). The club itself reminded him of a Beat Generation dive where Ginsberg and Ferlinghetti might have recited their poems.

It almost goes without saying that his determination to share the wonders of his best female friend's group with the readers of *Record Mirror* knew no bounds. Admitting that he'd been 'devoted' to the group since their 'masterly' *New Hormones* EP, he praised Linder's 'fascinating' voice and thought she relied on 'melodic jazz variation and unusual tone effects' to express herself.

Summarising the three lengthy bursts of experimental music that comprised Ludus' set, he informed *RM*'s readers that Linder delivered a 'wild melange of ill-disciplined and extraneous vocal movements, apparently without effort'. "An exquisite torture... from a valuable and special [band]," he added.

When Tony Wilson decided to open a rival club, The Haçienda, Morrissey and his friends remained loyal to The Beach Club, which had a homely feel compared to Factory Records' discotheque.

Recommended reading:
Morrissey's review of Ludus' gig, published in *Record Mirror* (May 10, 1980)

Recommended listening:
Ludus' 'Sightseeing' from their debut New Hormones-released EP, *The Visit* (1980)

SIGHTSEEING PART TWO

In August 1980, an irritated Cramps fan sends a letter to *Sounds* mentioning that he never received the membership kit that he was promised following payment.

I SENT OFF £1.50 to The Cramps' fan club in May to a Manchester address.
My membership cheque was cashed a month ago, but I haven't heard anything from them yet.
Can you get in touch with them for me?
Danny Loker, Bradford.

Sounds replied to the Cramps fan by essentially outing Morrissey's departure from the fan club's management (which was co-organised by himself and *The Next Big Thing* fanzine editor, Lindsay Hutton).

No PROBLEM. The Cramps' fan club, originally based at 384 Kings Road, Stretford, Manchester, and run by ace supporters Steven Morrissey and Lindsay Hutton, has now moved to Scotland. Lindsay attributes the breakdown in communication to a lost address during the transition across the border and has been trying to track down the origins of your cheque.

Meanwhile, Steven Morrissey has been waiting, fan club kit at the ready, for some sign of human movement from your direction.

You lost their address. They lost yours - but your full quota of membership stuff will be with you by the time you read this column.

Quotes from a Legion of the Cramped fan letter to *Sounds* and the magazine's response (Aug 1980)

Recommended listening:
The Cramps' 'What's Behind the Mask?' from their debut album, *Songs the Lord Taught Us* (1980)

SIGHTSEEING PART THREE

Morrissey revealed in his *Autobiography* that not only did he know Ian Curtis, but also that Curtis pestered him with poetry over the phone.

When the news came in on May 18th, 1980 that Curtis had committed suicide, it left such a numbness in the post-punk scene, that it almost killed it in its tracks, paving the way for the more optimistic New Romantics who had no time for bleak lyrics about 20th century urban decay.

Ian Curtis used to stay at his grandma's home on Milner Street, calling Morrissey to explore his vocabulary, to try out his poetry.

Until the revelation in his *Autobiography*, Morrissey would play down Joy Division and Ian Curtis' importance, possibly in an effort to establish himself as Manchester's sole miserable voice. In 1990 he said:

I saw them just before 'the death' and I was astonishingly unmoved. As were the audience, I might add. To me, it's all just... legend.

Quote from a Morrissey interview to Nick Kent with *The Face* (Mar 1990)

Recommended listening:
Joy Division's 'Ceremony', recorded at Ian Curtis' last gig on the 2nd May 1980, from their compilation *Still* (1981)

SIGHTSEEING PART FOUR

In the early hours of May 18th, 1980, Ian Curtis hanged himself in his house in Macclesfield. He had just viewed Werner Herzog's film *Stroszek* and listened to Iggy Pop's *The Idiot*. The surviving members of Joy Division struggled to find some way of coping with this tragic loss. Gillian Gilbert, girlfriend of drummer Stephen Morris, was enlisted to play keyboards, whilst guitarist Bernard Sumner took over lead vocals. They re-emerged as New Order, who would outlast Joy Division and become Factory Records' flagship band in their new dance music era.

Peter Hook: When we left Ian's funeral we said: "See you at practice." That Sunday afternoon I got the six-string riff to 'Dreams Never End', which we recorded as New Order. We just put Joy Division in a box and closed the lid, but it enabled the remaining three of us to establish ourselves as New Order. Through New Order people continued to become aware of Joy Division.

In an interview with *The Independent*, Johnny confessed to having been a Joy Division fan, especially guitarist Bernard Sumner. He followed New Order's career closely.
I first heard of Bernard through Joy Division's first album in about 1977 when I was 14. I'd not heard anything like it before. I didn't know where it was coming from, but I knew I liked it.
It kind of knocked me for six really.

In 1989, a couple of years after The Smiths split, Johnny formed alternative dance supergroup Electronic with ex-Joy Division/New Order guitarist Bernard Sumner. They would collaborate with Neil Tennant and Chris Lowe, of the Pet Shop Boys, and ex-Kraftwerk composer Karl Bartos.

Quotes from a Peter Hook-written article in *The Guardian* (June 14, 2011) and from a Johnny Marr interview with *The Independent* (July 18, 1999)

Recommended listening:
New Order's 'Dreams Never End' from their debut album, *Movement* (1981)
Iggy Pop's 'Mass Production' from his debut solo album, *The Idiot*, which he co-wrote with Bowie in Berlin (1977)

SIGHTSEEING PART FIVE

With the deaths of Ian Curtis and John Lennon, as well as the cutbacks and pessimism of Thatcherite England, the turn of the decade seemed more like a nightmare than a new dawn. Morrissey begins to suffer panic attacks on a daily basis. He is prescribed antidepressants, which only further burden him.

With the help and strength of his mother, Morrissey managed another trip to America in 1980, dumping himself on his Aunt Mary's couch for a seven-week stretch, in hope of securing a job and a new life in the promised land.

Recommended listening:
Joy Division's 'New Dawn Fades' from their debut album, *Unknown Pleasures* (1979)
The Smiths' 'I Know It's Over' from the album *The Queen is Dead* (1986)

SIGHTSEEING PART SIX

Steven Morrissey travels to the States to visit his Aunt Mary and his sister Jackie, who live in Arvada, a district of Denver, Colorado.
His aunt's family has grown since he was last there, while his sister is about to get married.

Writing to his friends back home, Morrissey would finally admit that there was no way he could actually survive living in the States.
It's dead here. Everyone walks like John Wayne, so starch and masculinist.

I wore a pink tie and everyone thought I was a transvestite. He would never again entertain the thought of returning.

Quotes from a letter extract by Johnny Rogan in *Morrissey & Marr: The Severed Alliance* (1992)

Recommended listening:
Ludus' 'I Can't Swim I Have Nightmares' from their debut EP, *The Visit* (1980)

SIGHTSEEING PART SEVEN

Returning from the States, Steven Morrissey visited his best friend, James Maker, who lived in Bermondsey in south London. He continued writing his manuscript on James Dean in order to pitch it to Babylon Books, who had just published his New York Dolls biography. James Maker's vast knowledge of James Dean's life and times was a great help in amassing information on Steven's hero. At this time he also began a pen pal friendship with a Scottish muso named Robert Mackie. The surviving letters have revealed a great deal about Morrissey's personality circa 1980–1981.

I'm going to London in about a month for a weekend with my friend Jimmy.
He has a huge flat and we often sit on the balcony looking for UFOs.
We're such a wild pair (yawn) ...one so modern as you would find us boring, but most people find us tres amusing.

During one of those lazy nights on James Maker's balcony, the pair sighted a flying saucer, an encounter that both have confirmed.

Writing to Lindsay Hutton, his former collaborator in The Legion of The Cramped fan club, he gave details of his close encounter:

The UFO was hovering low and slow over Bermondsey. At one point I stood on the balcony and stared directly into one hovering ship, and it STOPPED in mid-air above me.

Without a doubt, it was watching me.

Quotes from a Morrissey letter to Robert Mackie (1980)

Recommended listening:
David Bowie's 'Starman' from his concept album *The Rise and Fall of Ziggy Stardust and the Spiders from Mars* (1972)

SIGHTSEEING PART EIGHT

Shortly after Steven Morrissey's and James Maker's UFO sighting at the latter's Bermondsey home in south London.

James and his parents each had their own free-standing ashtrays in the living room.

Morrissey became James's confidante.

To James, Morrissey was a distraction from himself, from his self-doubt.

Recommended listening:
James Maker & Noko 440's single 'Born That Way', released under Morrissey's supervision via Attack Records (2004)

SIGHTSEEING PART NINE

Sporting all the sartorial, and musical, clichés that had befallen the punk movement, like leather biker jackets, spikey hair and shock rock lyrics, Mike Joyce kept on playing the drums in his first band, The Hoax, for another two years.

After self-releasing their *So What* EP and playing a gig at an Anti-Nazi League event at the University of Manchester, the group applied to perform at the council's Royal Wedding celebrations, albeit they forgot to mention that they were uncompromising anti-royalists.

The council had set up a battle of the bands event as part of the Royal Wedding of Charles and Diana celebrations. The Hoax would disturb everyone involved by spitting and sneering at the judges whilst performing songs such as 'Rich Royal' and 'Assassinate the Prime Minister'.

Amidst the furore caused by the band's performances and his aspirations to drum for a successful band, Mike quit The Hoax hoping for a better future.

Recommended listening:
The Hoax's 'Rich Royal' from their compilation album *...And So It Went 1979–1981* (2007)

SIGHTSEEING PART TEN

Shortly after leaving his first band, The Hoax, Mike Joyce found himself in a period of transition hoping to play with another punk band as soon as possible. According to biographer Johnny Rogan, at this exact moment Mike "received substantial compensation for injuries sustained in a car accident some years before".

He would use the money for formal drumming lessons and thus have a better chance of joining a bigger band. It is perhaps at this point that he bought his flashy drumkit, which, as Morrissey mentions in his *Autobiography*, he lovingly called Elsie.

The perks of rehearsing at TJ Davidson's studio meant that Joyce would be the first drummer to spot the advert that Irish punks Victim had placed in the studio. The band had just signed to local punk label TJM Records and were also on the verge of a breakup, but managed to survive and become a staple of Manchester's early '80s punk scene.

Victim became the resident band at the Portland Bar in Manchester's Piccadilly district and Mike soon found himself drumming for the first time in a semi-professional outfit.

Victim was a step up for me. The way I was playing in The Hoax was head down, no nonsense, mindless boogie. With Victim, I started looking from the outside.

Quotes from Johnny Rogan's biography *Morrissey & Marr: The Severed Alliance*, published by Omnibus Press (1992)

Recommended listening:
Victim's 'Cause or Consequence?' from their compilation *Everything*, featuring Mike Joyce on the drums (2003)

Recommended reading:
Morrissey's *Autobiography* (2013)

The World Won't Listen part one

Responding to an ad placed in *Sounds*, Steven Morrissey begins a pen pal friendship with a Scottish muso named Robert Mackie. Of all the letters that he wrote during this period to numerous pen pals, it is believed only Mackie's have survived, providing biographers with massive amounts of information about his personality in the early '80s.

He asked his new pen pal if being Scottish bothered him.

And told him Manchester was a lovely place 'if you happen to be a bedridden dead mute'...

...and ended by hoping Robert was an as unhappy as he was.

Attached to the letter was a photocopy of a James Dean photo, whilst the letter itself was signed off with a crude rendition of a Linder Sterling drawing from a Ludus cover and an unhappy face, keeping in theme with his lyrical pun on 'Ashes to Ashes', which had just been released.

Recommended reading:
Morrissey's letter, written to his pen pal, Robert Mackie (1980)
Recommended listening:
David Bowie's 'Ashes to Ashes' from the album, *Scary Monsters (and Super Creeps)* (1980)

The World Won't Listen part two

Addressing Robert Mackie as Paganini, Morrissey chided his pen-pal for calling him 'Steve', explaining that he preferred 'Steven', not that he was particularly fond of that either.

He went on to list his favourite musicians – Dolls, Jobriath, Nico and Magazine – and inquired whether Robert had seen vintage Bowie on *The Old Grey Whistle Test* 70's review.

He didn't share Robert's fondness for Kate Bush. 'The nicest thing I could say about her is that she's unbearable,' he wrote. 'That voice! Such trash!'

He claimed to have seen Bowie 14 times, beginning on September 3, 1972, and most recently on May 3, 1976, and appeared irritated that Robert didn't believe him.

He signed off as 'Natalie Wood', the actress friend of James Dean.

Recommended reading:
Morrissey's letter, written to his pen pal, Robert Mackie (1980)

Recommended listening:
David Bowie's 'Moonage Daydream' from his concept album *The Rise and Fall of Ziggy Stardust and the Spiders from Mars* (1972)

The World Won't Listen part three

Morrissey's letters to pen friend Rob betrayed an influence of Oscar Wilde's dry wit.
'It was a terrible blow to hear you actually worked,' he wrote. 'I didn't think anyone did so any more.' He expressed a preference for lounging around all day looking fascinating than having a permanent income, simultaneously questioning his own sanity.

He told Rob of his belief that only children, ie those without brothers or sisters, become psychopaths, then moved on to his liking for Eno's first and second albums and 'Backwater', a track from Eno's *Before And After Science*. He also said he thought Lou Reed's *Bells* album was his best ever, mentioning that he'd seen Reed four times.

Scathing in his condemnation of electronic music, he referred to Gary Numan as 'Miss Numan' whom he 'hated, loathed, detested, abominated and couldn't stand or abide'. He wasn't very partial to Orchestral Manoeuvres In The Dark either, suggesting that a liking for them was the result of having 'nothing to do'.

He closed this particular letter with a discussion on Art versus art; including in the definition films and books as well as music, then enigmatically cast aside Cliff Richard as someone undeserving of being raised to 'my level'.

Recommended reading:
Morrissey's letter, written to his pen pal, Robert Mackie (Oct 22, 1980)
Recommended listening:
Lou Reed's 'Stupid Man' from the album *The Bells* (1979)
Brian Eno's 'Backwater' from the album *Before and After Science* (1977)

In his next letter to Rob, Morrissey addressed his pen pal as 'Tugboat Annie' and opened with some barbed remarks about Rob's grammar. He enclosed a photograph of himself 'disguised as an artiste' which was 'suitable for framing'.

He'd just bought 'Love Zombies' by The Monochrome Set but felt he would enjoy it more wearing a long mac, of which he had three.

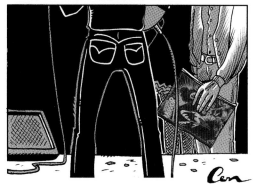

He accused Rob of taking acid, liking *Not The Nine O'Clock News* and masturbating to Anna Ford, and added that in his spare time he waltzed around Manchester 'looking sultry, overeducated and kinda deca (whatever that means).' This time he signed himself off as Ronald Reagan.

Recommended reading:
Morrissey's letter, written to his pen pal, Robert Mackie (1980)

Recommended listening:
The Monochrome Set's 'Love Zombies' from their second album, *Love Zombies* (1980)

Morrissey evidently spoke to Rob Mackie on the phone but seems to have been unable to decipher Rob's thick Glaswegian accent, about which he complained in his next letter.

He expressed a hope that Rob enjoyed *The Man Who Fell To Earth*, which starred David Bowie, adding that if he did he was the first person to do so.

Morrissey told Rob he was off to London soon to stay with his friend Jimmy – James Maker – who had a huge flat with a balcony on which they sat and watched out for UFOs.

He closed this letter with a complaint about rockabilly revivalists The Polecats who'd recorded a version of Bowie's 'John. I'm Only Dancing' that was not to his liking. 'If they REALLY had any imagination they'd shoot themselves,' he added angrily before urging Rob to go out and buy a Ludus record.

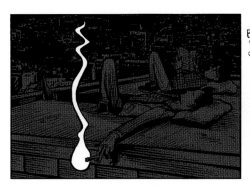

Ten years after Morrissey wrote the letter, Boz Boorer, guitarist of The Polecats, joined him when he assembled a new band in order to tour *Kill Uncle*. They have been together ever since, Boorer writing the music for the majority of Morrissey's solo albums. Along with Alan Whyte, Boz is credited with successfully blending jangle pop and rockabilly to create a new sound for Morrissey which helped revitalise his career. In 1995, Morrissey and his band would open David Bowie's *Outside* tour, fulfilling both his and Boz Boorer's wildest dreams, until Moz fell out with Bowie – but that's another story for another time.

Recommended reading:
Morrissey's letter, written to his pen pal, Robert Mackie (1980)

Recommended listening:
The Polecats' cover of David Bowie's 'John, I'm Only Dancing' from their debut album,
Polecats Are Go! (1981)
Simple Minds' 'I Travel' from the album *Empires and Dance* (1980)

In another letter to Rob, Morrissey spoke of his ambition to cultivate the State of Texas and recommended he watch the movie *The Last Picture Show* which was being shown on BBC2 the following Sunday. 'That film... was my first real sexual relationship,' he added.

He slagged off Generation X – 'appalling' – and didn't seem that impressed by The Motels either.

Moving on towards acts he liked, he said Nico's voice 'paralyses the imagination' and in response to an inquiry about Lou Reed live suggested that 'poor Lou was never "live"'. He also wondered how 'Walk On The Wild Side' had managed to get past the BBC censors and be featured on *Top Of The Pops*.

Dropping the cynicism for once, Morrissey admitted he 'almost cried' on hearing of John Lennon's murder. He said he didn't have any of his records or care much about The Beatles, but was still deeply disturbed when people who devote a part of their lives to peace are shot for it. 'It's always the wrong people,' he wrote 'Nobody would assassinate our dear prime minister'.

A few years later Morrissey would return to the above comments in a more controversial way. After the IRA attempted to assassinate Thatcher by planting a bomb in her Brighton hotel where she was staying during the 1984 Tory Conference, he notoriously stated: "The sorrow of the IRA Brighton bombing is that Thatcher escaped unscathed."

Recommended reading:
Morrissey letter, written to his pen pal, Robert Mackie (1980)

Recommended listening:
The Velvet Underground's 'I'll Be Your Mirror' from the album, *The Velvet Underground & Nico* (1967)
Orange Juice's 'Moscow Olympics', offered as a b-side to their single 'Falling and Laughing' (1980)

Morrissey's letter to Rob on December 4, 1980, opened with a few cutting remarks about religion. 'Wouldn't you just LOVE to kiss the Pope's feet,' he asked.

He moved on to alcohol, telling Rob that Pernod reminded him of Bowie's Aladdin Sane tour and nowadays he preferred Cinzano and vodka. He was troubled by the recent death of Mae West. 'And to think she was only 88 – such a waste'.

He wrote about his forthcoming trip to America, mentioning that he would visit New York and Colorado, but regretted that he'd miss *Coronation Street* and *Top Of The Pops*.

And closed on a rather personal note by inquiring whether Rob had a girlfriend and whether he liked girls. 'I have a girlfriend called Annalisa,' he wrote 'We're both bisexual. Real hip, huh? I hate sex,' he added.

Recommended reading:
Morrissey's letter, written to his pen pal, Robert Mackie (Dec 4, 1981)
Recommended listening:
The Smiths' 'Ask' from their second singles and b-sides compilation, *The World Won't Listen* (1986)
Brian Eno's 'Spider and I' from the album *Before and After Science* (1977)
...And The Native Hipsters' single 'There Goes Concorde Again' (1980)

Morrissey's next letter to Rob was written on March 10 after his trip to America. He talked about his book on the New York Dolls, of which he had only two so couldn't part with one, and mentioned his forthcoming book on James Dean.

He also said he was forming a group called Angels And Genderless and that they would be rehearsing as soon as he had got over his jet lag.

He complimented Rob's taste in liking *Desertshore*, Nico's 1971 album, mentioning the track 'All That Is My Own' – 'so refined' – before grumbling that in New York all the radio stations still played Beatles and Rolling Stones records, as well as Springsteen.

Morrissey was disappointed that Bowie wasn't as recognised in America as he was in the UK, observing that many people were still outraged at the mention of his name, and he admitted to singing along to his records, among them 'Cygnet Committee' and 'Unwashed And Slightly Dazed'.

Recommended reading:
Morrissey's letter, written to his pen pal, Robert Mackie (Mar 10, 1981)

Recommended listening:
David Bowie's 'Cygnet Committee' from the album, *David Bowie* (aka *Space Oddity*) (1969)
The Smiths' 'Rusholme Ruffians' and 'Barbarism Begins at Home' from the album, *Meat is Murder* (1985)

The World Won't Listen part nine

Morrissey and Rob had enjoyed another phone call in which Rob announced his intention of visiting Manchester. Morrissey's next letter asked Rob to describe himself so they wouldn't miss one another. Ever the joker, he said he was as 'blind as a bat', and advised Rob to look out for someone being helped across a street by an old lady.

Morrissey offered to put Rob up but stressed that he ran a 'respectable house'. 'No hanky panky,' he added.

Listening to The Monochrome Set as he wrote, Morrissey felt embarrased as Rob owned 22 Bowie albums, compared to his eight. He did point out he had lots of books, more books than records.

His tongue firmly in his cheek, Morrissey answered Rob's inquiry about what they might do together by stating that he would be tied a rack so the 'Texan sex ritual' would begin. 'You'd never believe what my sister can do with cotton wool and a tennis racket,' he wrote.

Recommended reading:
Morrissey's letter, written to his pen pal, Robert Mackie (1982)

Recommended listening:
The Monochrome Set's 'The Jet Set Junta' from their third album, *Eligible Bachelors* (1982)

The World Won't Listen part ten

From the tone of Morrissey's next letter to Rob Mackie, it would seem that Rob's visit to Manchester was not an unqualified success. 'I'm sorry your visit ended miserably,' he wrote, 'but that was your own fault.' Morrissey evidently took Rob to a transvestite club, a rash outing in view of Rob's inexperience in such places.

Rob had drawn Morrissey and enclosed the sketch in a letter, which impressed Morrissey enormously. '...everyone I've shown it to agrees that there's a great resemblance,' he wrote. 'Why have you kept your talents hidden? I had no idea I was writing to a genius.'

Morrissey offered to tape his Monochrome Set albums for Rob, and was deeply offended by Duran Duran. 'Girls On Film' he described as 'most chauvinistic, sexist piece of garbage I've ever seen.'

Recommended reading:
Morrissey's letter, written to his pen pal, Robert Mackie (1982)

Recommended listening:
Magazine's 'About the Weather' from their final album, *Magic, Murder and the Weather* (1981)

The World Won't Listen part eleven

Morrissey's next letter to Rob discussed the cold weather, snow evidently putting a damper on Morrissey *joi de vivre*, such as it was.

He scorned Rob for missing The New York Dolls and listed his current listening as Noel Coward, George Formby, Sandie Shaw and Cilla Black.

Moving on to literature, Morrissey claimed that he bought 30 books a week, then sang the praises of the James Dean film *East of Eden*. His latest ambition was to track down and interview the actor Richard Davelos who played Aron, 'the angelic brother' of Dean's character.

Morrissey closed this letter by writing off The Stranglers – 'absolute flimflam' – and the Bowie-Queen collaboration 'Under Pressure' – 'a spectacular disaster' – and informing Rob that Nico, who lived nearby, could often be seen 'whirling about Manchester in a black cape humming "Le Petit Chevalier".'

Recommended reading:
Morrissey's letter written to his pen pal, Robert Mackie (1982)

Recommended listening:
The Smiths' 'Accept Yourself' from their first alternate takes and b-sides compilation, *Hatful of Hollow* (1984)
Magazine's 'A Song from Under the Floorboards' from the album *The Correct Use of Soap* (1980)
Nico's 'Le Petit Chevalier' from the album *Desertshore* (1970)

The World Won't Listen part twelve

Studied for years by writers and fans alike, Morrissey's letters to his Scottish pen pal Robert Mackie provided a rare glimpse inside his psyche. The last letter was written a mere five months prior to the formation of The Smiths. The letters were not only filled with the quips and one-liners that would one day make him famous worldwide for his wit, but also artwork and collages, influenced by artist friend Linder Sterling, showcasing a rarely seen artistic side.

Morrissey quoted Oscar Wilde as saying:

"One should either be a work of Art or wear a work of Art.
It is only the shallow people who do not judge by appearances".

He poured scorn on Hazel O'Connor – a 'vile gorgon' – and felt insulted that Rob should even suggest that Morrissey might have been listening to her.

He again praised Ludus but admitted his record player was a museum piece, 'so don't expect any dazzling technology' should Rob visit again.

Morrissey closed his final letter to Rob in typically enigmatic style, quoting The Monochrome Set, advising him to put his money in a trust and signing off 'somewhere out there'.

Recommended reading:
Morrissey's letter, written to his pen pal, Robert Mackie (1982)

Recommended listening:
Ludus' 'My Cherry is in Sherry' from their first full-length LP, *The Seduction* (1982)
Ludus' 'I Can't Swim I Have Nightmares' from their debut EP, *The Visit* (1980)
The Monochrome Set's 'Ici Les Enfants' from the album *Strange Boutique* (1980)

CRAK THERAPY PART ONE

By early 1981 Johnny had left his home in Wythenshawe to pursue his career as a guitarist. The situation at home had gotten gradually worse after Johnny was arrested for possessing stolen LS Lowry prints.

They loved that I was passionate about music because they're passionate about music as well. They were proud of that, but I had to fight with them quite a lot as a teenager because I wanted to be a professional musician.
It must have been hard for my dad because I was kind of wild in a way. I was nice, but in my teens I was kind of wild. I was so idealistic and very energetic.

I always wanted to escape. I wanted to escape the world. I wanted to escape what I was around and what I was hearing... the conversations I was having with people... people's personalities – life.

Following a tip from a friend, Johnny lodged with Granada Television producer Shelley Rohde and her four children in a Victorian house.
He moved in with Angie, the first time.they had lived together, and was also allowed to use the attic as his rehearsal space.

I wanted to escape my consciousness, my feelings, what I was seeing. It's like how Wordsworth wrote The World Is Too Much With Us. I had a love of music and a love of melody and rhythm and sounds and all the things that make up pop music. I needed it to escape normal life. I still do, but I really did then. It's more of a need than just an attraction.

Aware that clothes shops were great places to meet other musicians, Johnny got a job at the goth clothing store Aladdin's Cave. By the end of the year he was working as assistant manager in another clothes shop, Stolen From Ivor, whilst Angie was a receptionist at the Vidal Sassoon hair salon.
For a while, things were looking good...

Quotes from a Johnny Marr interview with AskMeAskMeAskMe.com (May–July 2012)

Recommended listening:
Johnny Marr's 'New Town Velocity' from his debut solo album, *The Messenger* (2013)

CRAK THERAPY PART TWO

After being recommended by Wythenshawe friend Phil Powell, Johnny left Aladdin's Cave and started working at Perry Boy clothing headquarters, Stolen From Ivor.

I graduated from St Augustine's Grammar School a year early to form White Dice and record. I was qualified. My first job was in a clothes shop for Perry Boys in Manchester city centre, called Stolen From Ivor.

Johnny had told the owner of Stolen From Ivor that his best friend, Billy Duffy, was working at Johnson's, the fashionable rockabilly clothing shop in London.
The next thing he knew, Angie and he were on a train to London to buy some clothes for Stolen From Ivor.

Billy: *When I moved to London in 1980 I was working at Johnson's in the Kings Road and Johnny had got a very similar thing in Manchester.*

Billy: *I was part-time in the shop and the rest of the week in their warehouse, shipping clothes out and dealing with wholesale clients. I remember Johnny and Angie came down to look at the range and buy in bulk, which was pretty funny. It's ironic; we were both on a similar path trying to make it in bands whilst working in fairly cool clothes shops to supply ourselves with the required outfits!*

Following Billy's proven strategy if making contacts through the best clothes shop, Johnny had quit Stolen From Ivor by the end of the year and was working for the ultra-hip Manchester store X Clothes.

Quotes from a Johnny Marr interview with *Times Higher Education* (Oct 26, 2007) and a joint Johnny-Billy interview for Billy Duffy's *Stories* (Feb 2013) from his website BillyDuffy.com

Recommended listening:
Theatre of Hate's 'Do You Believe in the West World?' from the live album *He Who Dares Wins* (Live in Berlin) (1983)
Chic's 'Le Freak' from the album *C'est Chic* (1978)

CRAK THERAPY PART THREE

1981.

Johnny becomes a fully-fledged Nile Rodgers fan (of Chic fame) and decides it's time to form a new band: this time a funk band.

Chic really changed things in a way so few bands are able to. He's a genius in ways I'll never fully wrap my head around. He's an all-time great and a constant source of inspiration to me and as incredible a guy as he is a musician, and that's really saying something.

I was working in a clothes shop in Manchester called X Clothes. I'd pretty much left school the year before, moved out of my parents' place, too, so it was a very liberating time for me. Clothes shops, as I understood it, were where you worked if you were a musician trying to get a band together.

A classic for me is Nile Rodgers' guitar part on Chic's 'I Want Your Love'. All that is born out of an early love for Bo Diddley.

That beat is the root of all dance music. When I do sessions and I can't find a way into the track, I look for the Bo Diddley, whether it's half-time or double-time.

If you listen to The Smiths' 'The Boy with the Thorn in His Side', the rhythm part from verse two onwards – that chick-a-chick part – it's pure Nile Rodgers...

Rehearsing at Decibelle Studios, which was run by Dale Hibbert, the bass player of local band, The Adorables, Johnny once more recruited his best friend Andy Rourke to play the bass in his rhythm section.

This was the third band they had played in together following The Paris Valentinos and White Dice.

Quotes from Johnny Marr interviews with the *NME* (Mar 29, 2014), *The Times* (July 23, 2010) and *The Guitar Magazine* (Jan 1997)

Recommended listening:
Chic's 'I Want Your Love' from the album *C'est Chic* (1978)
The Smiths' 'The Boy with the Thorn in His Side' from the album *The Queen is Dead* (1986)

CRAK THERAPY PART FOUR

The three guitar players who influenced me were James Williamson from The Stooges, Bert Jansch and Nile.

When I was first getting my guitar style together, I was turned onto Nile Rodger's music and his songs and it was a game-changer for me. Really sent me down a road that has really stuck with me. He's been a massive influence since then and that's been on record over all the years of my career, which I think used to surprise people somewhat.

By 1981 Johnny and Andy had formed a third band, this time playing funk, naming themselves Freak Party after Chic's megahit Le Freak.

After disbanding Chic, Rodgers became an in-demand producer and session guitarist, laying down groundbreaking work for Bowie's *Let's Dance*, Madonna's *Like a Virgin* and more recently Daft Punk's 'Get Lucky'.

It's very interesting, because when I was a kid learning Nile's stuff, I thought that despite the fact that this guy I'm hearing is from New York and I'm from the suburbs of deepest darkest Manchester, something was calling me: the chord changes, the melody and the guitar style. There's a romantic aspect to the music and a sense of melancholy. I mean, 'At Last I Am Free' is one of the most affecting songs I've ever heard sung...

The time I grew up with for my generation of musicians — myself and what became the post-punk generation — we were done with the old rock clichés.

And people who loved guitar culture... Nile was a real guiding light for everybody because he was about songwriting. He wasn't about showboating and he had that beautiful technique in there. And everyone liked it: punks liked Chic, rockers liked Chic.

Everyone who had ears liked Nile's songs.

But yeah, when my son was born, we named him Nile. And he's turned out to be a pretty good guitar player and he's very, very happy to be named after him! Chic reconvened and put out Chic-ism just before my son was born... And now that Nile Rodgers and I are friends, and he and my son are friends, it's worked out very well. And Nile Rodgers calls my son his soul son.

Playing under the pseudonym Man Made in order to avoid attention, Nile Marr has become a guitarist and performer in his own right.

Quotes from Johnny Marr interviews with Drowned in Sound (July 29, 2012) and *The Observer* (June 30, 2013)

Recommended listening:
Chic's 'At Last I Am Free' from the album *C'est Chic* (1978)
Man Made's 'TV Broke My Brain' from his debut album *TV Broke My Brain* (2014)

CRAK THERAPY PART FIVE

Simon Wolstencroft on his bandmates in The Patrol, Ian Brown and John Squire.

I met Ian and John at "Alty" Grammar School in the first year when I was 11 in 1974. When the Clash album came out in April 1977 we were 14 and we became firm friends and talked about The Clash non-stop. Ian was into the punk thing but more into the Sex Pistols and he really liked The Adverts. There were other bands as well like The Specials. We went to the 2 Tone tours at the Apollo in Manchester in 1979.

Formed in 1979 by schoolmates Ian Brown, John Squire, Si Wolstencroft and Andy Watkins, The Patrol spent the most part of the '80s trying to find their own voice, before becoming the voice of a whole generation, years later, when they kickstarted Madchester as The Stone Roses. Ian Brown: I played bass in the band because it was the easiest thing to play. We got our own PA and sprayed it bright green because The Clash had one that was bright pink. I guess we were Clash copyists. That was what inspired us.

Right! This song's called:

Jail of the Assassins.

Ian Brown: I met Andy Rourke at a party when I was 16. The thing about The Smiths that never got written about was that the pre-Smiths groups that Andy and Johnny were in, the Paris Valentinos and White Dice, were funk outfits. When everyone else was a punk rocker, Andy was into The Fatback Band and Parliament.

I think that's what gave The Smiths the groove; Andy played the melody like a McCartney, but he had that funk undercarriage that he learned when he was a kid, when he first picked that bass up.

Soon after first meeting, Si Wolstencroft invited Andy and his mates over to his house for a small party, during which Andy's friends promptly trashed the place, leaving the young bassist alone to help Si clean the place up before his parents returned home.

Aw mate I'm fookin' wasted...

and on top of that I'm rehearsing with Patrol in a couple of hours!

I mean I really wanna play some funk or somethin' fresh ye'know?

Oi Si! I've got a great idea!

Wanna play in Johnny's and my band?

Soon after that fateful party, Si left The Patrol to join Johnny Marr's and Andy Rourke's funk outfit, Freak Party, as their drummer.

Quotes from Simon Wolstencroft and Ian Brown interviews with *Uncut* (Mar 2007), *The Clash* (Mar 4, 2011) and for John Robb's classic biography *The Stone Roses* (1996)

Recommended listening:
The Patrol's only surviving two-track demo tape, 'Jail of the Assassins' (1980)
The Stone Roses' 'I Am the Resurrection' from their debut album, *The Stone Roses* (1989)

CRAK THERAPY PART SIX

Simon Wolstencroft on becoming a member of Freak Party: A mate of mine, who used to drink in the Vine with Ian Brown and John Squire, said he knew a shit-hot guitar player who was looking for a drummer. I started smoking lots of weed and listening to lots of records. I really got into the funk thing. That's where I got my nickname. It was Johnny Marr who nicknamed me Funky Si because we were listening to funk through these huge great big speakers, Andy playing his bass along to it all. We were getting really stoned and I was getting really into the funk.

Johnny: I was getting the band together. We had somewhere to rehearse because Andy Rourke's mum and dad had split up and his mum went to Spain and left four teenage boys in this great semi-detached house. The house was like the Beverly Hillbillies with these kids running around with guitars with no adults and lots and lots of pot. We basically listened to Joy Division's Closer, Sextet by A Certain Ratio and Low by David Bowie. You listen to Sextet and Low and you will get a little bit of the feel of how Andy Rourke was such an unusual bass player.

Me, Andy and Si were cooking up post-punk funk and considering getting in singers. I was making these tentative forays to the microphone but I was not that keen.

Rehearsing for almost a year as a trio, Freak Party constantly again auditioned singers for their post-punk funk combo, but most of the candidates turned out to be bad John Lydon imitators. Of course, it didn't help that they were prompted by the band to audition to PiL's 'Flowers of Romance'.

To make matters worse, the lax environment at Andy's home had led him to start experimenting more and more with harder drugs.

Beyond smoking pot on a regular basis, by this time he had started smoking and snorting heroin.

Quotes from Simon Wolstencroft and Johnny Marr interviews for John Robb's classic biography *The Stone Roses* (1996) and Tony Fletcher's *A Light That Never Goes Out* (2012)

Recommended listening:
Public Image Ltd's 'Flowers of Romance' from the album *Flowers of Romance* (1981)
A Certain Ratio's 'Lucinda' from the album *Sextet* (1982)
The Byrds' 'Eight Miles High' from the album *Fifth Dimension* (1966)

CRAK THERAPY PART SEVEN

**Andy Rourke's home,
Hawthorn Lane, Ashton-upon-Mersey.**

The scene at Andy's started off being very much about teenagers with guitars, and then other people started to come around who didn't have a musical bone in their body.

The connection was drugs, and when it became nothing about music, then it was nothing about me.

Quotes from a Johnny Marr interview for Tony Fletcher's biography *A Light That Never Goes Out* (2012)

Recommended listening:
Chic's 'Good Times' from the album *Risqué* (1979)

CRAK THERAPY PART EIGHT

Disappointed by the lack of competent, and compatible, singers, Johnny Marr briefly flirted with the idea of getting Ian Brown in Freak Party:

That was when we got really tempted to go and personally talk to Ian Brown. I knew Ian Brown through Si. I knew John a bit. We were checking each other out, like you do. But there was an understanding that Ian and John were a musical item, so that's what stopped me asking Ian.

Meanwhile, the scene at Andy's house had changed and drugs were now being dealt from there. And as Johnny had been staying over with Angie, in order to rehearse, these changes began to impact on his friendship with Andy.

It was a slow, insidious thing that was much less to do with rock n' roll decadence than early '80s Manchester. And a lot to do with Thatcherism.

Johnny immediately broke up Freak Party, promising never to see his best friend Andy again.

Quotes from Johnny Marr interviews for John Robb's classic biography *The Stone Roses* (1996) and Tony Fletcher's *A Light That Never Goes Out* (2012)

Recommended listening:
The Stone Roses' 'I Wanna Be Adored' from their self-titled debut album (1989)

THESE THINGS TAKE TIME PART ONE

As ever, Steven Morrissey's circle of friends consisted of the New Hormones camp, which found itself competing with the Factory Records contingent.

In 1982 among his close circle of friends were Linder Sterling, Annalisa Jablonska and James Maker.

At Culture Club's northern debut, Morrissey watches as the audience visibly back away.

Boy George, encouragingly patronising, does not impress Morrissey.

Only a few months later, Culture Club reach number one in the singles chart, making it seem easy.

THESE THINGS TAKE TIME PART TWO

Despite his career as a music journalist never really taking off, Steven Morrissey continued submitting gig reviews to the *Record Mirror*, his final published pieces appearing in late 1981, covering gigs by Iggy Pop, Depeche Mode and, of course, Ludus.

He wasn't impressed by Iggy Pop – 'always there when we don't need him' – and described his stage antics as tiresome and as fearsome as a 'well-laundered' Klondike Annie.

He was a 'jaded gigolo' who sang tunelessly and whose next step would be the 'Golden Garter or, better still, retirement.'

Depeche Mode also came in for a roasting – 'perhaps not the most remarkably boring group ever to walk the face of the earth, but they're certainly in the running'. The scathing review described them as 'hilariously unimaginative', 'murderously monotonous' and 'sophisticated nonsense'.

As it happened, DM were supported by his friends Ludus – 'plainly wishing they were elsewhere' – whose music offers everything to everyone, wrote Morrissey. 'Linder was born singing and has more imagination than Depeche Mode could ever hope for,' he concluded.

Recommended reading:
Morrissey's two gig reviews, published in *Record Mirror* (1981)
Greil Marcus' *Lipstick Traces: A Secret History of the 20th Century* covering the influence of art movements on late 20th century countercultures (1989)

Recommended listening:
Iggy Pop's 'Don't Look Down' from his James Williamson-produced album, *New Values* (1979)

THESE THINGS TAKE TIME PART THREE

Morrissey's final piece as a journalist was a *Record Mirror* review of a Ludus gig, who shocked The Hacienda by performing in a dress made out of meat whilst also donning a black dildo. She also had every table in the club decorated with a paper plate containing a red-stained tampon and a stubbed cigarette. Her friends, The Crones, handed out packages of leftover raw meat wrapped up in pornography. By thrusting the dildo in the crowd's faces, she was making a protest against the club's policy of constantly displaying pornography.

As ever, Morrissey was fulsome in his praise for Ludus though he somehow sensed that their uncompromising message was unlikely to find acceptance beyond a narrow field of avant-garde followers like himself.

'Ludus are out to stretch the patience of the world to the very elastic limit,' he wrote. '...their music is unlike anyone else's.'

Linder: Bucks Fizz had just won the Eurovision song contest. At the end of their song the men pulled up girls' skirts, and that ticked off an outrage in me. Oh no, I thought, it's still going on. At the same time at The Hacienda they were showing lots of soft porn and they thought it was really cool. I took my revenge. I was a vegetarian, I got meat from the Chinese restaurant, all the discarded entrails. I went to a sex shop and bought a large dildo. I didn't tell anybody about it.

It's not just provocation. To be audacious requires a certain style also. I think it's ultimately about making one's mark, about what you would leave behind if you went under that No 8 bus. I remember being 16 in Wigan and reading about the original feminist protesters and thinking, "They left their mark. They threw their darts into the bullseye." Meat and tampons were supposed to represent "the reality of womanhood" and the dildo "here's manhood, the invisible male of pornography. That it can be reduced to this, a thing that sticks out like a toy."

I remember the audience going back about three foot. There was hardly any applause at the end. And that was a crowd who thought: nothing can shock us, we see porn all the time, we're cool. When that happened, when they stepped back, I thought, that's it. Where do you go from here?

Their most exciting and provocative moment was their creative peak and Ludus would break up soon after the Hacienda performance. Years later, acts like Lady Gaga would appropriate the statement, never once acknowledging Linder's contribution to protest art.

Quotes from Linder Sterling interviews for Lucy O'Brien's *The Woman Punk Made Me* (1999), *032c* magazine (Issue 11/ Summer 2006) and *The Observer* (Jan 12, 2014)

Recommended viewing:
The only existing video (sans sound) of Ludus' gig at The Hacienda, performing 'Too Hot to Handle' (1982)

THESE THINGS TAKE TIME PART FOUR

Morrissey sought to put his friendship with Richard Boon to good use by secretly giving him a self-recorded demo tape, possibly hoping to jump onto the New Hormones roster, alongside Ludus and the Buzzcocks.

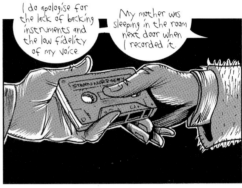

There were two songs on the cassette and Richard Boon remembered one being an early version of 'The Hand That Rocks the Cradle', with a different melody than the one recorded by The Smiths. This confirms that Morrissey has been writing lyrics before the band's formation.

The other number Boon remembered hearing on the cassette was a cover of the Bessie Smith song 'Wake Up Johnny'.

Years later, Tony Wilson also recalled Morrissey using the same tactic on him. A final, desperate attempt to escape his fate as an unknown Mancunian poet and join Factory Records.

Quotes from a Richard Boon interview for Nick Kent's controversial exposé for *The Face*, titled 'Dreamer in the Real World' (May 1985)

Recommended listening:
The Smiths' 'The Hand That Rocks the Cradle' from their eponymous debut album (1984)

Anna is Polish and lives on Stamford Street.

She wears vintage Victorian clothes, and Morrissey liked to hang out with her.

With a fortune of only seven pounds, Morrissey suggests they live together.

THESE THINGS TAKE TIME PART FOUR

Several months having passed since his last published gig review for *Record Mirror*, Steven Morrissey's journalist career was effectively over. Choosing to carry on, he finished his manuscript for his James Dean biography, *James Dean is Not Dead*, in which he curiously suggests that Dean survived his car accident.

He also wrote an extensive essay on the obscure silver screen heroes who influence him, titled *Exit Smiling*, and how the impingement of women rights shaped Hollywood.

Alas, Babylon Books, who had published his book on the New York Dolls, declined the essays, considering them uncommercial.

Left with no book contract for both his manuscripts, and *Record Mirror* declining his reviews, 1982 seemed like the bleakest year of his life.

Years later, when Babylon Books tried to cash in on Morrissey's fame by publishing the manuscripts, he would publicly dismiss the works of his youth.

Those weren't books, just juvenile essays, and thoughtless rubbish at that. I had no creative process, just pain, which I mistakenly assumed might be creative process. Well, it wasn't...

Quote from a Morrissey interview with *Rookie* magazine (Feb 26, 2013)

Recommended listening:
Molly Haskell's book *From Reverence to Rape: The Treatment of Women in the Movies* (1974)

For a long time, Morrissey doubted he would every find companionship, and waiting for it was too painful.

He was signing on, feeling at odds with his family, trying and struggling to keep going.

Recommended viewing:
The Smiths' 'How Soon is Now?', from their b-sides and singles compilation, *Hatful of Hollow* (1984)

Factory Records boss Tony Wilson enters X Clothes hoping to recruit Johnny as a replacement for Section 25 guitarist Paul Wiggin, who, suffering from a fear of flying, quit the band on the eve of their first US tour. Years later, Beth Cassidy, the current singer of Section 25 recalled the story as: I remember the story of when a 17 year old Johnny Marr was approached by Tony Wilson to join Section 25 after the first guitar player had left and he said no.

I thought that was hilarious and thought of course he was going to say no to a band that was far older and really grumpy.
He wanted to be in a band of his own age.

Confirming Billy Duffy's theory that hip clothing stores were hot spots for local musicians, Johnny Marr was also introduced to Matt Johnson, the brains behind The The.

Johnson had travelled to Manchester on the behest of Dave Hunt, a common acquaintance of his and Johnny's, in order to meet Johnny and possibly recruit him to the new The The line-up.

Quotes from a Beth Cassidy interview with *Louder Than War* (Oct 19, 2011)

Recommended listening:
Matt Johnson's (released later under the The The banner) 'Red Cinders in the Sand and Bugle Boy' from the album *Burning Blue Soul* (1981)
Morrissey's 'Reader Meet Author' from the album *Southpaw Grammar* (1995)

When record shop owner Pete Hunt left Johnny in charge of his vinyl record collection to travel abroad, Johnny not only had massive amounts of obscure '60s 45s to study but he also acquired a new friend in Matt Johnson.

I knew Matt Johnson from 1981, before I formed The Smiths. We wanted to work together then, that was before Soul Mining, so we were already friends and kept up with each other's work.

Sixties were great, mate...

but you should try listening to some more left field stuff—Residents, Zappa...y'know?

After performing for a couple of years as a solo act, Matt Johnson was in the midst of reforming his band The The in London. Having bonded with Johnny during his trip to Manchester, Johnson recognised Johnny's natural talent and officially invited him to join the group.

A band in London? Sounds fookin' great!

CHIC

Reluctant to leave Manchester, where for years he had been concentrating on building industry contacts, Johnny told Johnson that he would think about it but never actually got back to him. It took him a mere five years to respond to the offer.

Immediately after the demise of The Smiths in 1987, Johnny desperately wanted to join a new gang of musicians, ones he could call his friends. Within a matter of months he had finally joined The The.

It was something I was always going to do and I got around to being in a band with one of my friends...

It was nice meeting you, Johnny, mate.

I'll wait for your call, eh!

Dusk is my favourite thing I did with The The. I like 'Dogs of Lust', 'Slow Emotion Replay', 'Love is Stronger Than Death'...

Quotes from a Johnny Marr interview to *The Mouth Magazine* (July 29, 2012)

Recommended listening:
The The's 'Dogs of Lust' from the album *Dusk* (1993)

Recommended viewing:
The The, including Johnny Marr, performing 'The Beat(en) Generation' from the album *Mind Bomb*, live on *Top of the Pops* (1989)

Spring 1982.
Johnny spends most of his lunch breaks by closing X Clothes and heading next door to Crazy Face, a rival clothing store owned by Joe Moss. Moss' store might not be as hip as X Clothes, but Moss also manufactures most of the stock and therefore has a lead in the latest street fashions.

Crazy Face's top floor served as the storage room and was decorated with posters and framed photos of iconic rock and jazz stars, something that made a huge impression on Johnny, who at this point was getting over his funk phase and progressing into a full '60s and Motown obsession.

Joe Moss on meeting Johnny: They kept telling me there was this lad who wanted to meet me to talk about my photographs. He came upstairs and introduced himself. This lad walks in and sticks out his hand. He says: "Hi, I'm Johnny Marr and I'm a frustrated musician." And that's how it all began.

Johnny used to come in and teach me stuff on the guitar. To see him play was incredible. He always had his own approach. I found him really innovative. He was dead interested in the blues and the real roots music. He'd play Motown covers, things like Smokey Robinson's 'The Tracks Of My Tears'.

But he'd also perform the whole arrangement, including the vocal melody, all at the same time, just on guitar.
He started to come over practically every dinner time. It was a welcome break and he was a nice lad whom you could relate to instantly.

The two struck a friendship almost immediately; a friendship in which the older and wiser Moss took up the role of substitute dad, mentoring Johnny in the history of pop culture and music business.

Quotes from Joe Moss interviews for Johnny Rogan's biography *Morrissey & Marr: The Severed Alliance* (Omnibus Press, 1992) and Simon Goddard's *Mozipedia* (2009)

Recommended listening:
Smokey Robinson and the Miracles' 'The Tracks of My Tears' from the album *Going to a Go-Go* (1966)
Van Morrison's 'Crazy Face' from the album *His Band and the Street Choir* (1970)

Through his landlady Shelley Rohde, Johnny made his first TV appearance on the ITV talk show *Devil's Advocate*. After a series of inner-city riots broke out across the UK, ITV called 100 unemployed youngsters from Manchester and put them in a studio to discuss the causes of the trouble and the toll that the dole had been taking on their lives.

Around this time he started hanging out again with old Wythenshawe pal, Phil Fletcher, who had been crucial in bringing together Billy Duffy and Steven Morrissey, having hung out at their rehearsals during their brief tenure as T-Shirt/Nosebleeds. Johnny explained to Fletcher his need to find a new lyricist and vocalist, as people would never notice his music withouta talented frontman.

Upon hearing that the Buzzcocks were on the verge of breaking up, Johnny tracked down Pete Shelley and frantically tried to convince him that he was his ideal new writing partner. Pete Shelley on meeting Johnny: I was at Legends, the Manchester nightclub, and this kid came up to me and said, if you ever need a guitarist, I'm available... this kid it transpires was Johnny Marr.

Despite being frustrated at not having made it, according to Ian Brown Johnny was still telling everyone that he'd soon be a huge star.
Ian Brown: There's a great story of Johnny going into a pub in Sale called The Vine when he was 17 and telling everyone he was going to have a No 1 album – and a year or two later, he did! He always had that belief.
Johnny Marr: People always say I did that but I swear I didn't!

Quotes from young Johnny Maher's interview on *Devil's Advocate* (1981), a Pete Shelley interview for Mike Joyce's *East Village Radio Show* (June 2010), Johnny Marr and Ian Brown interviews with *Uncut* (Mar 2007) and John Robb's books *The North Will Rise Again: 1976–1996* (2009) and *The Stone Roses* (1996)

Recommended listening:
Morrissey's 'Reader Meet Author' from the album *Southpaw Grammar* (1995)

Johnny starts spending his evenings at Joe Moss' home.
Joe Moss: I'd known guitarists from '60s Manchester bands, and I'd never heard anything like this kid. My bloody tongue was hanging out. It turned to him telling me that he wanted to put a band together. I agreed to help him whatever he did. It was the most interesting relationship in my life.

The first person that popped into Johnny's mind was Billy Duffy, who had previously played with Steven Morrissey in T-Shirt/Nosebleeds. They had even attempted to revitalise Slaughter & The Dogs with him. Billy had since moved to London, become a member of Theatre of Hate and subsequently Southern Death Cult, who in time would evolve into seminal '80s hard rock band, The Cult.
Billy Duffy: Morrissey hated me because he thought we'd stolen some lyrics from him, which we probably had.

Joe Moss: He was loving my record collection and my book collection and I was loving just watching him play. My thoughts about this guy were pretty spot on. He seemed quite well-sorted for someone who obviously wasn't a wealthy lad, who didn't have any spare money at all. It was clear from the word go that Angie was a great, intelligent woman, a real source of strength to him.

Johnny subsequently turned his attention to his former White Dice bandmate Rob Allman, with whom he'd severed connections after leaving the band behind (and his life as a Wythenshawe lad). Allman briefly associated with Steven Morrissey via his close friendship with Billy Duffy, with whom he performed in various teen bands.

Allman suggested that Phil Fletcher, a Patti Smith fan who hung out with Steven Morrissey in the late '70s, was probably his best bet if he wanted to contact the young poet.
Frustratingly though, this connection too proved equally futile.

Quotes from a Billy Duffy interview with the *NME* (May 5, 1990), a Rob Allman interview for Johnny Rogan's *Morrissey & Marr: The Severed Alliance* (Omnibus Press, 1992) and a Joe Moss interview for Tony Fletcher's *A Light that Never Goes Out* (2013)

Recommended listening:
Studio Sweethearts' sole single 'I Believe' (1979)

I put a band together in 1982 and tried out a bunch of people. It is always the way when you are trying to get a band together with strangers that you go for people who you think have the right vibe, the right look; but I was always coming up against people who just weren't as into the hard work as I was.

They might have had the look. They might have been able to sing. But they didn't seem to have the passion or intensity that I had.

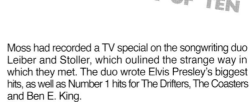
Through working at X Clothes I met Joe Moss because he ran the shop next door, which was called Crazy Face. Angie, my girlfriend back then, who is now my wife, and I and Joe were trying to get a new band together.

Moss had recorded a TV special on the songwriting duo Leiber and Stoller, which oulined the strange way in which they met. The duo wrote Elvis Presley's biggest hits, as well as Number 1 hits for The Drifters, The Coasters and Ben E. King.

Joe told me about this South Bank Show on Leiber and Stoller where one of them wrote music and needed a lyricist and heard about this guy and just went around and knocked on his door.

That's how I thought it would work out with me and Morrissey.

Quotes from a Johnny Marr interview for *Document and Eyewitness: An Intimate History of Rough Trade* (2010) and the excerpt published in *The Times* (July 23, 2010)

Recommended listening (some of Leiber and Stoller's greatest songs):
Elvis Presley's 'Jailhouse Rock' from the *Jailhouse Rock* OST album (1957)
The Coasters' 'Searchin', b-side to their single 'Young Blood' (1957)
Ben E. King's 'Stand by Me' from the album *Don't Play That Song!* (1961)
The Drifters' 'On Broadway' from the album *Under the Boardwalk* (1963)

I was watching this video, on Leiber and Stoller and they explained how they met. And I think with Mike Stoller, he knew of Jerry Leiber, or vice versa, from school, and he knew that he wrote music

One or the other... And he just thought, right, if this guy doesn't know me I'll go and knock on his door and say, let's write.

So the very next day that's exactly what I did. I phoned up a guy I hadn't spoken to for ages and I said, do you remember that guy Morrissey? Steven Morrissey. Do you remember him?

Stephen Pomfret: Johnny's personality is so strong that you feel you're completely consumed by him as soon as you meet him.

Journalist: *Morrissey was known in Manchester as Steve the nutter.*

Johnny: Yeah, that's right. Which attracted me to him no end! I was fascinated by this guy.

I wore a pair of '50s Levis on with proper American bike boots and a Johnson's sleeveless jacket and a Johnson's shirt and a real proper old American flying men's cap and a super quiff which was faultless...

Unlike Johnny's determination to control his fate, Morrissey seemed to be constantly waiting for a bus that never came. On May 22nd, 1982 he'd spend his 23rd birthday alone. I'm afraid I'm somewhat of a back bedroom casualty. I spent a great deal of time sitting in the bedroom

Everyone is, in fact, alone.

I see humans as essentially solitary creatures, and this is not changed by surrounding ourselves with others, because they too are solitary. Life is a very serious business for the simple reason that nobody dies laughing.

Quotes from Morrissey interviews with *Rookie* magazine (Feb 26, 2013) and the *Oxford Road Show*, BBC2 (March 1985). Johnny Marr interviews for *Document and Eyewitness: An Intimate History of Rough Trade* (2010), *Johnny Marr in Conversation, Talking Music* (1987) and John Robb's book *The North Will Rise Again: 1976–1996* (2009) and a Stephen Pomfret interview for Johnny Rogan's *Morrissey & Marr: The Severed Alliance* (Omnibus Press, 1992)

Recommended listening:
The Cookies' 'I Want a Boy for My Birthday', b-side to their single 'Will Power' (1963)

Quotes from Johnny Marr interviews for *Mojo Special Edition: The Inside Story of Morrissey & The Smiths* (May 2004) and Simon Goddard's *Mozipedia* (2009)

May 1982.
384 Kings Road, Stretford, Manchester.
Morrissey on Johnny's sudden appearance at his front door.

Johnny: I was pretty confident that he'd like me, but I was a bit worried in case he thought I looked too outrageous...

Morrissey: He pressed his nose against my window. Quite literally. It left a terrible smudge. I think he'd been eating chocolate or something.

Johnny: I had this really silly haircut at the time, this quiff. It looked like I had a French loaf sticking out of me head. I was afraid he'd think I was some kind of Gene Vincent freak. Pommy was there, but as soon as Morrissey came to the door Pommy took two very firm steps back, which is one of the things that got me to talk so fast. It was just plain exuberance. I began talking 300 words a second.

Morrissey: He seemed terribly sure of what he wanted to do, which I liked. He said 'let's do it and do it now' so we did. Then.

Quotes from a Morrissey interview with *Smash Hits* (Feb 16, 1984) and a Johnny Marr interview for Simon Goddard's *Mozipedia* (2009)

Recommended listening:
The Smiths' 'Reel Around the Fountain' from their debut album, *The Smiths* (1984)

Years after the meeting between Morrissey and Marr, Stephen Pomfret debunked many mythical details to biographer Johnny Rogan.

The mythical meeting was a fable and the chocolate stain on the window is bollocks. We got on the 263 bus and went around to Morrissey's. His sister came to the door and I asked if Steven was in. He took an age to come down the stairs. I said, Hi, Steven, I'd like you to meet a friend of mine, Johnny.

Johnny on the events upon arriving at Morrissey's room:

He let me in, which was a surprise – still is – and we sat in his room and he invited me to put a record on. I looked through his singles and found a Marvelettes record – I think it was Paper Boy. I was impressed that he had a bunch of Marvelettes singles, all on their original labels. I was aware it was a test, but I was pretty snotty about music as well and instead of playing the A-side, I played the B. I think we both had the match of each other, really. In fact, we got on famously well, it was like sparks flying.

When I came across Morrissey, in terms of influences it was pretty phenomenal that we were so in sync, because the influences that we had individually were pretty obscure. So it was absolutely like fucking lightning bolts to the two of us. This wasn't stuff we liked. This was stuff we lived for really.

We made an arrangement that he would call at noon the next day. But I remember leaving and thinking about those situations with frontmen before and I wasn't exactly skipping down the street because I worried he might not call, he might not be into it as much as I was.

Quotes from Stephen Pomfret's one and only interview with Johnny Rogan for *Morrissey & Marr: The Severed Alliance* (Omnibus Press, 1992), republished in the *Mojo Special Edition: The Inside Story of Morrissey & The Smiths* (May 2004), and Johnny Marr interviews for Simon Goddard's *Mozipedia* (2009) and *Document and Eyewitness: An Intimate History of Rough Trade* (2010)

Recommended listening:
The Marvelettes' 'You're the One', b-side to their single 'Paper Boy' (1966)

reel around the fountain **part one**

May 1982.
X Clothes, Manchester.

We made an arrangement that he would call at noon the next day. My feeling, as I left him was "well, yeah, okay. But I'll wait to see if he calls me tomorrow."

He called right on the dot and we were on and we arranged to meet the next day and from then on we started writing songs.

From then on, we kept in contact all the time. We just had this tremendous belief in ourselves, and since that day my life has totally changed, and I know that Morrissey's has, too. Right from the beginning we knew it was going to be brilliant. Morrissey agrees to meet Johnny in the attic he shares with Angie at Shelley Rohde's Victorian dwelling.

Johnny shows off his songwriting skills by coming up with a tune for the poem 'Don't Blow Your Own Horn', which Morrissey had given him on the day which they met. However, the partnership gets off to a rocky start: We were kinda half doing it but neither of us liked it very much. It was quite a jaunty, strummy thing. It didn't cut it and I don't think Morrissey really liked it either. We lived with it for about a week then decided not to bother with it.

Till this day 'Don't Blow Your Own Horn' remains unreleased.

Quotes from Johnny Marr interviews with *Melody Maker* (Apr 14, 1984) for Simon Goddard's *The Smiths: Songs That Saved Your Life* (2006) and Neil Taylor's *Document and Eyewitness: An Intimate History of Rough Trade* (2010)

Recommended listening:
The Smiths' 'Reel Around the Fountain' from their self-titled debut album, *The Smiths* (1984)

reel around the fountain **part two**

June 1982.
Steven Morrissey discusses Johnny's uncommon approach and the formation of their songwriting team with his best friends, James Maker and Linder Sterling.

On that first day when we were officially a partnership we had a conversation about many things and made a mental wish list and on that list was that we should sign to Rough Trade Records.

We rehearsed in Joe Moss' warehouse in town, intensely, three or four times a week. When I saw the words to 'The Hand That Rocks the Cradle', I just thought it scanned over the metre, the tempo, of 'Kimberly' by Patti Smith. Also it was terra firma, that was a real big touchstone for us. Remember we didn't know each other then so it was really important to the two of us that it worked.

So I played this chord progression for 'The Hand That Rocks the Cradle' and we decided that it sounded good. So good that we recorded it on my legendary TEAC three-track cassette recorder, which enabled me to put down two guitar tracks then a vocal on top. So after trying 'Don't Blow Your Own Horn', that was the first song we actually wrote.

Quotes from Johnny Marr interviews for Simon Goddard's *The Smiths: Songs That Saved Your Life* (2006) and Neil Taylor's *Document and Eyewitness: An Intimate History of Rough Trade* (2010)

Recommended listening:
The Smiths' 'The Hand That Rocks the Cradle' from their self-titled debut album, *The Smiths* (1984)
Patti Smith's 'Kimberly' from her debut album, *Horses* (1975)

reel around the fountain **part three**

June 1982.
Johnny's room in Shelley Rohde's Victorian home.

I was sat on the floor with these words that he'd typed out. As I was looking at them I just started to play this chord progression, this figure I'd been fiddling around with for a couple of weeks.

Straight away Morrissey said "Is that it? Keep going". So as I was looking at the lyrics, I didn't know how the vocal melody went, but I was getting a feeling from the words and just sticking with it. I thought it felt right.

Shocked as a child by the Moors murders whose victims were buried on Saddleworth Moor between 1963 and 1965, Morrissey wrote the lyric to 'Suffer Little Children' in hope of exorcising the demons of Manchester's past. Most of the victims were only a few years older than Morrissey and he would have a lifelong morbid fascination with the murders.

Having also read Emlyn Williams' book, *Beyond Belief: A Chronicle of Murder and its Detection*, which outlined the events, he also found himself equally fascinated with the protagonists: Ian Brady, Myra Hindley and, interestingly, the Smiths: David and Maureen Smith.

Quotes from Johnny Marr interviews for Simon Goddard's *The Smiths: Songs That Saved Your Life* (2006) and a Morrissey interview for the first book on The Smiths, Mick Middles' *The Smiths* (Omnibus Press, 1985)

Recommended listening:
The Smiths' 'Suffer Little Children' from their self-titled debut album, *The Smiths* (1984)

reel around the fountain **part four**

So any day if you walked into X-Clothes around 11am, you'd be hearing the Birthday Party Junkyard album, and if you came back an hour later, you'd be hearing Fireside Favourites by Fad Gadget. So all that melting pot, all that to me is what the early 80s is about.

Morrissey and I would do each other tapes, as you do when you meet a friend.
I can remember when he gave me Marianne Faithfull's 'The Sha La La Song'. It was like, wow!
That song really hit the jackpot for about two weeks.

You also can't underestimate the importance of Andrew Berry. He was one of the DJs at the early Hacienda and he knew everybody. Later, he helped me earn dough by DJ'ing with him at the Exit club just off Deansgate. We would play what became known later as rare groove.

Andrew brought into my life an awareness of what was going on in the gay scene in Manchester, whether it was Bobby O records or the fashions. He used to sit between me and Morrissey when we were writing songs. No-one else was ever allowed to do that.

Quotes from Johnny Marr interviews for Tony Fletcher's biography *A Light That Never Goes Out* (2012), Simon Goddard's *The Smiths: Songs That Saved Your Life* (2006), with the *NME* (June 24, 1989) and John Robb's *The North Will Rise Again* (2010)

Recommended listening:
John Lee Hooker's 'This is Hip' from the album of the same name, *This is Hip* (1980)
Marianne Faithfull's single 'The Sha La La Song' from the re-issue of her eponymous debut album, *Marianne Faithfull* (1965)

reel around the fountain **part five**

Andrew was someone I knew in Wythenshawe in 1976 and he very publicly decided he was going to be a hairdresser. At that time that meant saying, 'I'm a big poof,' which he was not; the graffiti went round Wythenshawe saying, 'Andrew Berry is a big poof,' but he was super hip.

Very importantly, Andrew brought me into gay clubs, and very important to me and the Smiths was a club called Manhattan, run by this fantastic guy called Dennis.
We would go up to the DJ booth and play the records we wanted.

When The Hacienda opened, Andrew quickly became one of the DJs. He was really into the electro scene coming out of New York. He had everything on the Ze label, like Suicide, James Chance, Was (Not Was), Lydia Lunch, James White and the Blacks, the Contortions, Mars.

He was a Roxy kid and a Bowie kid. You can't underestimate the importance of Andrew Berry. He furnished Bernard Sumner with his haircut and then he would do mine and eventually Morrissey's. He decided that his salon was going to be in the dressing room of The Hacienda.

Quotes from Johnny Marr interviews for John Robb's book *The North Will Rise Again: Manchester Music City 1976–1996* (2010). The extract was also republished in *The Quietus* (Sep 10, 2009)

Recommended listening:
Martin Rev's 'Mari' from his self-titled debut solo album, *Martin Rev* (1980)
Morrissey's 'Hairdresser on Fire', featured as a b-side on his debut solo single, 'Suedehead' (1988)

reel around the fountain **part six**

July 1982.
Pommy, Steven Morrissey and Johnny Maher rehearse above Crazy Face, Joe Moss's clothing shop.
In keeping with their sexually ambivalent outlook, they cover The Cookies' 'I Want a Boy For My Birthday'.

Later on, Joe Moss, Steven Morrissey, Johnny and Angie convene in Johnny's attic room at Shelley Rohde's home in order to talk strategy, specifically the future of the songwriting duo's partnership.

Recommended listening:
The Cookies' 'I Want a Boy for My Birthday', b-side to their single 'Will Power' (1963)

reel around the fountain **part seven**

July 1982.
After a rehearsal above Joe Moss' Crazy Face.
The time has come for Johnny to take some swift, yet harsh, decisions in order for his songwriting partnership with Steven Morrissey to flourish into a full-fledged band.

Sadly, he would have to let go of his friend, Stephen Pomfret, who was crucial in introducing Johnny to Morrissey, but whose skills with the guitar were not up to Johnny's standards.

I said, You'd like me to leave this band, wouldn't you — this band that doesn't yet exist?
Johnny said, Don't be silly, Pommy, you're part of it
I said, Don't talk crap, Johnny, I know when I'm not needed.
That was it...

All I can say to you is that I was not a member of The Smiths and I never wanted to be a member of The Smiths. I really didn't. When I knew they didn't want me to be, I didn't want to be. And I never regretted it.

Quotes from extra interviews with Stephen Pomfret for Johnny Rogan's biography *Morrissey & Marr: The Severed Alliance* (Omnibus Press, 1992), as printed in *Mojo Special Edition: The Inside Story of Morrissey & The Smiths* (May 2004)

Recommended listening:
The Smiths' 'Reel Around the Fountain' from their self-titled debut album, *The Smiths* (1984)

reel around the fountain **part eight**

Joe Moss: What was happening before then was very '80s. On one hand you had variants on the Spandau Ballets and Duran Durans, and all the epic bands – Orchestral Manoeuvres, typical '80s-type bands.

On the other hand, in Manchester you had indie bands like Foreign Press, The Chameleons, and all the Factory stuff, like A Certain Ratio.

It's strange looking back. There was nobody really attempting to come through thrashing at guitars.

Johnny: Morrissey and I almost had this unspoken relationship where we were both able to be ourselves, but both knew how important we were to each other.

What shouldn't be forgotten is that we really, really liked each other. It wasn't some business arrangement or relationship of convenience. There was intrigue and understanding because as different as we were, the thing that was paramount inside us was pop records and that absolute promise of escape. And he understood that without us ever having to talk about it.

But we didn't have to be absolutely magnetically joined by everything. If you live and work so closely together you observe the things you don't share – like peeking over the garden fence. Eyebrows were often raised from both sides! So stuff he liked that I didn't like Jobriath for example, I didn't have any violent objection to it. I thought it was kind of intriguing, it just didn't touch me.

I was inspired by Andrew Loog Oldham and his example. I thought that was really noble, someone who was able to make things happen. In my head I thought I was running around the Brill Building. But that's how I was, I wore hyperactivity as a badge of honour. With Morrissey, he didn't actually need to physically get involved in that side. I was happy finding group members, places to rehearse, places to record, clothes, haircuts, managers and record companies.

All he had to do was be brilliant and be with me, for us to be next to each other. That's what it was about.

Quotes from an interview with Joe Moss for *Mojo* magazine (June 2004), an interview with Johnny Marr for Simon Goddard's *The Smiths: Songs That Saved Your Life* (2006) and Gary Farrell's account in Johnny Rogan's *Morrissey & Marr: The Severed Alliance* (1992)

Recommended listening:
Jobriath's 'Inside' from his self-titled debut album, *Jobriath* (1973)

reel around the fountain **part nine**

I'd known Johnny for a while. I'd engineered a session for Freakparty (Johnny's and Andy's band), they rehearsed at Decibelle, the studio I worked and rehearsed at.
Due to the incestuousness of the Manchester music scene at that time, we had also shared band members, my drummer Bill Anstee, had also been Johnny's drummer in Sister Ray.
Johnny had also formed a physical attachment to my vocalist.

My band The Adorables had a bit of a following and minor interest from some of the independent labels. J approached me and asked if I wanted to play bass in his new band.
I'd never actually been in a band I hadn't put together myself, so was initially reticent. I can't remember the events that turned my indecision to a yes, but I eventually agreed, summoning my old band members to a meeting at my flat in Hulme, and letting them know.

I rode down to J's place in Bowdon. He had a room in the house of a local Granada TV presenter Shelley Rohde who presented Granada news and a smattering of current affairs progs from time to time. The first thing Johnny said as I was going to meet him was: "Whatever you do, don't call him Steve. He absolutely hates it. Always refer to him as Steven". I thought that was a really odd thing to say, but I went along with it. So Steven it was.

Steven and I got chatting, shared a few common interests (vegetarianism, Velvet Underground). J played me "I Want a Boy for My Birthday" on cassette, said it was likely to be the first single, and could I put a bass line to it. As it stood, it was just guitar and vox I took the cassette, promising to have the bass written for our next meeting. I was there a couple of hours, and we agreed to meet a couple of times a week to get things started.

I said I'd pick Steven up from Stretford, I was coming from Whalley Range, so I passed his door anyway.
I took him back home, Steven riding pillion, and that was the way we travelled for the next couple of months.

Quotes from Dale Hibbert's now defunct online blog DaleHibbert.blogspot.com (*The First Couple of Weeks*, Apr 21, 2007) and an interview by Dale Hibbert with Simon Goddard's *The Smiths: Songs That Saved Your Life* (2006)

Recommended listening:
The Cookies' 'I Want a Boy for My Birthday', b-side to their single 'Will Power' (1963)

reel around the fountain **part ten**

Why choose a name like The Smiths?

It's a very stray kind of name, very timeless. It's the most ordinary name in the universe. We christened the group at a time when many were hiding behind long names like Eyeless In Gaza or Orchestral Manoeuvres in the Dark. And when you meet these people they're so ordinary. Some haven't even read a book. Our basic message is you don't have to be cool. It was time to come down to earth and bare the soul.

July 1982.

After rehearsing in Johnny's attic room the duo decide that it is time to christen their band. Morrissey had written three names in his notebook: Smiths Family, Smithdom and The Smiths.

Meditating on it briefly, they unanimously decided that the band's name should be The Smiths.

According to Dale Hibbert, Morrissey and Marr named the band after Patti Smith, an icon they both adored and at whose gig they first met in 1978.

It has also been suggested that Morrissey might have been inspired by constant references to the Smiths, e.g. David Smith and Myra Hindley's sister, Maureen Smith, whose testimonies were crucial in the incarceration of the Moors murderers. Another strange coincidence is the fact that his namesake, Stephen Smith, co-wrote Viv Nicholson's 1976 autobiography, *Spend Spend Spend*, a book Morrissey has mentioned reading. Nicholson would also later feature on the covers of two Smiths singles.

Quotes from The Smiths' first interviews with the *NME* (May 14, 1983) and *Smash Hits* (Nov 10, 1983), an interview by Dale Hibbert for Simon Goddard's *The Smiths: Songs That Saved Your Life* (2006) and a Morrissey and Marr interview in which they explain the band's name live on *Datarun* (1984)

Recommended listening:
Morrissey's 'The Ordinary Boys' from his debut solo album, *Viva Hate* (1988)

While the search for a drummer was on we had fairly regular meetings. On one of these occasions names were discussed, not for the band, but for the band members. Johnny said I should adopt the surname Nelson, apparently Dale Nelson was a notorious American serial killer, and it would be a good choice for me.

The reason that they wanted to push band surnames was because they wanted to discourage the music press from using the surname Smith, as was a habit in those days e.g. Johnny Smith, Steven Smith etc.
This would have been predictable and highly likely given that the band name was The Smiths.

Quotes from Dale Hibbert's now defunct online blog DaleHibbert.blogspot.com (*Haircuts and Action Men*, Apr 21, 2007)

Recommended listening:
Morrissey's 'I Know Very Well How I Got My Name', offered as a b-side on his debut solo 7" single, 'Suedehead' (1988)

384 Kings Rd, Stretford, Manchester.
We agreed to meet a couple of times a week to get things started. I said I'd pick Steven up from Stretford.

I was coming from Whalley Range, so I passed his door anyway. I took him back home, Steven riding pillion, and that was the way we travelled for the next couple of months.

Quotes from Dale Hibbert's now defunct online blog DaleHibbert.blogspot.com (*The First Couple of Weeks*, Apr 21, 2007)

Recommended listening:
The Exploited's 'Sid Vicious Was Innocent' from their second album, *Troops of Tomorrow* (1982)

reel around the fountain **part thirteen**

A mod revival scene, influenced by the original 1960s mod subculture, developed in the UK in the late 1970s.

The revivalists became fascinated by artists who influenced their '60s idols and so became infatuated with the original rock 'n' rollers.

The purists started trimming their quiffs down to a flattop. Reacting against the New Romantics, a very hetero glam-meets-punk style, The Smiths purposely chose a more subtle approach to the deconstruction of gender roles.

In their first three months they experimented with their image.

The next event was getting my hair cut. I picked Steven up, and he directed me through various gestures to an old house on Paletine Rd fairly close to Fridays. Johnny was already there. The three of us had our hair cut in the flat top style, that stayed with the band for quite a while. I've been told John (sic) Moss was there, I can't remember him. I've seen him on TV, but he doesn't look familiar.

New Romantics:
Glam rock meets punk
Heterosexual
Synths

Roots revivalists:
1950s meets kitchen sink
Ambiguous
Guitars

Smile, Dale!

Much better!

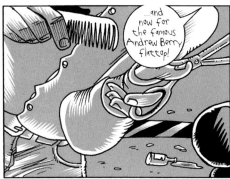

...and now for the famous Andrew Berry flattop!

I do remember a guy with heavy makeup, maybe this was him. There was a photographer who took shots of us outside and inside the house, he later turned up at rehearsals for more shots; the last I saw of him was at the Ritz.
I only visited this location once, and we had stopped rehearsing in Bowden and had moved on to Decibelle.

Quotes from Dale Hibbert's now defunct online blog DaleHibbert.blogspot.com (*Haircuts and Action Men*, Apr 21, 2007)

Recommended listening:
Morrissey's 'Hairdresser on Fire', b-side to his debut solo single 'Suedehead' (1988)

August 1982.

Over the next couple of weeks, we discussed the band's image.
Although I used the term "we", it was made clear that The Smiths were S & J only. That any contracts would reflect this, and I would assume the role of a more traditional bass player. It was odd to suddenly be a "band member", and not leader, but I took into consideration the fact that I'd had no success with any of my bands, so maybe it wouldn't be a bad idea to let someone else have a go.

S & J told me to buy some bowling shirts and turn up at a house near Fridays nightclub to get my hair cut.
I went to buy my shirts from the old army surplus store on London Rd. They had huge boxfuls of '60s bowling shirts, I made my choice and I had my shirts.

This store has long since gone, replaced by the Malmaison hotel. Above this shop was The Dolls Hospital, an amazing place lined with plastic body parts, a place where my Action Men turned up, when their injuries were beyond domestic repair, at a time when toys weren't disposable.

S & J told me that there was a strong possibility the band would project a gay image, more pretty boy than activist aka Tom Robinson. I'm not judging or commenting on Steven's sexuality, Johnny obviously isn't gay, and Mike wasn't on the scene yet. This has to be viewed in the context of a new band formation, where all sorts of ideas are placed on the table.

At that time, the first single was going to be 'I Want a Boy for My Birthday', and the band was going to have a gay identity. Weeks later it was never mentioned again.

Deserting the '60s US *Serial Killers in Bowling Shirts* image for a more subtle one, The Smiths also stopped insisting that Dale change his name to that of notorious murderer Dale Nelson.

By the end of the decade, the American band Marilyn Manson would successfully utilise the serial killer approach, as each member changed his name to a combination of the first name of an iconic female sex symbol and the last name of an iconic serial killer.

reel around the fountain part fifteen

By mid-1982 The Smiths were on a serious search for a drummer. Since they were rehearsing at Decibelle studios, in which Dale worked as an engineer, they stumbled upon Bill Anstee, who had performed both with Dale in The Adorables and Johnny in Sister Ray; they invited him for an audition alongside former White Dice keyboardist Paul Whittall. Johnny thought that he could try his experienced former bandmates, as well as listening to his songs accompanied by a keyboard.

Dale: We had arranged over a two-day period various drummers to turn up at Decibelle and audition. Bill turned up, he had played with both Johnny's bands and mine before, and although technically very good, was rejected on image.

Bill Anstee: Johnny showed me a phone book belonging to Shelley Rohde full of almost everybody you've ever heard of in the TV/record industry. To Johnny this was all he believed he needed to get where he was going.

Whittall and Anstee didn't stick around, the latter finding Morrissey especially irritating.

I didn't like the music they were playing, especially the lyrics. I would have had a total personality clash with Morrissey if I'd stayed around.

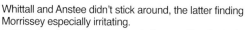

A notoriously guitar-centric band, The Smiths would sparcely use the piano on their recordings, their debut album featuring the keyboard on two tracks, 'Reel Around the Fountain' and 'I Don't Owe You Anything'. It is unknown whether Johnny's former White Dice bandmate had rehearsed these songs with them prior to the final recordings.

Quotes from Dale Hibbert's now defunct online blog DaleHibbert.blogspot.com (*Victim of a Hoax*, May 25, 2007) and a Bill Anstee interview for Tony Fletcher's biography *A Light That Never Goes Out* (2012)

Recommended listening:
The Smiths' 'Handsome Devil' from their first compilation, *Hatful of Hollow* (1984)

reel around the fountain **part sixteen**

August 1982.
Decibelle studios, Manchester.

Dale: After Bill Anstee was rejected on image, Tony, another one of my ex drummers gave it a go, but again was declined. A couple more turned up...

Finding a compatible drummer had become a nightmare and at some point Morrissey even invited a neighbour from Kings Road, Gary Farrell, who had played the drums in various local bands.

Johnny: Morrissey was by no means sat in his front room with the telly on. What connections he was able to draw on, he could. There was a guy in Stretford he'd known for a number of years who was a drummer. He got us all together one evening. This guy was really amiable and chatty, but he just didn't seem like a living breathing musician to me, just a nice guy with a drum kit, so obviously he wasn't in. But whatever could be done we both did.

It seemed that what Johnny and Morrissey were looking for was not just the stereotypical drummer who would simply bang away and accompany Johnny's orchestration. The drummer would also have to fit certain other criteria.

Feeling the pressure to record a demo in order to book gigs and contact record companies, Johnny thought that since he had already contacted former bandmates from White Dice and Sister Ray, he might as well call his recent ex-Freak Party drummer, Si Wolstencroft.

Contacting Funky Si was a touchy issue, as just six months before Johnny had severed all ties with both Si and his best friend, Andy Rourke, due to the debauched life his childhood mate was living at the time.

Quotes from Dale Hibbert's now defunct online blog DaleHibbert.blogspot.com (*Victim of a Hoax*, May 25, 2007) and from a Johnny Marr interview for Simon Goddard's *The Smiths: Songs That Saved Your Life* (2006)

Recommended listening:
The Smiths' 'Reel Around the Fountain' from their self-titled debut album, *The Smiths* (1984)

reel around the fountain **part seventeen**

August 1982.
Johnny's room in Shelley Rohde's home in Bowden.
Johnny decides to contact his former Freak Party
drummer Simon Wolstencroft (who he has nicknamed
Funky Si) in order to fill in the drummer slot in his new
venture, The Smiths.

Recommended listening:
The Smiths' 'The Hand That Rocks the Cradle' from their self-titled debut album, *The Smiths* (1984)

reel around the fountain **part eighteen**

August 1982.
Decibelle studios, Manchester.
Dale Hibbert manages to gain free access to Decibelle studios, in which he's been working as an engineer, for an all-night recording session so The Smiths can record their first demo.

Johnny has maintained for years that the band kept Dale as their original bass player due to his unlimited free access to Decibelle, yet Hibbert insists till this day that as a friend of Johnny's I would've given them that anyway whether I was in the band or not.

Utilising Si Wolstencroft's drumming skills and Dale Hibbert on the bass, Johnny had at long last a line-up for The Smiths. Morrissey sang the lyrics to the very first compositions he and Johnny had written together just a couple of months before, recording 'The Hand That Rocks the Cradle' and 'Suffer Little Children' in that single session.

Just as long as the hand that rocks the cradle is mine.

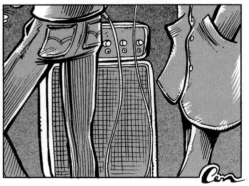

Quotes from Dale Hibbert's now defunct online blog DaleHibbert.blogspot.com (*Victim of a Hoax*, May 25, 2007) and from a Dale Hibbert interview for Simon Goddard's *The Smiths: Songs That Saved Your Life* (2006)

Recommended listening:
The Smiths' 'The Hand That Rocks the Cradle' from their Decibelle Studio demo recordings (1982)

August 1982.
Decibelle studios, Manchester.
As The Smiths record their two track demo, Morrissey invites Annalisa Jablonska, whom he had mentioned as his girlfriend in his letters to penpal Robert Mackie, to assist in the backing vocals of 'Suffer Little Children'.

Annalisa's cackling laughter and loud cries of the Moor victims' names, Lesley-Anne, John and Edward, created an eerie atmosphere on the already spine-chilling song. It came as no surprise that her vocals were downplayed in the later official releases.

Dale: That was a girl, a friend of Steve's (crying out the names of the victims). She turned up towards the end and did the weird laughing.

Johnny: Never saw her before, never saw her afterwards. She was nice. Very studenty. From what I remember she had an archetypical '60s vibe – a bob haircut and a duffle coat. Morrissey never being one to miss a sartorial angle!

The demo recording wasn't as pleasant an event as it could have been since their drummer, 'Funky' Si Wolstencroft, made it clear that he despised Morrissey's voice and demeanour.
I didn't like the cut of his jib.

There was a term for that kind of music at the time – the 'Raincoat Brigade.'
Looking at your shoes. Ordinary. Not very flash.
It wasn't jazz funk. I was Funky Si!

Quotes from interviews with Dale Hibbert and Johnny Marr for Simon Goddard's *The Smiths: Songs That Saved Your Life* (2006) and a Simon Wolstencroft interview for Tony Fletcher's *A Light That Never Goes Out* (2012)

Recommended listening:
The Smiths' 'Suffer Little Children' from their self-titled debut album, *The Smiths* (1984)

August 1982.
Factory Records, Manchester.
Morrissey and Linder visit Tony Wilson in order to hand over a copy of the recent Smiths two track demo, in the hope of getting Morrissey's band signed by this now legendary local independent record company.

Contrary to their later revisionist version of events, the band didn't think about signing to Rough Trade from the very start, but were in fact rejected by Factory Records on more than one occasion.

Johnny also did his part by trying to convince Wilson himself to get the band signed to his label.

Johnny: Tony Wilson came in to X Clothes one day and unravelled the plans for what was gonna be The Hacienda... I was Johnny from the shop, I knew everybody. They'd nearly all had to suffer The Smiths' demos I'd play on a practically daily basis in the shop!

The truth was that, having been pestered for years by a desperate Morrissey, Wilson had no intention of signing the young poet's musical venture.

Tony Wilson: In 1980, Morrissey told me he was going to be a pop star and I said, "Steven, write your novel." I was very dumb that afternoon, I thought there was no way he'd make a pop star.

For years Wilson would come to regret not signing The Smiths, admitting that the band would have saved Factory Records from its downfall.

Quotes from interviews with Tony Wilson and Johnny Marr for *Mojo* magazine (June 2004)

Recommended viewing:
Michael Winterbottom's *24 Hour Party People*, in the finalé of which Wilson admits his mistake in not signing The Smiths (2002)

August 1982.
New Hormones Records, Manchester.

Steven Morrissey and Johnny Marr visit Richard Boon's office where Morrissey had spent a great deal of time in the past years helping out with various tasks, as Boon had signed his best friend's band, Ludus. Having been rejected by Factory Records the band's last chance in town was Boon's label, New Hormones.

Foreseeing the band's meteoric rise, Boon insisted that The Smiths stop pursuing Manchester-based record companies and that they should instead focus on getting signed by a London-based company.

Boon: Morrissey came in saying right, we've got this track could I help? And I said 'No, because you need more resources than I could possibly, possibly offer.'

If that initial series of bad luck wasn't enough, their drummer, 'Funky' Si Wolstencroft, finally decided that he just didn't like being in a band whose sound he detested.

I decided not to join The Smiths not just because of Morrissey's voice, which I disliked intensely, but because by this time I was listening to British jazz funk and early '80s soul/disco.

He seemed to be doing the polar opposite of the records I was spinning back then.

After briefly helping out his former Patrol bandmates, Ian Brown and John Squire, in their new band, The Stone Roses, Funky Si formed the band The Weeds with The Smiths' hairdresser, Andrew Berry. He soon became one of the longest serving drummers of The Fall and later reunited with his former Stone Roses bandmate, Ian Brown, on his second solo album, *Golden Greats*. He has since regretted declining the drummer position in The Smiths.

Quotes from an interview with Richard Boon for NewHormonesInfo.com (*Indie Originals: The New Hormones Story*, Feb 3, 2008) and an interview with Simon Wolstencroft for the *Lancashire Telegraph* (May 10, 2012)

Recommended listening:
The Fall's ninth studio album, *Bend Sinister*, in which Simon Wolstencroft first stepped in on the drums (staying until 1997) (1986)
Ian Brown's 'Golden Gaze', co-written by Simon Wolstencroft, from his second solo album, *Golden Greats* (1999)

September 1982.
Johnny's room in Bowden.
Johnny and Morrissey's hairdresser, Andrew Berry, is so infatuated by The Smiths' vision that he agrees to pull some strings to enable the band to open for Blue Rondo à la Turk, who would be playing at The Ritz in Manchester on October 4th.

Johnny: We knew Andrew Berry and John Kennedy, who were general faces about town.

They'd staged a couple of fashion show-type things in Manchester, and because they'd already done something at The Ritz and had journalistic connections with The Face in London, they'd managed to book both the venue and Blue Rondo – though their ulterior motive was to put us on.

With the gig booked for the next month, the pressure was now really on for Johnny to find a permanent drummer for The Smiths.

Mike Joyce: I moved to Chorlton-cum-Hardy which is a kind of enclave, a bit of a bohemian place.

I lived with a guy called Pete Hope who knew this lad Johnny Marr who used to work in X Clothes in Manchester. Johnny asked Pete if he knew any drummers and Pete said:

Quotes from a Johnny Marr interview for *Mojo* magazine (June 2004) and from a Mike Joyce interview for *Swine* magazine (Mar 2006)

Recommended listening:
Blue Rondo à la Turk's 'Klacto Vee Sedstein' from their debut album, *Chewing the Fat* (1982)

Mike Joyce tours the UK playing the drums in the Irish punk band, Victim, enjoying being part of a group that's well respected.

First band I joined was a band called The Hoax and they were based in Manchester. Once I started working with them that was my first introduction really into being in a proper band.

Straight after that I joined a band called Victim, who were a massive influence on me as friends, as well as musicians. They were from Northern Ireland and they were just a great bunch of lads to be with.

In autumn 1982 Victim entered the studio to record a single, scheduled to be released by Illuminated Records. However, problems meant that their best track, 'Cause or Consequence', went unreleased. It was at this stage that Mike began to consider his options and other bands.

A mate of mine that I was living with at the time, a guy called Pete Hope (I'd moved out to Chorlton by that point), he told me about this lad called Johnny Marr that was getting a band together and they were looking for a drummer and did I fancy it? So I was like:

What the hell are old men doing....

messin' with our lives?

Yeah, yeah. I'll have a bit of that.

And some of that magic mushroom, thank you very much!

Quotes from a Mike Joyce interview for *Inside the Smiths*, a documentary dedicated to The Smiths' rhythm section, directed by Stephen Petricco and Mark Standley (2007)

Recommended listening:
Victim's 'Cause or Consequence', featuring Mike Joyce on the drums, from their compilation album, *Everything* (2003)

September 1982.
Spirit Studios, Manchester
Dale Hibbert had left Decibelle and set up a Spirit
Studios with some new partners. It was there that
Johnny invited Mike to audition for the band.
Dale and Mike immediately recognised each other,
as Victim had shared the same bill with The Adorables
on quite a few occasions.

*So I went down to an audition, I suppose, in Tariff Street,
at Spirit Studios.*

Mike also recognised Johnny from the few times he'd
bought some punk clothing at X Clothes.

*I'd seen Johnny working in X Clothes. He was so cool I didn't
dare buy the clothes. He'd been to London and had biker boots,
the perfect fade on his jeans and a big white poloneck.
He looked like a 1960s pop star; he was destined to be in a band.
I was more into punk so used to buy these fluffy mohair jumpers
whereas Johnny was more into the biker gear they were selling.
In the morning he'd had a Roger McGuinn bowl cut, but in
the band his hair was up, like an Elvis quiff.*

*Johnny was there and a bloke called Steve and a guy
called Dale playing bass. Morrissey was walking up and
down. He had a long coat on. He didn't look at me.
He just walked up and down. Kind of like a caged animal.
Just kinda striding up and down. Walking backwards
and forwards. A couple of furtive glances over at me.
I felt as though he just thought I was stupid. I just felt
a bit intimidated by him.*

*I thought: "Right —Weird! I won't speak to him, I think I'll
stick with Johnny!" Just prior to that (I didn't tell them
at the time but I think I was going out later, it must have
been a weekend, 'cause obviously I mean I went out on the
weekends) I had partaken of a few mushrooms — just to help
me concentrate. At the time, I was having a bit of fun with
the old experimentals It was all a bit hazy. As far as I was
concerned I was meeting people.*

Quotes from Mike Joyce interviews published in *The Guardian* (Jan 23, 2012), *Mojo* magazine
(Aug 1997), Simon Goddard's *Songs That Saved Your Life* (2004), for the documentary *Inside
the Smiths* (2007) and Tony Fletcher's biography *A Light That Never Goes Out* (2012)

Recommended listening:
The Byrds' 'Eight Miles High' from the album *Fifth Dimension* (1966)

September 1982.
Spirit Studios, Manchester.

Johnny: Mike was tripping out of his head. I thought, 'Right, you're in, you've got balls.'

Mike: I stopped playing for a second and of course I didn't realise how long it was going to take for the mushrooms to take effect.

As I was playing I looked down and I saw a Saturn V rocket going underneath the right side of my leg round and down the left side. It wasn't even a straight Saturn V rocket! It was a bending one - like a Dali one.

And I thought 'Right, okay, what's the next song!'

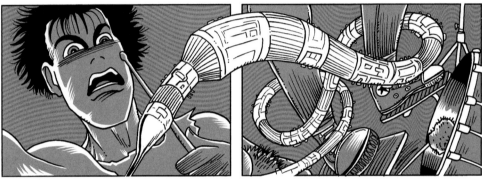

And I think it was over cause Johnny said "Right that's okay, thanks very much" and he spoke to Morrisey (who said) "Yeah alright" and I thought 'Well thank goodness for that! I'll get on me rocket and go home now!'

Quotes from a Mike Joyce interview for the documentary *Inside the Smiths* (2007) and a Johnny Marr interview for Johnny Rogan's *The Smiths: The Visual Documentary* (Omnibus Press, 1994)

Recommended listening:
The Smiths' 'Handsome Devil' from their first compilation *Hatful of Hollow* (1984)

I had the audition and went back to a friend's house and said, "They're going to be the next big thing, they sound fantastic." I was so into what they were doing, but it was very difficult to judge what a group could do. I remember saying to my flatmate: "I think they could be the next Psychedelic Furs!" I was well into them. That was as big as I could see then. I thought that was huge!

September 1982.
Andrew Berry's salón behind The Haçienda.
Mike Joyce officially joins The Smiths and is given a flattop haircut by their hairdresser and promoter, Andrew Berry, just before the band's first gig at The Ritz, opening for Blue Rondo à la Turk. The next step was to inform his best friends, his bandmates in Victim, that he would be leaving them in order to join The Smiths.

I had to make a decision and it took me a week or two. I remember Johnny saying: "Come on! Join the band! Don't be daft! Go for it, now!" I said, "Oh, I don't know. I'm not really sure if I should." Then The Church played the Gallery in Manchester and Johnny and Angie were there. I went down and said: "I've decided to leave Victim and join The Smiths." Johnny said, "Yeah, fantastic!" The next day I saw Victim's equipment for sale down at Al Music.

At this point Morrissey invited his best friend, James Maker, to join the band as a proto-Bez type dancer, in order to introduce them to the city's gay scene and shock the rest of the audience.

I was living in London and travelled to Manchester to attend a couple of early rehearsals. I'd heard the songs on cassette. I wasn't there to rehearse. The idea of me going through dance steps whilst Morrissey sang I Want a Boy For My Birthday would have been just a little too Diana Ross & The Supremes.

I was there to drink wine, make extraneous hand gestures and keep well within the tight chalked circle that Morrissey had drawn around me.

There was no discussion on how I would fit into the stage show. My involvement was not part of any long-term plan.

The Smiths' second lineup now consisted of Dale Hibbert, Mike Joyce, Steven Morrissey, Johnny Marr and James Maker.

Quotes from a Mike Joyce interview with Johnny Rogan for *Mojo* magazine (Aug 1997), conducted for Rogan's biography, *Morrisey & Marr: The Severed Alliance* (Omnibus Press, 1992), and a James Maker interview for Simon Goddard's *Songs That Saved Your Life* (2002)

Recommended listening:
The Church's 'Almost With You' from their second album *Blurred Crusade* (1982)
The Psychedelic Furs' 'Love My Way' from their album *Forever Now* (1982)

October 4th, 1982.

The Smiths play their first gig at The Ritz in Manchester, opening for headliners Blue Rondo à la Turk.

Mike: Blue Rondo were bastards to us. They were the 'in' group, we were the local support. We couldn't use any of their equipment.

Johnny: Blue Rondo were a bunch of dicks really rude and quite aggressive. They were all midgets too – which probably explains the attitude. In between soundcheck and going on stage, one of their turned-up-jean-wearing Wag Club dudes came up to us and said, "Touch any of our gear or move any of those fucking microphones and we'll be doing you afterwards"... so Morrissey spent most of the gig crouched down at a preposterous angle, singing into their midget-height microphone.

Chris Sullivan (Blue Rondo): The Smiths went on immediately after Hewan, a Latin jazz DJ, and looked out of place, because the audience was largely groovers in zoot suits with pencil moustaches.

Johnny: Blue Rondo was the epitome of that early '80s Hard Times/Demob scene which I was very aware of 'cos I was in the modern clothing industry. I was into a harder style, an R&B bohemian thing, and Morrissey was into a '50s aesthetic, which was very much ahead of its time. So when we saw these guys who were just trendy in a very mainstream sense we knew we were going to wipe the floor with 'em.

Just before their opening gig, a Smiths tradition began as the house DJ played a tape provided by Morrissey featuring Klaus Nomi singing 'The Cold Song'.

Right after the song ended James Maker introduced the band to the Ritz crowd in French. Dale Hibbert definitely did not expect what happened next.

Dale: Steven said, "We're going to be a gay band, but not in a Tom Robinson, effeminate kind of way, but more in an underlying kind of macho type way." It was a very strongly manufactured image that was being prepared.

We actually played on the floor in front of the stage, but there was this other guy that came out with us, wearing stilettos and a leather jacket.

James Maker: They were black court shoes! I wouldn't be seen - on a kidney machine - in white stilettos. And they were not props, I assure you. I was given a pair of maracas - an optional extra - and carte blanche. There were no instructions. I think it was generally accepted that I would improvise.

Johnny: I liked James; he was a friend of Morrissey's. They were very alike - very literate; men of letters but with an exhibitionist streak...

Quotes from Johnny Marr, Mike Joyce and Joe Moss interviews for *Mojo* magazine (June 2004), Dale Hibbert, Johnny Marr and James Maker interviews for Simon Goddard's *Songs That Saved Your Life* (2002) and from a Mike Joyce interview for *The Guardian* (Jan 23, 2012)

Recommended listening:
The Smiths' 'The Hand That Rocks the Cradle' from their debut album, *The Smiths* (1984)

October 4th, 1982.

The Smiths play their first gig at The Ritz in Manchester, opening for headliners Blue Rondo à la Turk.

Mike: The first gig we ever did, was supporting Blue Rondo a la Turk, with palm trees behind them. My snare drum went through, and I asked to borrow theirs. They said no, so I had to play with hardly a sound.

Johnny: I knew there'd be a lot of people who'd never heard anything like it before, or wouldn't get us, especially with James Maker stood next to us. Because I was out all the time seeing whatever groups there were. So I knew we absolutely did not fit in.

Everything seemed to be going as planned for Johnny and Morrissey, except that their bass player, Dale Hibbert, started having a strong sense that the band was indeed taking a pro-gay direction

Johnny: Well I'm guessing if I was Dale and you're stood on the stage with a guy in woman's shoes, playing 'I Want a Boy for My Birthday', around a very effete little guitar player and an unfathomable singer, then he's probably on the money isn't he.

But we didn't sit down with Dale and say "Hey Dale – get with the programme!" I think that's a bit clumsy that whole area and we just weren't and aren't that clumsy.

Us doing that Cookies song was absolutely echoing The New York Dolls who everyone had forgotten about but Morrissey hadn't and I hadn't. We wanted to bring something to our audience that the Dolls and Patti Smith had brought to us. That was it.

Joe Moss: It was stunning. Morrissey was just 10 foot tall – I had no idea he was going to be that kind of stage performer. In rehearsals he'd been active and putting kind of a show on, but nothing like this, the intensity of it was just – blimey! You realised it was someone who was totally unique there in front of you.

Johnny: The most significant reaction I remember from the first show came from Joe Moss. He went into this very uncharacteristic gush about the way I played guitar and that meant an enormous amount to me. It was an important confidence boost and a real foundation stone in the story of the band. We knew we were on to something.

Quotes from Johnny Marr and Joe Moss interviews for *Mojo* magazine (June 2004), a Johnny Marr interview for Simon Goddard's *Songs That Saved Your Life* (2002) and a Mike Joyce interview for *The Guardian* (Jan 23, 2012)

Recommended listening:
The Cookies' 'I Want A Boy for My Birthday', b-side to their single 'Will Power' (1963)

reel around the fountain **part twenty-nine**

November 1982.
Following their debut gig at the Ritz, perhaps through their well-connected friend Andrew Berry, The Smiths landed their first interview. It was through this *i-D* interview that Morrissey and Johnny's differences with Dale Hibbert came out.

How difficult has it been for you not being part of the Manchester sound?
Johnny Marr: It's like fashion. All these stray 'perrys' are nightclubbing now, which puts others off going out. It's not necessary to move to London, but what bothers me is that whole 'Joy Division' thing. It's very patronising being a Manchester band.
The music up here is pretty trashy. It's got direction ut it's the wrong one.
Everyone is trying so hard to be innovative and original.

Why the Smiths?
Steven Morrissey: The name doesn't mean anything, it simply serves its purpose. I think it's very important not to be defined in any one category. Once you're defined you're limited and musically that petrifies me.

How important are clothes to you?
The don't have the relevance they once had, like in the '60s you could look at someone and assess their personality. That's not the case anymore. Clothes are no longer the window of the soul.

What does the word soul mean to you?

Are you tempted by the power to influence people through music?
Steven Morrissey: I think the best power you could have is to get people to think about themselves with a reflective influence because people are so complacent about everything.

Quotes from the first interview The Smiths ever gave, published months later in *i-D* (Feb 1983)

Recommended listening:
The Exploited's 'U.S.A.', from their second album, *Troops of Tomorrow* (1982)

December 1982.
Spirit Studios, Tariff Street, Manchester.
Dissatisfied with Dale's skills on the bass and his reaction towards Morrissey's dream of Smithdom it fell on Johnny to give him the sack, shortly after their debut gig at The Ritz and their first press interview.

Dale: I can remember it well. It was on the stairs as I was going out Johnny said something like:

And I thought they meant they wanted to rehearse somewhere else. So I said:

It fell to him to tell me because he was the one that introduced me to the band. But there was no way that I would have made it with them.

There was no way I'd have gone on tour and done all that stuff because I was married with kids. I just didn't suit the image that was being prepared.

Quotes from Dale Hibbert interview for Simon Goddard's *The Smiths: Songs That Saved Your Life* (2006)

Recommended listening:
God's Gift's 'Discipline' produced by Dale Hibbert at Spirit Studios and released by New Hormones (1982)

December 1982.

Through contacts provided by now manager Joe Moss, Johnny booked a recording session at Drone Studios in Chorlton in order to record a demo for EMI. The session would also serve as an audition for Andy Rourke, with whom Johnny had reconciled after sacking the band's original bass player, Dale Hibbert.

Andy: The first time we played together, we recorded the demos for 'Handsome Devil' and 'Miserable Lie'. That was also the first time I met Morrissey and Mike.

Out of the blue I got this call from Johnny that he's met up with this guy Morrissey, they've got this thing together called The Smiths and would I like to come down and play with them. I was made up, know what I mean? I was straight down there!

Morrissey had this long overcoat on and he looked a little bit aloof, very pleasant and all that — he shook me hand — but you could tell he was a bit nervous — I was nervous as well. I don't think he was called Morrissey then, he was just Steven, know what I mean?

The Smiths was the fourth band Andy and Johnny would have played in together after The Paris Valentinos, White Dice and Freak Party.

We just ran through the three or four songs. Johnny just kinda jammed them out and then 10 minutes later that was it, we were doing a take. We got three or four musical tracks down, which sounded great to me. I was just buzzin' off 'em, know what I mean? We all were!

And then, as always, Morrissey went in and sorta did his thing over the top.

It was the first time it had all kinda come together, with me and Johnny sorta playing against each-other and stuff like that. That's when I kinda found my niche and I don't think that ever changed throughout The Smiths; I kind played on Johnny's melodies and accentuated them the best I could.

Quotes from Andy Rourke interviews for *The Guardian* (Jan 23, 2012) and the documentary *Inside the Smiths* (2007)

Recommended listening:
The Smiths' 'What Difference Does It Make?' from their May 31, 1983 John Peel session, released on their compilation *Hatful of Hollow* (1984)

December 1982.
Drone Studios, Chorlton, Manchester.
Andy auditions for The Smiths whilst recording a
new demo.
Andy: It was like it wasn't me actually playing the bass.
It was like I was kinda possessed and this kinda demon was playing this stuff. It was nothing I'd rehearsed before
or anything - it just kinda came out. It was a pivotal point I did kinda know at the time because when we started
playing together the energy was just there and it was just right, you know what I mean?

And everybody - we were all looking at each other going
"fucking hell!" - we were all nodding at each other.
It quite rarely happens, you know what I mean, when
these three musicians get together and it all kinda
works, especially when you've just met!

Johnny: We hadn't seen each other for about a year.
So later I asked him round to mine and it was good to see
him again. But he was a bit confused, I think, because he had
to put up with me playing The Drifters, whereas a year and
a half before, me and him were listening to David Bowie's Low
and A Certain Ratio!

At that point the band realised that their recently sacked
bass player, Dale Hibbert, was in Drone Studios' control
booth, observing Andy's audition and the recording of
their new demo.
Mike: We could see Dale giving us quizzical looks through
the glass from the control booth.

Dale: That story's absolute rubbish.
It's true I did see them at Drone, but only because I was an
engineer and a partner in Spirit Studios, so I was there checking
out the competition. I already knew Andy because I'd recorded
the demo of Freak Party and he was far, far superior to
me as a bass player. I honestly didn't mind.

Quotes from an Andy Rourke interview for the documentary *Inside the Smiths* (2007) and
interviews of Johnny Marr, Mike Joyce and Dale Hibbert for Simon Goddard's *Songs That
Saved Your Life* (2002)

Recommended listening:
The Drifters' singles 'This Magic Moment' and 'Save The Last Dance For Me' (1960)

January 23rd, 1983.
The Manchester Sound gay club.

Johnny: Our second gig really was rammed... and that was when all the Factory people turned up and we did a full set for the first time.

Tony Wilson: I was there with Richard Boon and I was blown away, it was fantastic. As we were leaving Richard asked what I thought of Morrissey now and I said, "I take it back completely, he's amazing." He already had that arrogant thing.

Andy: Morrissey was this very quiet, unassuming person, but as soon as he went on he became something different. It took your breath away. He had a pocket full of confetti and threw it over the audience, which none of us expected. We did about eight songs. There were about 300 people there, which wasn't bad for my first gig.

Mike: Morrissey had started yodelling by then, and he'd get down on his shoulders and put his legs straight into the air. It was theatrical, quite balletic. None of this was rehearsed. I remember watching the faces of the people at the front. It was just shock: "What the hell is this?"

Andy: James Maker introduced the band in French and danced wearing stilettos and playing maracas.

Andy: He was the gay Bez. But I think we realised it was gilding the lily a bit; we already had a frontman — who was this strange, exotic creature no one could understand.

Joe Moss: The reason James only did one more gig was because of me. He detracted from Morrissey and didn't really have a function. I was just protecting the band.

James Maker: My guest appearances with them were quite superfluous, really. I never belonged with The Smiths and I didn't wish for it.

I was 21. The maracas-shaking go-go dancing was just a silly and enjoyable, temporary diversion. I very much had my own plans and went on to formulate them.

Soon after The Smiths started making it, James formed Raymonde. Morrissey would invite them to open for most of the dates on the triumphant *The Queen is Dead* tour in 1986.

Quotes from Andy Rourke and Mike Joyce interviews for the *The Guardian* (Jan 23, 2012), Johnny Marr and Joe Moss interviews for *Mojo* magazine (June 2004) and a James Maker interview for Simon Goddard's *Songs That Saved Your Life* (2002)

Recommended listening:
The Smiths' 'Miserable Lie' from their eponymous debut album, *The Smiths* (1984)

January 1983.
Johnny's home in Wythenshawe.

I was at my parents' house one Sunday evening and my little brother had a guitar knocking about. I started to play some chords and quickly came up with this riff. I got very excited about it as I knew it was good. But I didn't have anything to record it on...

So my girlfriend Angie (who's now my wife) ran around to her house and snuck her dad's car out.
I got in the car with my guitar, playing the riff over and over again so I wouldn't forget it!

We drove to Morrissey's. I got there, and I'm holding this guitar outside his door in the rain, unannounced. "Oh, hello," he says, "what have you got there?" I said: "A new song." "Well, you'd better come in then." So in I went, and Morrissey pulled out this tape recorder, and we recorded the music. Then I went home.

He called me the next day and said:

Quotes from a Johnny Marr interview with the *Daily Mail* (May 4, 2013)

Recommended listening:
The Smiths' 'Hand in Glove' from their first compilation, *Hatful of Hollow* (1984)

January 1983.
Above Joe Moss' Crazy Face boutique.
Following their second gig at Manchester Sound, The Smiths have been rehearsing intensively. Joe Moss convinces the band to drop James Maker and tone down the overtly gay imagery.

The strategy would prove one of the cornerstones of the band's success, as Morrissey's lyrics would in turn become even more ambiguous and cryptic, yet always retaining his liberal attitude.

February 1983.
Strawberry 2 Studio, Stockport.
Joe Moss agrees to finance the recording of The Smiths' debut single, 'Hand in Glove', hoping to find a way to distribute it or use it as a sample to record companies.

Morrissey's mother visits them during their rehearsals to express her gratitude to Joe Moss for overseeing their progress. She slipps a note to Joe, thanking him for his commitment.

Reference:
Joe Moss mentioned the contents of the note to Johnny Rogan for his biography, *Morrissey & Marr: The Severed Alliance* (Omnibus Press, 1992)

Recommended listening:
The Smiths' 'Hand in Glove' from their first compilation, *Hatful of Hollow* (1984)

February 4th, 1983.
The Smiths perform at The Haçienda.
Joe Moss: There were less than 12 people to see them that first time. By the time they came back a few months later, there were 2,400 people there, and thousands more standing outside, unable to get in. They were magic that night, and we recorded the gig, so that was the version of 'Handsome Devil' we used on the single straight off the sound desk. That shows you how good that gig was, how fully formed the band was already – after just three gigs.

Andy: I think Morrissey may have had gladioli in his pocket. When we played a few weeks later, there were more of them. By the third Haçienda gig I remember Interflora bringing 30 boxes of gladioli at that gig. The whole place just stank. By this time we were being mobbed. I remember Tony Wilson saying: "Nothing has ever happened like this at the Haçienda. This is a first." It was absolutely insane.

Morrissey: The flowers actually have a significance. When we first began there was a horrendous sterile cloud over the whole music scene in Manchester. Everybody was anti-human and it was so cold. The flowers were a very human gesture. They integrated harmony with nature something people seemed so terribly afraid of. It had got to the point in music where people were really afraid to show how they felt – to show their emotions. The flowers offered hope.

However successful the gig, things came to a head later on when Rob Gretton had a huge row with Morrissey in The Haçienda.
Peter Hook: There was a lot of competition in the early days. Morrissey was very outspoken about Joy Division – which our manager Rob Gretton hated. He really did fucking hate Morrissey going on about Ian.

And they had a wonderful, wonderful upset in The Haçienda, when Morrissey was mouthing off about Joy Division... Rob Gretton said to him, "Fucking trouble with you Morrissey is that you don't have the guts to kill yourself like Ian!" Morrissey went fucking mad! He went mad and stormed off!

Quotes from interviews with Joe Moss for *Mojo* magazine (June 2004), Andy Rourke for *The Guardian* (Jan 23, 2012), Morrissey for the *Melody Maker* (Sept 3, 1983), Peter Hook for *Rock Cellar* magazine (Mar 4, 2013) and a Marr/Morrissey interview with *Canal 33* (Catalonia TV), where they voice their opinion on Joy Division (Nov 18, 1985)

Recommended listening:
Joy Division's 'Atmosphere' from their compilation of b-sides and singles, *Substance* (1988)
The Smiths' 'Handsome Devil', recorded live at The Haçienda, and offered as a b-side to 'Hand in Glove' (1983)

Johnny: Most days we'd jump in our little van and go off to do a gig somewhere, buying 100 quids worth of flowers on the way. There'd be news everyday too – Radio 1 were going to give us a daytime play, I was buying a Rickenbacker... Really fucking exciting.

We all piled in a van, there were no windows or seats – just a a mattress. We filled it full of fags, joints and laughter. We had the same humour, the same impenetrable lingo – this truncated kind of English made up of obscure bits of the Young Ones, Beatles documentaries and other nonsense.

People get the wrong impression about Morrissey. He was different, of course he was, but we were a real band. When you're driving back from Carlisle at half-five in the morning in a smelly van, day in, day out for months, it's impossible to remain aloof. We were all very tight as people, Morrissey included.

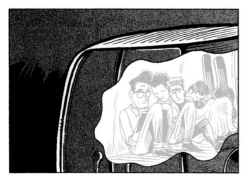

Unbeknownst to the venue, James Maker was not part of the band anymore, so London's Rock Garden advertised The Smiths as a Magazine meets the Velvets five-piece. Nonetheless, their first gig in the capital proved a triumph generating a loyal following. Having recorded a demo of 'Hand in Glove' just prior to the gig, Johnny thought it would be a great chance to give a copy to indie label Rough Trade Records.

I went in on a Friday. Rough Trade was this very shambolic, super-busy hive. The first thing that struck me was that there were records everywhere and lots and lots of people running around. Someone asked me if they could help me and when I said I wanted to see Geoff Travis I was kind of bustled out.
Did I have an appointment? Would he know what it was concerning? Was he expecting me? I got the picture.

Quotes from Johnny Marr interviews for Document and Eyewitness: An Intimate History of Rough Trade (2010), *The Inside Story of Morrissey and The Smiths – Mojo Special Limited Edition* (2004) and the *Daily Mail* (May 4, 2013)

Recommended listening:
The Smiths' 'These Things Take Time', from their first compilation, *Hatful of Hollow* (1984)

I was kicked out and stood outside for 10 minutes, when I noticed this car go back and forwards full of boxes of records. So I walked around the back of the building and there was a loading bay open, with a couple of hippies loading records into this car.
I climbed into the loading bay and pretended I was working, and got into the building that way.

I found my way to Geoff's office. He looked really busy. I hung around until he was on his own.
Then I made a break for it, and just at that point he came out of his office. I just grabbed him and said, "Hey Geoff, uh, hi, my name's Johnny.
I'm in a band from Manchester and you won't have heard anything like this..."

It was inevitable that The Smiths would eventually be signed by a record label. But what mattered most to the band at this point was not commercial success, but creative freedom and... Friendship. That was what had changed in Morrissey's and my life.

We had met each other, were working together, and we were in love with each other, in the best possible way. And 'Hand in Glove' came out of that.
To Morrissey the band proved a life line of sorts, as his desperate cries for companionship were answered in the form of The Smiths.

Four northern souls working hand in glove with each other, their lives entwined through poetry and music.

Quotes from a Johnny Marr interview with the *Daily Mail* (May 4, 2013) and Simon Goddard's *The Smiths: Songs That Saved Your Life* (2006)

Recommended listening:
The Smiths' 'Hand in Glove' and 'Still Ill' from their first compilation, *Hatful of Hollow* (1984)

The band found their place as advocates of marginalised youth, as well as poster boys for the rising independent music scene. However, they also courted serious controversy early on, with accusations of paedophilia and glamourising the Moors murderers – accusations the band strongly denied. They overcame these initial obstacles to produce four albums, which are considered amongst the most important and influential ever recorded... but that is another Tale. And for another time.

GALLERY

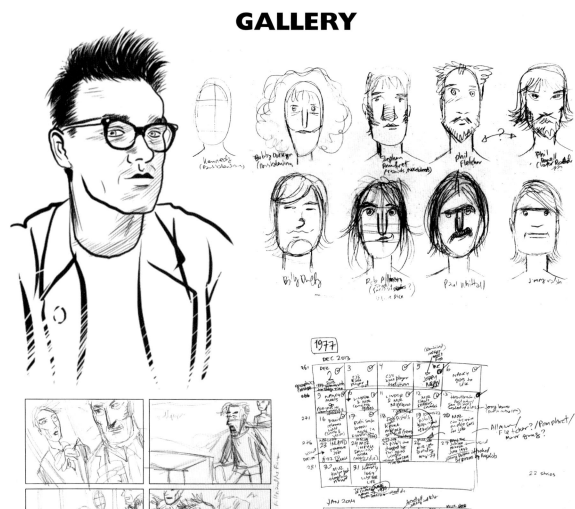

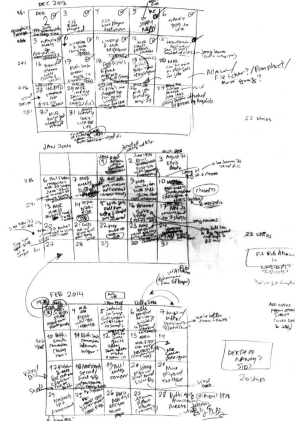